THE LONGEST KILL

THE LONGEST KILL

THE STORY OF MAVERICK 41, ONE OF THE WORLD'S GREATEST SNIPERS

Craig Harrison

ST. MARTIN'S PRESS ☙ NEW YORK

www.stmartins.com

The Library of Congress Cataloging-in-Publication Data is available upon request.

ISBN 978-1-250-08523-8 (hardcover)
ISBN 978-1-250-08524-5 (e-book)

Our books may be purchased in bulk for promotional, educational, or business use. Please contact your local bookseller or the Macmillan Corporate and Premium Sales Department at (800) 221-7945, extension 5442, or by e-mail at MacmillanSpecialMarkets@macmillan.com.

First Edition: February 2016

10 9 8 7 6 5 4 3 2 1

Author's Note

This is a true story, though some names and details have been changed.

For my loving wife Tanya, Dani and Leslie,

who loved and supported me in the dark days,

and a big thank you to Paul and Sue.

Contents

THE LONGEST KILL

Prologue: Life or Death

Helmand province, Afghanistan, November 2009

My index finger was resting on the trigger of my Accuracy International AWM .338 sniper rifle. It was the best sniper rifle in the world and was topped off with the best telescopic sight in the world: the Schmidt & Bender 5-25. I'd been taught that the effective range of this rifle was 1,600 yards. Today, I was going to get it to reach a lot further.

I'd been a sniper for ten years. I'd been in firefights where my odds of surviving seemed slim to none, but I'd never had to make a shot like this before. I'd never had to shoot so far and to factor in so many variables, while under so much pressure. The pressure of life or death.

The three Jackal armored vehicles I was commanding had set out from our base at 0400 hours. By daybreak we'd been in position on high ground, about two and a half miles south of Talajan's district central. We were tasked with providing observation and protection to a joint British Army and Afghan Army foot patrol clearing a village in a valley below. Once I was happy that the Jackals were covering all the Taliban's potential approach routes, I'd grabbed my sniper rifle and positioned myself behind a crumbling old wall made of mud and straw—the only half-decent cover the area offered.

The area was crawling with Taliban and as soon as the

sun came up they started their attack. For three hours I'd provided oversight, acquired and taken out Taliban targets. By now I was sweating, stripped down to a T-shirt under my body armor, even though it was a mild winter's day. Then I watched as a vehicle-borne patrol from my regiment was dispatched to help the foot patrol. They'd done their bit but now they were in a precarious position themselves, their Jackals bogged in and the crews—my mates—under attack from all flanks. They had good firepower on the vehicles but they were in a gulley and couldn't see what was happening around them. They were dangerously exposed and fighting for their lives. From my vantage point I could see the enemy machine gun that was pouring fire down at them. I'd witnessed too many casualties being loaded on the back of a Chinook in this war. I had to take out the machine-gun crew.

To my mind the sniper is the ultimate professional soldier, one of the only true force multipliers in the British Army's inventory. A sniper pair can wreak havoc that is completely disproportionate to their number. They can slow battalion advances and turn attacks. They can enhance the defensive battle by making the attackers' lives hell. We neutralize commanders and key equipment. As the hackneyed phrase goes, "one shot, one kill." Snipers don't just kill though. They are trained to observe and report, carry out reconnaissance and can also adjust mortar and artillery fire. They are the masters of the shadows.

The British Army has had a sporadic relationship with sniping, continually having to relearn lessons. The sniper pair was conceived and developed in the First World War, and its basic principles have not really changed that much to this day. Unfortunately, in the interwar years snipers drifted out of fashion and in the Second World War sniping had to be re-established. The same thing happened when that war ended and after Korea. It wasn't really until after the Falklands War in 1982 that the British Army realized that their snipers needed to be permanently established and better equipped.

My regiment, the Blues and Royals, didn't have a history or culture of sniping in the way that other regiments do, particularly the Parachute Regiment, the Royal Marines and the Special Forces. I had to fight to become a sniper and I had to fight to bring my sniper rifle on operations. On this day it would turn the tide of a battle.

All the evidence said that it couldn't be done, that this shot was impossible. It was far outside the recognized range of the rifle, I was out of adjustment in my scope and my position was appalling. Every time the rifle recoiled a little chunk of wall broke away and I had to hold the bipod with my left hand just to stop it falling off. Accurate shooting is all about the minimal transference of interference to the weapon. I was struggling with that one today.

Four pounds of pull is all that it takes to cause the trigger to "break." Once the hammer falls, the .6-ounce bullet will leave the barrel at a speed of around 3,000 feet per second. I calculated that the bullet would take almost six seconds to reach the Taliban machine-gun crew. At this range every variable came into effect: wind speed, temperature, humidity; even the earth's rotation in that six seconds would all affect the trajectory of the bullet. That's a lot to think about. And underneath all of that was a twisting sense of urgency, knowing that time was running out.

I pushed all of the information and background noise out

of my mind and focused again on my breathing. As the crackle and bang of gunfire from the valley faded away all I could hear was the thud of my heart. Through my scope I saw the gentle rise and fall of the cross hairs on the target and with each exhale I settled my aiming point on to the Taliban machine gunner. Even with the magnification of the scope the target was tiny, but I could clearly see the gunner and the weapon firing.

On my final exhale I paused and my world went still, perfectly still. I was like a statue with only the very tip of my index finger able to move. I willed my finger to start the pull and felt the briefest of resistance before the 4lb was taken up. The trigger "broke" and the rifle fired. It recoiled solidly into my shoulder and the scope rose off target before settling back down. Cliff, my spotter, had a telescope with far greater magnification than my telescopic sight and was able to see more detail. While staring through my own scope my right ear was straining, waiting to hear what Cliff said. The seconds slowly ticked by. Count six seconds now and you will see what I mean. At lot can change in that time; most importantly the target could move.

After what seemed like a lifetime, Cliff suddenly spoke. "Miss."

I cursed before getting a grip of myself. I cycled the bolt, chambering a fresh round, and started my firing sequence all over again. I got control of my breathing, took up the slack in the trigger and got my aiming point back on the target.

I know I can make this shot . . . I have to make this shot.

1. Guns Are a Boy's Best Friend

I was crouching behind a small bush in a copse, struggling to bring my breathing under control. My heartbeat was thumping in my ears, so loud I was convinced the sound would give me away. I clutched my rifle close to my chest. The smell of gun oil was strangely soothing and it steadied me.

The footsteps were getting closer now. I turned my head an inch or two until I could see my companion, hidden behind a nearby tree. He gave me a nod—he was ready. I waited until the last moment, forcing myself not to move, staring through the branches until I saw the outline of a man to my front. Then I stood, raised my rifle and pointed it straight at him.

"Bang!" I shouted. The dog walker jumped in the air, clutching his chest in fright.

"You little shits!" he screamed at my brother and me, as we tore off into the woods, laughing.

My brother and I rarely saw eye to eye, but we did come together for our favorite game of scaring dog walkers and other unsuspecting ramblers in the woods near our home in Cheltenham. The gun, a deactivated bolt-action rifle, was a present from my dad.

We had been living at the Lincoln RAF base when he came home with it one day. "It's from the Second World War," he'd told me, before handing it over as a present. My brother got a PKM machine gun, but he wasn't that interested in it. I, on the other hand, loved that Springfield rifle like an old friend. Dad taught me how to strip the rifle down in order to to oil and clean it, and I carefully looked after it. I'd spend hours outside with it, playing on my own in the woods, pretending I was a soldier.

I was born at Cheltenham Hospital in November 1974, the younger of two brothers. I was a small kid with big ears—something the bullies liked to pick on as I grew up. When I was young we moved around a lot, as my dad was a dog handler in the RAF. Mum had been a kennel maid in the RAF, but the rules back then meant she had to leave the Forces when she married my dad.

Dad split when I was little. I can't actually remember how old I was but it was probably for the best. He made Mum miserable, although I didn't see any of their problems at the time; they kept all that from me.

With Dad gone, the three of us finally settled in a caravan park in Cheltenham and Mum got herself a job as an ambulance driver. Her true love was dogs—and it showed. I didn't have a bad childhood, but my brother and I definitely ranked below the family pets.

My mum had taken the rifle off me by then. "You need to grow up," she told me. I was devastated but I still managed to get into mischief without it. We lived in the caravan site for about a year and a half and I remember the elderly caretaker, a miserable old sod who was always having a go at the kids on the site for riding our bikes or walking on the grass. In retaliation some of us—me included—used to jump out at him. He had a heart attack and died while we were still living there and I've always assumed we scared him to death!

We moved again, to a flat above a chip shop, which had some obvious bonuses. Our neighbors were a woman called Liz and her son Jamie, who was about the same age as me. She used to hang a sign around his neck when he'd done something wrong. The first time I met him, he was wearing a sign saying: "I must not steal biscuits." The awful thing was that this first meet actually took place at school. His mum used to ring the headmaster and tell him to make Jamie wear the sign all day. If Jamie had done a number of things wrong, he had to wear multiple signs.

After school, Mum would instruct me and my brother to go out and play by ourselves, so that she could have the flat to herself. Mum sometimes treated us as a hindrance and then it was best to keep out of her way. We never sat around as a family watching TV or having dinner. I remember one night being woken up by a fireman while I was in bed; an alarm had gone off in the chip shop and they were evacuating the building. He got me outside and on the lawn, where Mum, my brother, the dogs and the budgie were all waiting alongside Liz and Jamie, who had a sign round his neck that said: "I must not shout, 'Fuck.'" I looked at Mum as I ran up to them.

"Shit, I forgot about you," she said.

To be fair, though, I was no angel when I was young and my mum did work hard to provide for us. She just used to snap every now and then. I remember not folding my trousers properly and she started smacking me. I literally pissed myself and had to sleep in my stained clothes. She came in during the middle of the night and said sorry. The next morning, she realized you could see her handprints and she packed me off to my granddad's house for a week to hide.

My granddad, Reg Harrison, became a father figure to

me. My grandma died when I was young and I don't really remember her, but my granddad I will never forget. I loved him with all my heart; he provided the stability and love in my somewhat turbulent life. He had been in the RAF as well, leaving as a sergeant, and he was one of the most decent and kind people I have ever met.

He used to take me driving in his blue Ford Escort; when we drove around a disused quarry, he'd let me steer. I remember being at his house one Halloween, looking out of the window, when I thought I saw a ghost. It frightened the life out of me. I grabbed a walking stick, ran outside and started beating it. It turned out to be my granddad in costume. When he came back in, he had a cracked nose and a black eye— but he was still laughing. He thought the whole thing was hilarious. That was my granddad all over.

By the time I was seven, we'd moved home a few times. As a result, I changed schools a lot, which really didn't help me. I was constantly the new kid and therefore constantly picked on. I became more and more of a loner.

Luckily, Mum then met Keith, whom she married when I was ten. He was in the RAF but you really wouldn't have put the two of them together. He was fun and very "country"; he would take us to game fairs, where I'd be engrossed by the guns and the strange leafy get-ups. These turned out to be something called ghillie suits—a uniform with which I would, in time, become very familiar.

It was around this age that I started to develop a real interest in nature. Just as I had in Cheltenham, I loved being out in the woods, and I now spent more and more of my time there. I saved up money and bought a Black Widow catapult, which I kept hidden behind the shed. I used to go into the woods and shoot cans with it. Never animals; I had a genuine respect for animals.

Mum was working as a dog warden in Cheltenham when a better job offer came in. Keith's brother ran an animal shelter for a charity but was moving away—and Mum was asked if she wanted to take on responsibility for the shelter. It had two on-site bungalows, stables, three massive kennels for ten to fifteen dogs, ten sheds, outbuildings and a lot of land. It was a fantastic opportunity for all of us, but for me in particular there was one added bonus. As well as homing cats and dogs, it also cared for horses.

It must have been through the country shows that I had developed a real thing for horses. Not long after we moved into the animal shelter, Mum gave me my first one: Kipling. Just like that old Springfield rifle, Kipling and I were inseparable. I'd gladly get up early to sort him out, sit impatiently through my lessons at school counting the minutes until I could race home and then take him out across the fields. He was a great horse, very loyal. Once we were out in the countryside, I'd dismount and walk, and he would just follow me; he never ran off.

It wasn't long before I started to compete in jumping and team-racing events. Kipling was just a hacking pony, unsuited to jumping, so I decided to borrow a bigger horse for my competitions, and I lent Kipling to a girl called Helen.

"Please don't jump him; he's only a hacking pony," I pleaded with her.

She jumped him and jumped him. By the time I got him back he was fucked and we had to put him down. I hated her for that.

Next, we got a bigger horse called Ginger, a thoroughbred with a showjumping background. That's when my skill really took off and I entered more and more competitions—and actually started to win. All this brought Mum and me closer together. There had always been a barrier between the two of us but our love of horses was the one thing that could break through.

We ended up with more horses, a donkey and a Shetland pony, plus all of the dogs and cats. I used to spend most of my time in the sheds mucking out. Mum paid me £5 a week in return, which was good money for a kid.

One day at the shelter, I walked in to find that Keith's brother had come to say hello with his other half and their son Richard, who was a year older than me. For some reason, I started calling him Tom—and it stuck. He was also a bit of a loner yet we instantly clicked and from the moment we met, we started doing everything together. He would spend every weekend at our bungalow and we'd go out riding and walking. His mum didn't really like him hanging out with me, as she thought I was a bad influence, but that didn't stop us. In hindsight, I *was* a bad influence but, regardless, we stayed (and remain) very close friends.

We added shooting to our weekend activities after I stumbled across a huge rifle with a telescopic sight and a silencer leaning against the living room wall. I knew that Keith had a rifle for vermin control around the shelter, but had only ever seen it from a distance; I'd never had the chance to touch it. He usually kept it in a secure cabinet and must have forgotten to put it away. Knowing Keith was safely asleep in bed (he had been working nights), I picked up the rifle and started to examine it. Thoughts of my Springfield came flooding back as I turned it over, looked through the scope and then touched the trigger.

Boom.

It had been loaded. The shot wasn't too loud due to the silencer but I stood there dumbfounded, staring at the rifle and waiting for Keith to leap out of bed and come racing in. Luckily, he hadn't heard the shot—but I wasn't out of the woods yet. Mum had a collection of Beatrix Potter and Wind in the Willows plates that were worth quite a bit of money, and one of them was now in bits on the floor. I spent the next hour trying to glue it back together but I've always been crap at jigsaws. It ended up with the rat's head on the mole's body and the frog upside down, so I threw it away instead. Somehow I got away with it!

Over the next few weeks I craftily worked on Keith and eventually he agreed to let Tom and me use the rifle. We'd grab some eggs for targets, and gradually work further and further back as our aim improved. It took a while to figure out how the scope worked but once I had that sussed I became quite a good shot. Tom would wrap the rifle in cloth and strap it to his bicycle handlebars so we could take it further afield. How we didn't get caught I will never know.

When I was fourteen I started competing in tetrathlons, which involve running, swimming, riding and shooting. As I'm left-handed, Mum got me a left-handed pistol for my events, and after that Tom and I quickly forgot about the rifle.

We'd often blow off lessons to go shooting. Being "late developers" at school, stuck in the special-needs classes and picked on by everyone else, we preferred to head out into the country to shoot rabbits, not for fun but to eat. My grandfather had given me a small pocket knife, and that, along with a box of matches, was all I needed. We'd get water from a stream, light a fire and then boil the rabbits up. We learned our skills through trial and error. I was developing a good education out in the country.

One day, Tom and I were exploring a farmer's field when I noticed a blue pipe. I stabbed it with my knife and it must have been under pressure because a stinking liquid sprayed out all over Tom. He walked around like a zombie, groaning and trying to get chemicals out of his eyes. Eventually he tripped over and fell face down in the river, where he started to float off. I couldn't control my laughter but eventually managed to fish him out and get him cleaned up.

I lit a fire and we tried to dry his clothes. Good old Tom got his trousers too close to the flame and, as they were polyester, they went straight up.

"How am I going to explain this?" he asked me, staring in disbelief.

"Bad day at school?" was all I could come up with.

If ever we went down the high street, we'd head to the lower end, which was full of secondhand shops, the only places Tom and I could afford. One day I found a book called *Sniper*. The title appealed to me so I bought it. Both Tom and I devoured that book, which was full of photos, and I started to dream that one day I would be a sniper.

As practice, we started to stalk each other in the long grass. I used rubber bands to attach grass to my clothing, like it said in the book, and then we would both work toward each other and see who was spotted first.

One afternoon out in the country, we spied a couple kissing and cuddling on a blanket out in a field, so we decided to stalk up on them. It was a great feeling, silently creeping up on someone and them having no idea that we were there. It was also a great feeling that we might see some breasts. As we got closer, I realized that the woman was the mum of one of the lads from school.

"It's Smithy's mum," I whispered to Tom.

"What should we do?" he whispered back.

"Smithy is one of the wankers who picks on us for going to special needs—so let's keep watching."

We didn't see any breast but we did see some bra, which was better than nothing.

As the couple headed off, Smithy's mum dropped a letter. We read it: it was to Smithy's dad, saying that she was leaving him and taking her son with her.

The next day at school, breaktime saw us, as per usual, being picked on. People were calling me and Tom names and shoving us around for being "retards." I spotted Smithy in the group of bullies—and marched straight up to him.

"Sort your own life out before picking on others, you cunt," I told him, and thrust the letter in his hand. I had no idea what the "C" word meant but I'd heard it on TV and thought it had a good ring to it.

Unsurprisingly, that didn't make me more popular with Smithy or his mates.

It was just as well that the headmaster boarded his dog and cat at our kennels so Mum was friendly with him. I think that was the only reason he let me stay, rather than excluding me for truancy. When I did go to school, I used to spend all day staring out of the window, waiting for lessons to end. I hated every minute I spent there. The "special needs" part of the senior school was in the middle of the building, in a large glass classroom, so everyone could see you, which gave the bullies plenty of ammunition.

In our spare time, Tom and I started weight training and we both got big quickly. We thought that if we gained muscle it would stop people picking on us.

At last our purgatory came to an end. We both left school at sixteen and Tom immediately joined the Army. There wasn't much discussion; he just did it. Without him, I felt like my right arm had gone and the house suddenly felt very, very empty.

2. Joining the Army

"Get fucking moving. You're not on your mummy's tit now!"

I was standing with a group of new recruits on the platform at Brookwood Station while the welcoming committee—a line of soldiers—screamed at us. Chaos quickly ensued as they shepherded us over to the waiting trucks, still yelling. Our bags were thrown on roughly and we clambered in after them. Everyone sat in silence, nervously glancing at their feet, as the vehicle moved off. Eventually, the truck squealed to a halt in the car park at Pirbright Barracks—and then the shouting started again.

"Grab your bags and follow me!" a soldier barked at us before running off.

We scrambled to obey.

"You run everywhere. Don't let us catch you walking!" he yelled over his shoulder as we hurried to keep up.

Once inside, they lined us up and asked which regiments we were going to. I was joining the Cavalry, and us Cav soldiers were made to stand in a separate group while a short fat officer who looked like a relic from the Boer War walked down the line.

"Blues and Royals or Life Guards?" he asked each of us, making a note of each person's choice on his dilapidated clipboard.

I had no idea. "Blues and Royals, sir," I told him, when he came to me.

That was it: I was joining the Blues and Royals. What a crap way to choose a regiment—but that was, unfortunately, the sort of thing I would come to expect from the Cavalry.

When Tom had left, I'd made up my mind: I was going to join the Army as well. My brother had joined already and was in the King's Troop, Royal Horse Artillery. His choice had surprised me as when we were younger he had shown no interest in horses whatsoever. I wish he had expressed more enthusiasm back then; then he could have given me a hand with the mucking out in the mornings.

Tom had gone into training to join our local infantry regiment, the Glorious Glosters, but I'd decided that I wanted to be a farrier, a noncommissioned officer who looks after horses. I had thought long and hard about which regiment to join and in the end my love of horses won out. I also remembered that my grandfather had told me it was important to get a trade, and a farrier seemed perfect for me. My decision meant that I would have to join the Household Cavalry, as they were the only regiment who had them.

It felt like a very long and lonely walk to the recruiting office in Cheltenham, the day I signed up. I paused at the door, then I took a deep breath and walked in. There were four lads in the waiting room, some in suits and some looking like tramps. I was somewhere in the middle, wearing my old school blazer, which was so faded you could clearly see the darker patch where the badge had been. It was all I had in the way of smart clothes.

A sergeant from the Green Jackets led me into a room with a desk. I sat where I was told.

"So, what can I help you with?" he asked.

"I'd like to join the Army, please."

"Any particular part?"

"Household Cavalry. I want to be a farrier."

"Okay," he replied, sliding a load of forms across the desk to me. "That sounds fine—but first we need to check if you're bright enough."

I didn't know this at the time, but certain educational standards are required for different parts of the Army. I had just failed all of my GCSEs, so I hoped I could pass these exams.

"Do I sit the test now?"

"No. Can you come back next Wednesday?"

"Okay."

I stood up and shook his hand before heading home. I carried myself differently walking back. My shoulders were back a bit and I felt good. I found myself counting the days before I could head back to the Army office to sit the test.

The day before the exam, I was sitting in my room when Mum came in.

"Tom's been kicked out of the Army," she said. "They found out about his hearing."

My heart sunk; I knew how much joining the Army meant to Tom. He had always had poor hearing, but he'd kept quiet about it during the interviews and had managed to bluff his way through the medical.

Wednesday, the day of the test, arrived and I was about to leave when there was a knock on my door. It was Tom, fitter than the last time I saw him and with a new look in his eyes. One I would come to know well, a sort of hunger. He told me all about the basic training and the dos and don'ts. It was clear that he'd loved it and he walked with me to the recruiting office through the driving rain, not bothered one bit by the weather as he told me all of his stories. We stopped just outside the building.

"What about joining the Foreign Legion together?" I asked him, wanting to give him some hope for the future. We had talked about this idea in the past.

"Let's see how things go with you first, mate," he replied. "Go on then—in you go. I'll wait outside."

I took a breath and walked in. The same sergeant as before met me and led me to a classroom where the same four lads were waiting.

"Am I late?"

"No, take a seat; we have a lot to get through."

The room was deathly quiet. I could hear the clock ticking on the wall and the rain lashing against the window. Another sergeant then walked in with the exam papers.

"No talking," he announced, fixing us all with a look that was not to be messed with. "If you get caught cheating, you'll be asked to leave. You have one hour. Begin."

I looked at the clock, the exam booklet and the chewed pencil in front of me. I glanced out the window—only to see Tom grinning and giving me two thumbs-up. The sergeant walked over to me.

"Do you know that guy?"

"Yes."

"Okay, well, you better get on with it now."

I started looking at the questions, but got distracted when I realized that some fucker had left chewing gum under the desk—which was now stuck to my trousers.

"Forty-five minutes left," the sergeant announced.

I'd forced myself to concentrate. After what seemed like only seconds later: "Thirty minutes left."

Fortunately, it was multiple-choice, so I started ripping

into the questions. Some of the other lads had finished already.

"Time. Pencils down."

We were led downstairs and told to wait while our papers were marked. After a nervous half an hour or so, my name was called and I went back into the office.

The sergeant didn't mince his words. "You've done well and made it into the Cav," he told me briskly. He shook my hand and told me to be back next Wednesday for medicals. I felt such joy at passing, but also really sad for Tom. There would be no Foreign Legion for us now.

A week later, I had some random man's cold hands around my balls, telling me to cough. I passed the medical and was then led to see an officer, who congratulated me before I went through the procedure of swearing allegiance to the Queen. I was given £15 and told to await a reporting date. "That's my shilling taken," I thought to myself.

The first person I told was my granddad, who kept telling me how proud he was, while gently taking the piss out of me for joining the Army rather than the RAF; the Navy, Army and Air Force all love to hate each other. Mum was less enthusiastic; she just wanted to know when I would be leaving. Tom and I went out and celebrated with the £15.

A formal letter arrived a week later, telling me I needed to report to Pirbright, and giving me the date. When the big day came round, in February 1991, Granddad gave me a big hug and told me how proud he was of me once more, before I headed to the station. Mum came with me, and she started to cry as the train pulled up. I wasn't sure if she was emotional because I was leaving—or upset that there would be no one round the house to do all the jobs anymore.

As the train pulled away, I realized that I hadn't ever

really traveled that far in my life, especially on my own. It was a three-hour journey, and I spent most of it feeling like a dick as I saw other lads, also clearly on their way to join up, who were wearing suits, while I was dressed in my old school blazer and a pair of trousers with a whiteish sticky patch where I'd failed to get all the chewing gum off.

But all that was forgotten by the time I was standing in line, standing to attention and answering, "Blues and Royals, sir," to the Boer War relic. My Army career started right there and then.

I was put into Pirbright Platoon on that first day in the Forces—and it would come to represent everything I love about the Army. A different bunch of lads, all thrown in together and fast becoming friends. There were four of us going to the Cavalry and we became particularly good mates. Nick was a clean-cut guy with very nice hair, who would become a very close friend. Mark was your classic stereotype Jock—never happy. Terribly, his family had been killed in the Lockerbie air crash. And then there was Paul, from Thetford, who reminded me of Pig-Pen, in *Peanuts*, the kid who always had the dust swirling round him.

Once inside our assigned accommodation, the four of us were put in the corner. My bed was next to the door, which banged into it all the time—and it was freezing. Not the best start.

The first week of training was pretty straightforward. There was no need for an alarm clock as someone came in to wake us every morning. We were being looked after by a soldier from the Scots Guards.

"Everyone into the showers," he ordered us on our first day.

We all walked into the shower room to see a naked man in there, who proceeded to give us a lesson in "how to shower properly." After that was the "how to shave" lesson. Not too bad—but our instructor was the naked man again, and he hadn't bothered to put a towel on.

Getting our kit issued involved running round the various departments in camp. I looked at the boots that were passed over the counter to me.

"These boots are different sizes," I pointed out.

"Don't worry, you'll grow into them," the storeman answered.

Once back in the block, we were taught how to iron, and then left to sort out our kit.

The next day, we had a swimming and fitness test. The swimming test was run by a civilian (civi) called Pat, who had one leg bigger than the other. I had no idea how he didn't swim round and round in circles. The test started with us kneeling by the pool while Pat walked along the line, slapping us hard on the back, at which point we were expected to roll into the water. He called these "Bloody Marys."

The group was split into strong and weak swimmers. The weak swimmers did the test first, while the strong swimmers were taken to the end of the pool and made to create waves by pulling back and forth in unison along the edge of the pool. I noticed my new friend Paul struggling. When he sank underwater I broke ranks, swam over and dragged him out. Pat made me kneel on the edge and gave me four Bloody Marys for that. Lopsided twat.

Once the swimming was done, we were sent on a run around camp. We had nine minutes and thirty seconds to run a mile and a half. Some of the lads didn't do so well after the swimming, but I passed the test.

The medical center came next and, yet again, I found a

strange man cupping my balls and asking me to cough. I swear his thumb was stroking the edge of my ballsack while he talked to one of the nurses.

Finally, we had our hair cut. With my head shaved I looked ill—and it made my ears stand out like a wing nut.

That night, the instructors gave us hell. We stood at the ends of our beds while they screamed and shouted at us, throwing our kit around the room. I quickly formed the opinion that the instructors loved themselves, and as the course progressed I was not proved wrong.

The chief instructor was from the Irish Guards and he seemed to hate the Cavalry. He made a beeline for me and whacked me over the head with his pace stick. It hurt like hell.

"Say, 'Night, Sergeant,'" he said to me, as my skull throbbed painfully.

"Night, Sergeant," I muttered.

"Good. Be in the same place in the morning," he told me as he walked out the door.

The next morning, he walked in and hit me over the head with his pace stick again. He did this every day for the whole course.

What goes around comes around, though. A year later, I met him in a bar in Canada, while on exercise. I walked straight over to him and knocked him out. As he was picking himself up off the floor, I leaned over him. "Be careful who you kick on the way up—as they will kick you twice as hard on your way down," I told him, before walking off.

Back in training, days turned to weeks, weeks turned to months. I loved it; it was only being hit on the head twice a day that got me down. I phoned home just once during the whole period.

We got paid in cash every two weeks. There was a snack

wagon called Taffy's that used to drive around camp, and it knew exactly when we had been paid; the prices would double overnight. The instructors used to take their cut as well. This money was apparently going toward the end-of-course party but a lot of the lads were too young to drink.

After a number of weeks, we got our first decent leave: two weeks off. Heading back to Cheltenham, I expected things to look different, that things would have changed. Of course they hadn't; the place was still a shithole.

As I approached the house, I saw my granddad letting himself in. He used to come round each night for his tea. He gave me a huge hug and I could see the pride in his eyes.

Once inside, I sat there with Mum and Granddad and told them all about basic training and how it was all going. Mum then showed me my room, which was now full of dog cages.

"That will be £50," she said.

"What will be?" I asked.

"Rent."

"Fine."

I didn't mind paying the rent, but I did mind her just walking in all the time to let the dogs in and out. It was quite annoying when I was trying to enjoy a bit of private space.

I rang Tom and felt like a millionaire. I met him outside McDonald's with the biggest, daftest grin on my face. It was great to see him.

As we headed inside, I saw that the Manton brothers were there, all four of them. There was a long-standing feud between them and us. Tom went off for a piss and I headed up to the counter to order the food.

That's when it started.

"Not seen you for a while. Give us a burger," I heard from behind me, as a thrown straw bounced off the back of my head.

"Craig, are you fucking deaf?" one of them shouted at me.

I ignored them, placed my order and went to find a table. As I passed the stairs that led down to the toilets, a lad called Pete, part of the Manton "gang," was coming up them. He barged straight into me, while pushing me backward.

Something just snapped inside of me. I kicked him straight in the center of the chest, sending him flying back down the stairs. I followed him down, kicking him as hard as I could. The remainder of his gang started to follow, so I grabbed a mop and started jabbing at the chest of the lead guy, forcing them back up the stairs. I didn't want to get blocked in.

As I popped back out the stairs, I was hit from behind and from the side. I charged at the nearest guy and drove him over the table, using the mop handle to push down on his throat. Once he hit the floor, I really applied the pressure. His eyes started to bulge. Maybe being hit over the head all the time with a pace stick had messed with my mind, but rage was pouring out of me.

I got punched again on the back of my skull and, fortunately, this diverted my attention. Without that, I think I could have killed the guy.

I let go of the mop and punched the guy who had just hit me in the neck. He dropped like a sack of shit, so I kneed him in the face on his way down, before grabbing his hair and smacking his head into a table.

Meanwhile Tom was at the door, letting people out and keeping an eye out for the police.

"Come on, we need to go," he shouted.

"Hang on," I replied.

I ran over to the counter, threw a tenner down and grabbed our food, before running out with Tom. He led us down disused railway lines and various paths until we were sure we had got away. We ended up in a pub.

"What the fuck was that all about?" he asked me.

"I don't know, mate. It was like I was taken over."

I had a black eye, a black ear and a split lip—but I knew that I had not come off second best.

That night, I headed round to Granddad's. It was great to spend time with him. He got his RAF photos out and told me about some of the really amazing stuff he'd got up to when he was in the Forces. Just before I headed home, he gave me some wise advice.

"Slow down, be careful with your money and don't drink too much."

Wise words indeed.

The two weeks' leave went quickly and—completely ignoring Granddad—I have never been so drunk or spent my money so fast. The night before I had to go back, I realized I was out of money, so I asked Mum for some. She went nuts and threw me out of the house, following up by chucking my clothes out of the window. The new stereo I'd bought myself crashed down next to them. I grabbed my kit and walked to the station, planning to sleep there and then jump on the train the next day.

I was cold and hungry by morning. As the train departed the station I didn't feel like I was leaving home. I knew that the Army was now my family and it felt good to be back in camp. We were lined up and our names called out to check if anyone had gone AWOL.

"What do you say?" I heard from behind my head.

"Morning, Sergeant," I replied in a normal tone of voice.

"Just because you have been on leave, it doesn't mean you can stop answering properly, you horse-shagger."

"Yes, Sergeant!" I shouted out.

"So, you're a bit of a fighter, are you, Harrison?" the sergeant asked, pointing at my black eye.

"Sort of, Sergeant."

"Well, report to the gym and fucking run."

I tore off across camp and stopped just outside the gym, where I was met by an old-school PTI (physical training instructor).

"Harrison, is it?"

"Yes, Sergeant."

"Good. You're now on the boxing team. Looks like you've started already."

I loved being on that team. One thing the Army likes is boxing. I got my own room and extra food at mealtimes because of the additional training I was doing. There were ten of us selected for the squad, but only five would get to box in the one-off fight night we were training for, so we were all trying to prove ourselves. I became incredibly fit. The instructors also taught me how to control my rage and direct it, so I didn't lose it when the "red mist" descended.

Before long, it was weigh-in time—and time to find out if we were fighting or not. When my name was called as one of those selected, I was delighted.

The whole of camp turned out to watch the evening of boxing. We were fighting the Royal Artillery. The instructors were there in their formal mess kit and the gym was absolutely packed. I was due to fight last so I watched each one of my team members head off from the locker room and then heard the screams and claps muffled through the wall. Once you had fought you were taken to a separate room, so eventually I ended up on my own.

The coach came in and put some pads on so he could get

me warmed up. Just as we finished, there was a knock at the door. That was my cue.

I headed out to the ring. The screams and shouts were almost deafening. I'd never been in an atmosphere so electrifying and primeval before. It was rhythmic and tribal—people baying for blood. The more I absorbed it, the more amped-up I felt. I kept my calm, though. Just as I had been taught.

Once in the ring, I ended up sitting waiting for the other dick to arrive. I looked up to see him dancing and pointing at me, while mouthing, "You're going down." He was muscular and about my height, but all of his prancing around and flashy overconfidence made him look nervous to me.

We were called into the middle of the ring while the referee said his bit. As I turned around to head back to my corner, I was pushed from behind and struggled to keep my balance. The prick had shoved me.

The crowd went mad. There was beer getting slung everywhere and fights breaking out in the crowd. I was escorted back to the dressing room while they sorted things out.

I kept warming up—until there was a knock at the door again. The crowd were swearing and chanting as I walked back into the ring, keeping my head down. The referee repeated his bit.

"Fuck it, let's just fight before this place blows up," I thought to myself.

As I headed back to my corner, I was shoved again from behind. The referee took a point off the twat for that.

Then the bell rang and that was it.

I couldn't hear the crowd. I couldn't hear the shouting. All I could hear was my own heartbeat echoing in my head. Time started to slow down, as if I was moving through treacle.

The other guy laid into me. He was good. I didn't even manage to throw a punch in the first round.

Round two saw us trading blows more evenly. I was starting to get my pace up now. It continued this way until round six—when I managed to get him into the corner and started pummeling his body. He slammed his head forward and head-butted me in the eye.

As I stepped back, he managed to catch me with a good hit. I slammed him back into the corner and smashed him twice with a haymaker. He dropped to the ground with a dull, heavy thud. The referee started his count—but the lad didn't get up. I'd won.

The next morning, I was sore. I felt like I'd been run over, in fact. I found out that our team had drawn on the night, overall. It was quite nice walking through camp with black eyes; everyone knew I was on the boxing team and I felt like my bruises were badges of honor. We all got one more week on the team before it was disbanded, which gave us a chance to recover. I wasn't looking forward to going back to my platoon and being hit on the head twice a day.

Once back with the lads, after the boxing comp was finished, the thumps on my head continued but the instructors seemed to be going a bit easier on us. All we were doing now was training for our pass-out parade. We got our smart No. 2 dress—our official parade uniforms—tailored, then spent the whole time on the drill square. The camp sergeant major took responsibility for the parade rehearsals and spent most of the time sending people to the camp prison for who knows what; the bloke was a lunatic.

At the final dress rehearsal he went nuts and sent me to the nick. I can't even remember what I'd done wrong; something minor. Surprise, surprise, it was all of the Cav lads spending our last night in the regimental prison.

The jail was a small building with individual holding cells. It was old school: wool blankets; gray bricks; high, barred windows. The place reeked of polish as it was continually being cleaned by the prisoners. It was run by a huge Irish Royal Military Police (RMP) sergeant, who was six foot six and built like a brick shithouse. He went to town on us, making us run round and round with yellow helmets and crappy old webbing on. He marched us out to this sandhill and made us pound up and down it while carrying weights. We had old boots on that didn't have any laces in so the whole thing was an epic.

Once we got back to the prison, Nick muttered something under his breath to me and the RMP took it the wrong way, deciding both Nick and I were taking the mick out of him. He punished us both, making me stand with an old artillery shell pushed out above my head while Nick had to clean the ceiling with the floor bumper. We were there for six hours being thrashed, before being sent back to our cells. We didn't manage any sleep that night as we still had to sort out our kit for our passing-out parade.

The big day arrived and Granddad was there beaming at me. Mum, Keith and my brother came to it as well. I felt such pride marching onto the drill square. It had been a long hard course, but I had a real sense of achievement now that it was over.

I won the prize for the fittest recruit, which really made my day. The rest of the occasion passed in a blur.

Before I knew it, I was back at home—and waiting to go to the riding school in Windsor, just outside of London.

3. Too Much Energy

When I arrived at the riding school in Windsor, the brief was pretty simple: keep your head down; don't get in trouble. But as a lad growing up in the country I'd led a sheltered life. While everyone else was doing sex, drugs and rock and roll, I was mucking out stables. Now the bright lights of London were calling me and, before I knew it, I was on a train heading into the "Big Smoke" for a night out.

Just a few hours after that, I was in Sam's nightclub in Regent Street, so drunk that the room was swaying and I couldn't keep track of the conversation going on around me. I'm not sure what happened next but it kicked off. Since that first fight in McDonald's, when I'd found out that I was actually quite handy with my fists, I hadn't exactly gone looking for trouble—but I never felt the need to back down either. Now, I ended up with four bouncers going at me. I steadily worked through each one, punching and kicking them until only one was left. I punched the last one and, as he dropped to the floor, I kicked him in the head to make sure he didn't get up.

I was feeling pretty pleased with myself but in the background I could hear heavy breathing and then the crowd parted like the Red Sea. The fifth and final bouncer had arrived. Standing in front of me was the biggest guy I have ever seen in my life. His head was dropped and his chest was heaving; he looked like a buffalo.

"You," he said, pointing at me.

"Fuck it," I thought to myself. I drew back as if I was about to run away—and then charged straight at him. I jumped in the air and then whacked him as hard as I could on the head. I tried to pile-drive his head into his shoulders. By the time I'd hit the ground, he had collapsed in a heap. I stood there stunned, thinking, "I can't believe that worked."

The sound of sirens broke my trance and I realized all of my mates had already legged it. I started running—but the police were quickly on my tail and they caught up with me at Piccadilly Circus. Now, anyone who says that the police treat you fairly can fuck off as far as I'm concerned. They rammed me with their car and drove with me on the hood for over thirty feet until I slid off. Then they got out and kicked the shit out of my ribs with their knees, so that no one could see what they were doing. After that, they bundled me in the back of the car and did a slow drive-by of the club, so that the doormen could ID me. The big guy was up on his feet and he ran over and started rocking the car until we sped off.

I'd never been arrested before so didn't know what to expect, but for some reason the police decided not to charge me and I was handed over to the Royal Military Police. They took me to Knightsbridge Barracks and moved me from cell to cell before handing me over to my regiment. I was on my regiment's books but I hadn't even formally arrived yet as I was on the riding course. I was flapping, convinced I'd be thrown out before I even got to my regiment.

The next morning, I was marched in front of the regimental second-in-command. He looked up from his paperwork and said, "Welcome to the Household Cavalry Regiment. This is your last warning . . . Dismissed."

That was it. All very bizarre, but a big relief. I did a bit of shopping in London and then headed back to Windsor to finish the riding course.

The course was largely a basic equestrian program: how to ride a horse and how to look after it. It was designed to build confidence in your riding ability, so there were some unique aspects to it—like going over jumps without holding your reins. I was already experienced with horses so the course passed pretty effortlessly for me and soon enough I was back at Knightsbridge Barracks, where I found out that I was posted to the 2 Troop of the Blues and Royals.

The 2 Troop is known as the Farmyard Troop. Initially I thought it was because we were all country boys—but it turned out that it was because all of the lads were maggots who couldn't give a fuck.

Unfortunately, the Army has a bit of a tradition of always picking on the new guys. One morning, I was quietly minding my own business, grooming my horse, when one of the senior troopers, who was running late, arrived flustered. He had just started to groom his horse when the handle snapped off his brush.

"Here, you can use mine if you want," I said, offering him the brush.

"Fuck off," he replied.

I went back to brushing my horse. Suddenly, I became aware of another trooper moving toward me. He punched me from behind and started whaling on me, punching me over and over again. I tried to protect myself but other troopers were joining in and, before I knew it, four of them were holding me down while the other one punched me.

"You live on the fourth floor, don't you?" he asked.

I nodded.

"Tonight, I'm coming to your room. Leave your door open. I'll fix you," he said, pointing in my face.

The lads all drifted off and I was left on the floor, thinking, "I was only trying to help."

I've always hated bullies and was more than ready to fight back. That night I waited in my room, door open.

He never came.

Ceremonial duty—the bulk of my job as a member of the Household Cavalry—was, I soon discovered, repetitive and tedious. We spent the whole time preparing for the next parade: Trooping the Color, the State Opening of Parliament, the routine guarding of Buckingham Palace. It was never-ending and all of it involved polishing kit and rehearsing. After two years of working with dross and a skull-crushingly boring routine, I'd had enough. All I wanted to do was soldier but I knew that was never going to happen in Knightsbridge.

So one sunny autumn day I packed my belongings into my rucksack and went AWOL, catching the ferry from Dover to Calais, where I headed to the nearest police station.

"I want to join the Foreign Legion," I said to the duty constable.

I was convinced that I'd read somewhere that this was what you were supposed to do but the constable just stared at me, then waved at the door in a gesture that said, "Go away." I walked out of the police station, now unsure of my next step. In the end, I caught a ferry back to Dover and stayed in a hotel for the night, before heading back to France the next day. I walked into the same police station and stated my intentions again. This time he at least acknowledged my presence. It turned out that they got so many people trying to join the Legion in haste that they gave them the brush-off at first to see who was really committed.

He explained in broken English that the Legion wouldn't come and collect one man, so I would have to wait until there were more of us. He took all of my belongings and gave me a boilersuit and a blanket before showing me to a cell and telling me that I could sleep there. I spent the next week mopping out the police station and weeding an old people's home for cash, which gave me enough money to buy some food. By the end of the week, two Germans, a Frenchman and a Spaniard had rocked up, so there were now enough of us.

Early on Saturday morning, a legionnaire arrived in a crappy army truck to collect us. All of our personal belongings were loaded into the back in clear bags and then he gestured for us boilersuited recruits to get in the back too. The police constable gave us a bottle of water and an apple each and then we were sealed in.

We drove for hours. It was freezing and no one spoke English. I must have dropped off because I woke with a start as the tailgate crashed down and the legionnaire started shouting at us in French. I had no idea what he was saying but I could get the gist of it: "Get the fuck off my truck."

I had no clue where we were but there was a really strong smell of oak. As I rounded the truck I could see why. There was a set of huge wooden gates in front of us and as we approached another legionnaire opened them. Passing inside, I could see the guardroom to my left but I didn't want to stare so I kept my head down and went where pointed.

We were herded into a big waiting room with beds. I got the impression we would be there for a while. I sat on the end of a bed, staring at my bag of belongings. Everything I owned in the world was in that bag. "What the fuck am I doing here?" I thought to myself.

We were told to have something to eat, and a large pot of soup arrived. It literally looked like shit floating in a toilet. I decided to pass on the shit soup and eat my apple. The next dinner course arrived. This time it looked like little bits of shit in water. I was convinced the legionnaires were watching us through peepholes to see if we would eat it.

When we all turned in I picked a bed next to a wall. That way, if any fucker came for me, they had only one way to make their move.

It felt like I'd only just closed my eyes when I was jerked awake by a legionnaire banging a dustbin with a nightstick and shouting at us in French. We weren't allowed to leave the waiting room and there were only two sinks and one toilet with no cubicle. By picking the bed next to the wall, I had put myself next to the toilet. I looked over to see a half-naked German having a dump next to me. He wiped his arse, gave me the thumbs-up and then walked off.

Breakfast arrived. It looked like the same stuff from last night but now it had some color in it. I was too hungry to care anymore so I wolfed it down.

My boilersuit stank. When the door opened and fresh air and sunlight poured in, I felt like I'd been released from prison. A legionnaire gestured for us to form a line outside, in front of a hatch in the wall that looked like a barn window. He showed us how to stand properly. Back straight, head up, look straight forward, arms down by your sides, palms touching your legs while your fingers are locked straight. The hatch banged open and we were gestured forward in turn, handing over our personal belongings and being given a tracksuit, eighties-style school trainers, three white T-shirts, six pairs of socks, a metal cup, plate and water bottle. We were also allowed to keep our wash kit, less "smellies."

Once we all had our kit we were shown into another room

with twenty beds in it. The room was full of other "walk-ins," as they are known, from all over France. I befriended a Scottish lad called John, who seemed like a good guy. He was a freelance skydiving photographer who had sold all of his kit to join the Legion.

There were now twenty of us in yellow tracksuits, mainly Germans and Eastern Europeans. We were led off for the obligatory haircut and waited silently in line. One lad started talking and a legionnaire casually walked over and punched him in the sternum. The lad collapsed to his knees in pain and was dragged out of the line. Fortunately, John spoke some French so he kept me on the straight and narrow.

The food was still terrible and it looked like the officers ate better than us.

It was a long day. We had lectures on the dos and don'ts, the same speech delivered in the native tongue of everyone present. Despite the mattress being full of hay and the bed being as hard as stone, I slept like a log that night.

In the morning, a few people were sporting cuts and bruises to their faces. I headed to the bathroom to shave and bumped into John, whose nose was halfway across his face. He quickly told me that he'd been jumped in the toilets the previous night and beaten up by some Poles and Germans. Some of those lads were big units so I decided that I wouldn't use the toilet at night; I'd piss in my water bottle instead. I just needed to remember to empty it out when I was in a rush.

Theft was happening all of the time. Every morning something else had gone missing. They lined us up and gave us a warning about not stealing kit. Then a legionnaire walked down the line and punched each of us in the sternum to reinforce the point.

The first week was all interviews and medicals. We rolled

into the second week—and that's when things started to get nasty. They introduced us to the training complex, which looked like a relic from the Roman Empire. There was an oval sand track round the edge and in the middle a sort of coliseum, with all kinds of gym kit on it. They absolutely thrashed us. Funnily enough, it was the large Poles and Germans who suffered the most. They might be able to beat people up in the toilets but they couldn't run for shit.

I was in the dinner queue with John when a huge legionnaire came over and introduced himself. He was a Brit, an ex-paratrooper, and he was massive. He took us to one side to give us some warnings and advice, and although I thought he was being friendly I was still slightly wary. Suddenly, he dropped his trousers and showed us his arse. It was covered in cigarette burns.

"What the fuck?" I asked.

"Just a heads-up," he said. "When the Legion pays you, they take most of the money back; it means that you don't have any money to desert with. They give you it back when you go on leave. Anyway, I decided to hide my money up my arse in a cigar tube. That didn't go down well. They pinned me down and used cigarette burns to loosen up my arse cheeks."

He pulled up his trousers and walked off. John and I just looked at each other. I could see the Germans and the Poles staring as well.

I must have been one of the lucky ones—or not seen as weak—because I soon got tired of pissing in my water bottle and started using the toilets at night, but I never got done over. I don't know how the Germans had the energy to beat people up anyway; I was exhausted every night.

*

Once all of the interviews, medicals and fitness tests were over, we were sent to the Farm, which is where the Legion conducts its basic training. I wanted to go to 2 REP, the 2nd Foreign Parachute Regiment, which is airborne, but I was told that only the top two recruits were allowed to pick where they go. The rest go where they are sent.

On Wednesday morning I was marched into the interview room. It was a bleached white room with three people in suits sitting behind a table. They had all the paperwork I had filled in laid out in front of them. One of the suits spoke.

"We made it clear that we don't take men who are AWOL; we have checked with Interpol and you are absent from the British Army."

"I know, but I was hoping you might bend the rules," I replied.

"Well, we don't."

That was that. Before I knew it I was back in the original corridor in front of the barn window in my boxer shorts, feeling sick to my core; I didn't want to leave. The hatch opened and I gave back my pile of issued clothing as they handed me my clear plastic bag. I could see everyone else's clothes were separated into piles. It turned out they sold the clothes to charity shops.

I got dressed. A legionnaire opened the big gates and I walked out, inhaling that oak smell for the last time. They gave me some travel money to get back to England, and directions; we were just outside Paris. The gate closed behind me. My Foreign Legion dreams were over.

By late afternoon I was back in England. My money was gone, I was starving and I needed a drink. I was planning to jump on a train to London to rejoin my regiment; I couldn't see what other option I had. I started walking across fields, hoping for a short cut to the station, but soon got lost. It was raining and I was cold and wet. Eventually I found a road and started walking down it. An HGV lorry passed in the other direction, turned around and pulled up behind me, flashing its lights. The passenger door opened.

"Where are you going?" asked the driver.

"The station," I replied. "I'm trying to get to London."

"Hop in; I'll give you a lift."

I wouldn't normally but I was soaking, covered in mud and frankly having a shit day. I clambered in. Once we started moving, the driver introduced himself as Butch.

"You know the station will be shut at this time of night."

"That's all right; I'll just sleep there until the morning."

"I bet you don't have any money, do you?"

I shook my head.

"Look, why don't you come back with me?" he said. "Do some odd jobs and I'll pay you. Get yourself a bit of cash to get back to London. What do you say?"

I didn't really have much choice at that stage. I nodded. "All right, then."

We pulled up at a depot full of lorries. Butch lived in a static caravan on site and things looked all right, quite a nice setup. I could see myself doing odd jobs round there.

It turned out that Butch was an ex-para. He'd moved into the caravan after his wife had left him.

He gestured me inside and the first thing I noticed was that everything was burned. He had half-melted picture frames scattered around, half-burned books; even the door on his microwave was warped. It couldn't have been very safe. He obviously noticed my reaction.

"House fire: that's why I had to move into the caravan," he said. "Right, let's get you a change of clothes. I can wash the others before you go back to London."

"Cheers," I replied, as he headed off to the back of the caravan.

I was hoping that he might have a spare tracksuit, but he returned with two pairs of shorts: one set Lycra and the others the tiniest set of tennis shorts I had ever seen. I picked the Lycra ones and got changed while he started cooking.

"Chicken in red wine sauce," he announced, handing me a bottle of Bud. Soon I was sitting at a melted picnic table, with a melted knife and fork in front of me, wearing Lycra shorts and a white T-shirt, drinking my beer and tucking into a plate of hot food.

"Do you like porn?" he asked.

"What man doesn't?"

He pressed play on the video player and two blonde lesbians servicing each other popped up on the screen. I suddenly remembered that I was in Lycra shorts; there was no way I could hide an erection. "Green, green grass," I started thinking to myself. "Buses are red, Margaret Thatcher on a wet day."

Butch snapped me out of my chanting. "The job I want you to do is clean my oven," he said, placing a duster and a can of Pledge on the table. "I'll give you thirty quid."

"Don't take the piss," I replied. "You can't clean an oven with a fucking duster and Pledge."

I didn't want to stand up as I was trying to keep my boner under the table. There was a pause before Butch just shrugged. "Right, I'm ready for bed," he said.

"I'll just crash here," I said, tapping the hard seat.

"No, there is a spare room," he replied, gesturing to a door.

I headed over, opened the door and saw one bed and my clothes dumped on the floor. As I turned around, Butch closed in on me and grabbed my bollocks.

"Do you want some fun?" he breathed, his excitement plain in his voice.

"Fuck off," I screamed, and head-butted him.

He collapsed to the floor, his head bouncing off the side of the sink. "Fuck," I thought to myself. "I've killed him."

I tore off out of the door and was halfway across the lorry park when I remembered that I was in Lycra shorts with a semi-boner. I ran back into the caravan, where Butch was still in a heap on the floor, moaning and rolling slightly. I grabbed my clothes, took fifty quid out of his wallet and kicked him in the nuts for good measure.

"Have fun with that, you wanker," I said to him. "No wonder your house got burned down, you fucking pervert."

I walked for a bit and then flagged a taxi down. I slept at the station until it opened and then I got the first train back to London.

My regiment gave me fourteen days in jail for going AWOL. After my time in the regimental prison, things pretty quickly went back to the way they were, and I was reminded of all the reasons I went AWOL in the first place. One day, I was called into an office by a senior NCO (noncommissioned officer).

"Do you want to earn some extra money debt collecting?" he asked.

He gave me the afternoon to think about it. Having looked at my empty bank account, I returned. "The answer's yes," I told him. "Where and when?"

He told me to go to a certain nightclub at a certain time and date where I'd be meeting a massive black guy. Apparently I couldn't miss him. I got to the club at the right time, bought a drink and waited, keeping my head down. A mountain of a man approached me.

"Craig?" he asked.

"Yes," I replied.

"I'm Terry."

The first meeting was short and sweet. A chance for him to see if he liked me.

"I'm the one that does the bulk of it and I do all of the talking," Terry explained. "You're just there to lend a hand if need be. I'll be in touch."

He walked off.

A week later I got a phone call and Terry told me he had his first job for me. Fortunately, I had the day off. I met Terry two hours later in the Bunch of Grapes pub near Harrods, where he told me the job was in Ilford and the guy owed him a lot of money.

We climbed into his big black Warrior four-by-four; it was pretty much the only car he would have fitted in. While driving, he explained that this guy had mucked him about for three months and had had enough warnings. Forty-five minutes later, we were there.

Terry wasted no time once we arrived, laying into the guy. I was not that impressed with what I saw, to be honest. It was just old-fashioned bullying. Back in the car, Terry didn't look like he'd even broken a sweat and he certainly wasn't show-ing any remorse. He handed me £400. As I had been told: easy money.

"You okay?" he asked.

"Yeah, I just haven't seen anything like that before," I replied.

"If people don't pay and keep fucking around . . . that is when they call me in."

"I bet they pay up then."

"Normally."

I just stared at the floor.

"You don't want me coming round to your house twice," he said.

We drove back to London in silence.

I didn't hear anything for a month and was about to go home on a forty-eight-hour leave pass when I was told there was a message in the guardroom for me, to meet Terry in the Bunch of Grapes. I walked in and spotted him at the bar.

"I need someone I can trust for a job," he said. "Tomorrow. It's in Oxford; £400 again."

"How do you know I've got the weekend off?" I asked.

"I've got my ways."

This was all slightly worrying. I didn't want to moan that I had a forty-eight-hour leave pass and was heading home. He didn't strike me as the sort of bloke who would give a shit. He picked me up in a Mercedes four-by-four this time and I slept for the entire journey. Terry woke me up ten minutes before we arrived.

We drove down a cul-de-sac and it looked like there was a guy waiting outside for us. I began to worry about an ambush and I started checking behind us, and to the left and right. My heart was in my mouth.

"That's strange," said Terry, spotting the guy. "Don't worry. This should be quick. In and out."

Terry swung open his car door and headed to the front of the Merc. As I got out, I was hit from behind by a second bloke who appeared from nowhere. My face slammed into the car door and I started to fall, getting kicked in the gut on my way down. Blood was pouring from a cut on my forehead and I was winded. I needed to get up fast.

My attacker was middle-aged and overweight, but fast and powerful. He came in to kick me again and I lashed out, kicking him in the shins. He went down. By this point, Terry had spotted what was going on and ran over, clothes-lining the fucker as he tried to get up. He went down again and stayed down, moaning a bit.

Terry stormed over to the first guy. "Pay up, you cunt," he screamed into his face. The bloke disappeared into one of the houses, coming back with a large envelope, which he reluctantly handed over.

"Let's go before the police arrive," I said urgently. The last thing I needed was to get in trouble with the regiment again; I doubted I had any more lives left to lose.

After driving for a while, Terry pulled into a lay-by. He looked me in the face. "This isn't for you, is it, Craig? I can see it in your eyes."

"No," I admitted, shaking my head.

Nothing more was said as we drove back. He dropped me off where he'd picked me up. I was covered in blood.

"If you ever need me, just call," Terry said, handing me a business card. "Oh, and I don't have to remind you to keep your mouth shut about what you've seen, do I?"

He really didn't. I was planning to forget I'd ever laid eyes on him. He drove off and I never saw him again. I found out subsequently that he went to prison for shooting someone. I'm glad I left when I did, although it was a shame to give up the sideline in some ways, as the money was really handy.

Months passed and it was total fucking Groundhog Day. On guard duty: one day on, one day off. Sat on a horse, outside a national monument, with tourists taking your picture for hours at a time. On your day off, you were expected to clean and polish your kit. We called it "doing the bounce." I wanted to be a farrier; that's why I joined the fucking Cavalry. But with all the trouble I kept getting into, my face never seemed to fit and they wouldn't give me the chance.

Then in August 1993, when I was up in Edinburgh for the Military Tattoo, Granddad died in his sleep. He'd had a couple of strokes and become quite frail, but it was still a shock. I never got the chance to say goodbye and I couldn't shake the feeling that there was something he'd been wanting to tell me. I still wish he was alive, especially so that he could see all that I've achieved. I owe so much of it to him. The loss tore my soul apart and, coming on top of my frustration with the Army, I could feel the pent-up rage growing inside me.

I had a friend in the squadron called Steve, who always had a black eye or broken nose. Although I kept asking what had happened to him, he would never say. Then, one evening, he took me to a gym in Euston. The gym in camp was rubbish—one dumbbell, a bench and a wonky mirror that the Army wives liked as it made them look slim. I thought maybe he was taking me to a flashier joint, but as we walked up the stairs I could see it was a proper spit-and-sawdust affair. There was good kit, though; my kind of gym. We kept walking to what I thought would be the changing rooms. People were saying hello to Steve as we passed through a door and then made our way down a corridor, through another door and then down some stairs.

I found myself in a huge room with a boxing ring in the middle, with seating all around it. There was blood on the canvas and sawdust on the floor. The room was absolutely packed with people and was a real sweatbox.

Steve turned to me. "You want to know what I do?"

I nodded, although I had an inkling.

"This," he said, sweeping his hand across the room. "Prize fighting."

"How does it work?" I asked, my brain already whirring.

"You can choose if you want to have someone in your corner or go alone. You have three fights a night. No head-butting, kicking or biting. Four rounds of five minutes until someone is knocked out or quits. You can use elbows, knees and—of course—fists."

I looked round the room, taking it all in. Steve continued, "You get £350 per fight. Top tip, though: lose the second or the last fight. If you don't, the pikeys will think you're a cocky fucker, fill you in outside and take the money back. They break your hands as well."

Steve pointed to a small hole in the wall. "That's where you get your money or place your bets."

You would never know any of it was there. Decent gym upstairs and a shitty, sweaty boxing ring downstairs. There were some right dickheads in the crowd, flashing their cash around. I could see the pikeys watching them.

A whistle blew and two fighters came out of opposite doors and approached the ring. They weren't in boxing gear, just tracksuits and jeans. The noise of people cheering and booing was deafening. There was a referee who started the fight and I watched for a few minutes before Steve tapped me on the arm.

"So, do you want a bit of it?" he asked.

"Fuck it," I thought to myself. "Yes, mate," I replied.

Steve introduced me to a short man called Nigel, who ran the business. He looked me up and down, smiled and nodded.

"You look all right," he said. "Can you fight next Wednesday?"

I was stammering a bit so Steve answered for me. "Yes."

For the next two years, I fought. I won and lost; that is the nature of the game. My opponents got bigger and better— Bulgarians and Poles with hard heads and harder fists. I had to have my nose reset four times and I lost a few teeth—but I inflicted more damage than I took.

My regiment got utterly sick of me. I was constantly on parade with black eyes and a broken nose. In the end, they realized that they had to do something to bleed off my excess energy and calm me down.

Their solution was to off-load me on to P-Company, which is the physical selection process for the airborne forces. Three weeks of endurance marches, assault courses and generally getting thrashed.

Beforehand, I found out as much as I could about what the course involved, through books and literature, to make sure I was prepared. From my research, I thought it sounded much more like my cup of tea than bloody guard duty. The airborne forces have a reputation for being tough and I thought I would fit in. This was my chance to get away from all of the bullshit. I couldn't wait to get started.

There are no hills in London, so to prepare I trained at a local tower block. With a rucksack weighing thirty-five pounds on my back, I ran up thirty-two flights of stairs, and then ran down again. I did this for hours at a time. I was the first person from the Knightsbridge regiment to attend P-company—and I passed with flying colors.

Once I had passed, the regiment decided it was time to get me out of London, away from all the drama and the fighting. In 1995, they posted me to Windsor. Windsor is known as the "green" side of the Cavalry. While Knightsbridge is all about shiny boots and parades, Windsor is all about soldiering.

I finally felt like I was on my way.

4. The Balkans

Bang, bang, smack.

I fell back over a bale of hay. Opening my eyes, I saw blue sky above me. There was a taste of copper in my mouth, so I turned my head to spit out a mouthful of blood. I could feel myself being lifted up . . . my vision came into focus just in time to see a fat hairy man covered in blood lifting me high up off the grass. I smacked him in the guts, got to my feet to move to my left and then followed up the gut punch by smashing him in the back of the head.

It didn't work; this fucker just wouldn't go down.

I smacked his face and then his ribs, but it still didn't seem to register. I had to think fast if I was going to win this fight.

I was in a farmer's field, in a makeshift ring made out of hay bales, and things weren't looking good. As long as it was fist to fist I was coming out on top, but now that the fight had turned dirty the odds seemed to be swinging in my opponent's favor.

He stepped into my space and landed a head-butt right in my face. I crashed to the ground and watched helplessly as things went dark.

Seconds later, the light came back—but I knew it was over.

I tapped out and then dragged myself to a hay bale, where I sat and took stock, before heading back to my car. I was used to patching myself up by now and always carried a first-aid kit. I rummaged around until I found some gauze, and then sat on the hood and tried to stop my lip from bleeding.

A couple of the spectators drifted over and one of them shook my hand.

"You had that, mate, right up until he nutted you."

I could only nod in agreement.

"That bloke got beat a week ago and was told in no uncertain terms that he needed to win."

In this business, there were no unsubtle hints. I spat out some more blood and wiggled a few teeth, just to check that they were staying in there . . . this time, at least.

I'd been at Windsor for a few months now. I was in the Guided Weapons Troop. There were twelve of us and we had four Spartan armored vehicles, each equipped with a Swingfire wire-guided anti-tank rocket. These light armored vehicles required a three-man crew. They were small and space was tight, but they were highly mobile.

It was a good bunch of lads and the whole troop was quite old school. Minimum bullshit and problems dealt with in a grown-up way. I liked it.

The main reason they sent me to Windsor was to get me away from the fighting. It didn't really work, though. It wasn't long before I was on leave and a bit low on cash, so the offer of a few fights seemed quite appealing. But after getting thrashed in the field, I climbed into my white Rover. Looking in the rear view mirror, I straightened my broken nose. Again. Seeing the cut over one eye and my bleeding gums, I thought, "That's it, that's the last one. I'm too old to keep doing this. I'm fucked." And that was my last prize fight.

While on leave, I was staying with Mum. I only had a few weeks before I would be heading off to Bosnia for my first tour, so I thought it would be okay. It was fine being at hers at first, but after a while she started to make me feel more and more unwelcome. I think she felt that I had left home now and so shouldn't be staying for weeks on end. The problem was that I had nowhere else to go.

I spent most of my time trying to stay out of her hair, hanging out in the local gym or going on the piss with Tom, who was working at the animal shelter. On my last night of leave, Tom convinced me to go to Church. Not the nice variety where you kneel down and pray, but the nightclub version in Cheltenham: an old church that has basically had a bar added to it.

I ended up talking to a girl at the bar who told me she was there with her sister. Tom was shitfaced by this point and, as I looked over the girl's shoulder, I could see that he was on the dance floor with a girl in a wheelchair, pushing his foot into the back of it, wheeling her around and bumping her up and down in time with the music.

"Where's your sister?" I asked the girl next to me, shouting to be heard over the music.

"She's in a wheelchair and I think she's on the dance floor; I hope she's strapped in."

As she finished speaking she looked over toward the dance floor and saw Tom and her sister. Her jaw dropped open.

Tom came over to us, sweating and grinning, pushing the girl in the wheelchair. He leaned in to speak into my ear. "I think I'm in here."

I just smiled and nodded.

The girls had a quick chat and then told us they both needed the toilet.

"I'll help," said Tom quickly.

He wheeled the girl off, with her sister in tow, and then proceeded to drag her, still in the chair, backward up two flights of stairs. Ten minutes later, they bumped back down the stairs and joined me at the bar. The poor girl looked all over the place, her eyes a bit glassy with shock.

"Fucking hell, that's hard work," Tom told me.

Looking down, I could see blood on his shirt.

"Where did the blood come from?"

"There was a queue for the ladies so I carried her into the men's. When we came out, some bloke was sat in her wheel-chair. I put her on the floor and, er, *convinced* him to get out. I think one of the wheels might be buckled, you know."

"Of course it's buckled; you dragged it up two flights of stairs."

I could see the girls talking to the door staff and they didn't look happy. "Mate, I think it's time to go," I told Tom.

We nipped out a fire exit and made a clean getaway.

The next morning, I woke up with a pounding head, still in last night's clothes. I had lunch with Mum and we were having quite a pleasant time, avoiding the fact that I was off to Bosnia, when I destroyed the mood.

"Mum, I need some money to get back to camp. Could you lend me some?"

It was like flicking a switch. She went nuts, screaming and shouting, and threw a plate of hot food at me that went straight over my head and hit the wall.

"Fuck this," I said, standing up to leave.

She was still yelling as I grabbed my bag and walked with my head down to the station, planning to jump the train to London and then Windsor as I had no money.

I was sitting on a bench at the station with two black eyes

and a broken nose when Mum suddenly appeared, walked straight up to me and gave me a hug.

"I'm sorry," she said. "Stay safe."

She thrust £60 into my hand and walked off.

As soon as I got back, I was summoned to the squadron leader's office. I marched in and saluted.

"You've been fighting again, haven't you, Harrison?" he said straight away.

There was a painful silence.

"You were sent here to stop the fighting and it's obvious you have been doing it again."

"Think fast, Craig," I thought to myself. "No, sir," I told him, as straight-faced as possible.

"What?" he asked incredulously. "Look at your face."

"It was my horse, sir. While on leave I went riding and I fell off."

That would have to do. The squadron leader just stared at me.

"I better not find out you're lying to me, trooper."

"Yes, sir."

"Dismissed."

I marched out of his office. The sergeant major cornered me in the corridor.

"Fell off your horse?"

"Yes, sir."

"What happened to your knuckles?"

I just stared at my boots.

"Go on, fuck off and stay out of trouble."

Our troop spent the next two weeks sorting out the vehicles, which were going to be shipped to Split and then driven on low loaders to Banja Luka. We would meet the vehicles there.

Once the vehicles had gone, we did some training—PT (physical training), going on the ranges and mine-awareness packages—plus the inevitable administration and paperwork. People wrote letters to family and left them sealed in camp, in case they didn't make it back. I couldn't be bothered with all that, as now that Granddad had gone I didn't think anyone would particularly mourn my passing. I did actually receive a letter from Mum, a single piece of paper with "fuck off" written on it.

We were allowed out over this period so, of course, we spent every spare minute in the local pub getting drunk. The Lord Raglan was right next door to camp and did lock-ins all of the time.

Departure day arrived and all of the families and girl-friends turned up to wave us off. Obviously no one came for me, so I climbed straight on the coach and stared at the scene, wishing it was different.

We were bussed to Brize Norton. We'd been told we would fly by TriStar aircraft, which looks like an easyJet plane but is gray and held together by tape and chewing gum. But on arrival at the airfield we walked straight past the TriStar and headed toward a C-130 Hercules. No luxury flight for us, just six hours of webbing seats and the stench of aviation fuel. The last time I was on one of these I was jumping out of it on my parachute-training course with P-Company.

The noise is deafening in the back of a Hercules, so much so that it's pointless trying to listen to music as the drone of the engines drowns it out. You also have to hope that no one throws up because if one person does it starts a chain reaction. Before you know it most of the aircraft will be being sick.

We had a safety briefing and then took off. Once we'd stopped climbing, the loadmaster opened the back ramp a bit to let some air in (the plane was flying low enough that it didn't need to pressurize). I needed a piss so I clambered down to the ramp where there was a little tube to pee in. I started the flow, closed my eyes and leaned back a touch, enjoying the sensation.

Over the drone of the engines I suddenly heard shouting. I opened my eyes to see people yelling and waving at me. The draft from the opening on the back ramp was causing my wee to spray into the aircraft—all over the lads near the back.

"Sorry," I shouted, and waved an apology. Great, I was relatively new to the squadron, and I'd just pissed over half of them.

It was a long, cramped flight and—for some mysterious reason—there was a stench of urine. Once we landed, we all tried to get the feeling back in our legs. As I stepped off the back ramp, the heat hit me straight away.

We were crammed in a bus with no air conditioning and driven for about an hour and a half to Banja Luka. The country was a real mixture in terms of its landscape. We drove through a lot of wooded areas and then through a village that was very alpine in appearance. More woodland and then suddenly a really developed town with apartment blocks dotted over the hillside appeared. It was like a mini Swindon dumped in the middle of the Forest of Dean.

We were to be based out of a place nicknamed "the Potato Factory," an old building on the outskirts of Banja Luka. As we arrived, we could see that our vehicles were already there and were now painted white with "SFOR," for Stabilization Force, written in big black letters on the side.

We had a few briefings upon arrival and were then shown around. Out the back of the factory were two converted shipping containers: one for washing in and the other with toilets. The accommodation was on the second floor and was cramped, with bunk beds jammed into each room and not much space to store our kit. The ops room was downstairs. Just over the road was the cookhouse and next to that was the tank park. That was it for the next six months.

It was hot even at night. The bunk beds squeaked. I felt like I was on a boat if the guy on the bottom bunk rolled around a lot. Nighttimes quickly drove me mad: the heat, the squeaking, the movement.

By the time we arrived the country was coming out of almost three years of bloody conflict. The whole Balkan area was in a state of turmoil after the break-up of the former Yugoslavia. The Bosnian war had kicked off in 1992, after Bosnia-Herzegovina declared independence, with the Bosniaks, Croats and Serbs fighting over territory. Although the war was now over, in theory, the locals needed a bit of encouragement to stick to the peace treaties, so SFOR, a NATO-led multinational peacekeeping force, was deployed to deter hostilities between the warring factions. Basically: stop them all fighting so that the country could redevelop. Our job was to conduct patrols around the local area to "show a presence." Basically: convince people not to do bad things and leave each other alone—by trying to be in the middle. Also: to provide reassurance, just by being there. It was fairly tenuous and very hard to measure success. We headed out every day in the vehicles, drove around, waved and had a chat.

Initially, we had to learn the area, and quite quickly discovered a waterfall and a river nearby. This became our troop secret; we didn't tell anyone else about it. We started sending false location reports to the ops room and would then head to the river to freshen up and cool off. Our cunning plan quickly unravelled though. We had been told not to pee in the water but one of the lads did and something swam up his dick. He was in serious pain so we had to tell the medics where we'd been. That put a stop to that one. It was good while it lasted though.

There wasn't a huge amount of threat to us. The aggression and anger we saw in the Balkans was directed toward the other warring factions. There was no threat from IEDs (improvised explosive devices) and although we heard that the Serbs had mines it was unlikely they would use them against us. We did hear stories from Kosovo about the Serbs stringing up mines in trees with activation rods and then making Albanians run through them. That must have been horrific.

Shelling took place—but over our heads. We were down in a valley occupied by Serbs on one side and members of the Army of the Republic of Bosnia on the other: the two sides liked to lob shells at each other. Although they wouldn't deliberately target us, we nevertheless remained on a state of high alert. One day I was in the basement of the Potato Factory in our improvised gym, working up a sweat on the punchbag, when I heard a commotion outside. I tried to ignore it. Suddenly, there was a series of bangs in succession so I grabbed my rifle and ran outside.

A couple of locals had thrown some hand grenades over the wall; luckily none of them had gone off. The QRF (Quick Reaction Force) had caught two of the lads. The banging was the lads from the QRF running across wooden pallets, which had then fallen over and hit the wall.

My first patrol on "operations" came around quickly. My troop was tasked with going down to a river and retrieving a dead body. All four vehicles would go. I was driving one of the Spartans and the troop was commanded by a corporal of horse called Dave (corporal of horse is the Cav's equivalent of sergeant). Dave was a top guy who never seemed to get stressed about anything.

He might not have been stressed—but I was. My heart was in my mouth as we pulled up next to the river. I'd never seen a dead body before so there were a lot of emotions rolling around in my mind: fear, anxiety, yet also a macabre sense of curiosity.

There was a crowd of locals gathered at the scene. "Take the interpreter and tell them all to pull back," Dave told me.

I did as instructed. Once we got them back a decent distance and the troop was in all-round defense, Dave turned back to me. "Grab your rifle and helmet and come with me."

I followed him for about thirty yards down a dirt track to the river. The first thing that hit me was the smell; it practically burned my nostrils. I'd smelt dead animals before but this was multiplied by ten.

As we got closer, I could see the body on the river bank: a man dressed in a tracksuit sat upright, braced against a tree. His arms had been tied behind his back, stretched round the trunk, and his stomach had started to bloat. His face was blue and dark red. There was a very small hole on one temple where a bullet had entered . . . and a fist-sized hole on the other temple where the bullet had exited. His brain had fallen out and part of it was next to his shoulder; the rest must have washed away in the river.

As I got closer still, I could see that his eyes were open. They were bloodshot, cold and lifeless, like doll's eyes staring at me. I don't know why but I wanted to feel him. I reached out and touched his cheek with the back of my hand—it was cold and hard.

We had to wait for the military police to arrive. They charged in like a SWAT team, waving their weapons around and shouting "move" to each other while bounding forward.

"This man's been dead for days," one of them said.

"No shit, Sherlock," I replied.

"This is a crime scene," another one shouted at us.

Dave and I just looked at each other and raised our eyebrows.

"Right, fuck this," said Dave, walking off. "We're out of here. Come on, Craig. Let's leave the experts to it."

Two months went by and not much happened. We patrolled a bit, guarded our little base, ate, slept—that's about it. All of the British forces moved to a new, big base called "the Metal Factory," which had proper living compartments with three beds in, a decent gym and a much better cookhouse. We didn't have to wear our helmets and body armor when we moved about and our weapons were kept in an armory, so it was a pretty easy life.

The only downside was the smell. The displaced locals had a camp on the other side of the road to the factory and as time went on the smell got worse and worse. A few of us were tasked to find out where it was coming from. It turned out that the locals were burning dead bodies wrapped in plastic.

Two weeks later, our troop was ordered to set up a base north of Banja Luka. It was two hours' drive away and we did a rotation of two weeks there and two weeks back at the Metal Factory. The change of scenery helped the time go faster and it was nice to get away from the rat race of the main camp.

One day at the Metal Factory, I was tasked with driving the commanding officer (CO) to a meeting at the SFOR headquarters at Camp Ilidza, which was based in a Sarajevo suburb. It was a long, tedious drive. Once we got there I dropped him off and found somewhere to park the Land Rover. I settled down to wait, absent-mindedly watching a small group of Gurkhas about twenty yards away, who were stacking mines into piles. It looked like old, dilapidated ordnance from the war. An officer approached and started shouting at them, while pointing. All I caught was, "Not here . . . over there."

"Poor fuckers," I thought to myself. It was a tough enough job stacking heavy objects in this heat without some knob coming over to gob off at you.

I was just starting to close my eyes, thinking I might have a little nap, when there was a huge explosion. The Land Rover rocked, my window shattered, and I heard a *thunk* as something smashed into my door. There was a pattering sound, like rain pouring down on the vehicle.

All I could see was smoke where the officer and the Gurkhas had been standing just a moment ago.

I opened my door and stepped out, my ears ringing slightly. Glancing down, I saw what had smashed into my door: a boot, with a foot still in it. I picked it up, put it on the hood and ran over to where the guys had been. There was just a huge crater—no sign of anyone.

Looking around, I could see that my Land Rover was peppered with shrapnel and covered in blood. The three guys had been vaporized. The sound of "rain" had actually been blood and body parts hitting the vehicle.

I stood there feeling helpless, almost unable to take the scene in.

People started to arrive within seconds, although it felt longer. A medic ran over to me.

"Are you all right?" he asked.

All I could do was nod. I went back to my Land Rover and retrieved the boot. It was still smoldering. I found the medic and gave it to him, and then I went to sit down. The image of the foot in the boot was burned into my brain.

Dave, the troop leader, came to get me. He drove me back

to the Metal Factory and they gave me two days off. On the third day, I was summoned to speak to the RMPs. They wanted to find out what had happened and obviously I had had a ringside seat.

I went through it all again. It was only two days ago, but already it seemed like a lifetime. I described the sound of the rain hitting the roof, rain that turned out to be blood; that never leaves me. Even to this day, every time I am in the car and it starts to rain, I am instantly back there. I can't help but think of those poor fuckers, getting vaporized.

Midway through the tour, the locals decided that they wanted to thank us for helping them—so they dropped off a freezer's worth of pig and chicken feet. The chefs couldn't really think of anything to do with them, but I was keen on trying some local cuisine, so I asked the interpreter to make me a local dish using the chicken feet. It tasted absolutely terrible and I spent the remainder of the tour pretty much living on Scotch pies.

You get R&R (rest and recuperation) during a tour, and in Bosnia, instead of letting us go home for two weeks, they sent us off to a British Army base in the coastal town of Split for some adventure training. There was a whole spectrum of activities available and, like everyone else, I wanted to do something fun, relaxing and not too hard. I picked white-water rafting, as did most people, and much to my surprise I got it.

There were four of us going rafting. Dave, Ronnie, Paul and myself. Ronnie was from Newcastle and had one of the strongest Geordie accents I have ever heard. Paul was very quiet and into *World of Warcraft* games, which made him a bit odd in my books. We were told to wait outside the camp for a pickup.

We were mooching around the car park, waiting, when we heard a car backfire and then a crappy old yellow hatchback with a fake leather roof screeched to a halt in a cloud of dust. A bloke got out. "Iz youz here for ze trip?" he asked in broken English.

We just looked at each other.

"White-water rafting?" Ronnie asked him.

"Yez," he replied. "Jump in."

We all clambered in and he raced away. About forty-five minutes later he stopped in the middle of nowhere. We were next to a field and at the end of the field was a very small river, more of a big stream. You could cross it in six or seven strides and I could probably piss faster than it was flowing. The guy dragged a canvas bag from the boot and pulled out a deflated boat. He got an air canister and started inflating it.

"Go to ze back and chooze a helmet," he told us.

We looked in the boot and saw a big bucket full of helmets. There were a couple of cycling helmets, a hard hat from a construction site and one proper skateboard-type helmet. I ended up with a cycling helmet as it was the only one that fit.

We put on our swimming trunks and waited while the raft continued to inflate. About twenty minutes later it was ready and we put it on the water.

"Climb in," the bloke said, waving at us.

We all got in what could loosely be described as a dinghy. We weren't really going anywhere as the current was so slow and the water was so shallow that we were actually touching the bottom. The guy jumped in his car, reversed up to us and wound down his window.

"I meet you about two milez downriver," he announced, and then drove off.

There was a loud siren going off in the distance. We all just stared at each other.

"Well, this sucks," I said, sitting down in the boat. "This isn't exactly white-water rafting."

"Hold your horses," said Dave. "I think I've heard about this. They open the floodgates of the dam at certain times of the day to release water."

We sat there for about ten minutes. After that, we started to hear a rumbling sound off in the distance. As one, we turned and looked upstream. A wall of water was hurtling down the valley toward us. We all started scrabbling around, trying to get our feet into the foot straps, to find something to hold on to. Paul, the quiet guy, was shouting at the top of his lungs. I was now very, very scared, feeling completely helpless as a twenty-foot-high wall of water bore down upon us.

It hit us like a train. We were immediately launched downstream. Spinning, bobbing, dipping, moving at a frighteningly fast pace—it was absolutely terrifying. We hadn't got any oars so we all started desperately paddling with our hands, while trying to hang on. Huge trees passed us by in the water; at one point an old shed went zooming by.

"Hang on and paddle, hang on and paddle," Dave was frantically screaming.

Off in the distance, I could see the battered old yellow car. The guy was standing on the roof with a pair of binoculars, watching us. After ten minutes of sheer fear, fighting to keep the raft upright, we beached in a field near the car and the guy ran down to meet us.

"Good time . . . yes . . . good time . . . yes?" he kept repeating, nodding hard. He immediately undid the valve on the boat and the air rushed out, while we were still standing in the dinghy on shaking legs, speechless.

He packed everything away and then drove us back to the camp.

Not long after our trip, they stopped the white-water rafting. It was far too dangerous and just incredible that no one had been hurt. I spent the rest of my R&R doing as little as I could get away with. Frankly, I felt lucky to be alive.

Toward the end of the tour, HQ organized for us to shoot some captured weapons at a range they'd improvised in a valley. There was an array to choose from, mainly AK47s but also an old elephant gun. As I walked down the firing line, seeing what was on offer, the gun toward the end caught my eye. It looked like an elongated AK.

"What's that?" I asked the corporal who was running the range.

"Druganov SVD," he replied. "It's the Soviet sniper rifle."

It was the first sniper rifle I had ever played with. I had to say, I liked it. I liked it a lot. I got set up on the firing point and once I'd worked out the scope I quickly got my eye in. I fired at a solid tree trunk a couple of hundred yards away, practically splitting the tree in half.

The next rifle I had a go on was the AK47. The trigger was very, very sensitive and it made me even more worried about the way the locals casually walked around with their fingers on the mechanism.

The final weapon was the elephant gun, a double-barrel rifle with bullets that looked like they were meant for an anti-aircraft cannon. Ronnie decided to go first.

"What shall I aim for?" he asked me.

I grabbed a set of binos and looked downrange.

"Go for the tree I was firing the Druganov at," I told him.

He shouldered the rifle, and I trained the binos on the tree again. There was a huge boom to my left as the rifle went off. Nothing hit the tree.

"Ronnie, you dick, you've missed."

He didn't reply.

I looked over into a huge cloud of smoke. As it started to drift away, I could see that there was no one there. Ronnie was about twenty feet behind the firing point, lying on the floor with the elephant gun pointing directly up. He was gasping for air and looked pretty shocked. We all ran over to him.

"Are you okay?" I asked.

"Your turn," he said, handing me the gun.

It turned out that he had fired both barrels at once and it had launched him backward like a rag doll. He had also dislocated his shoulder.

"Fuck that. I'll stick to the Druganov," I told him.

It wasn't long after that our tour drifted to a close. We were soon packing up and heading home. It had all seemed pretty pointless, really. It didn't look like we'd achieved anything—and it certainly didn't look like the violence was calming down.

For me, though, it was a tour of firsts: my first operational tour, my first exposure to dead bodies, my first exposure to soldiers losing their lives in front of me.

It was also my first time firing a sniper rifle.

5. Kosovo and Out

An hour into our journey, the train lurched to a stop. I looked out of the window: a small, bald, fat guy was running past the train, sweating and panting.

"What the fuck?" I thought to myself.

The next minute, the windows of the carriage shattered, pelted with hundreds of stones.

"Helmets on!" someone shouted, and I fumbled to get my helmet on and the chinstrap done up.

I knelt up from where I lay crouched on the floor and cautiously looked out of the window. Outside, there was a TV crew and about thirty people swearing, throwing stones and trying to smash their way into our carriage through the end doors. I ran over and held the handle down on the door nearest me. Rocks started to hit my shoulder and my helmet as I desperately tried to keep the attackers at bay.

Through the window, I could see three men. One was grunting as he tugged on the door handle, another was hitting the glass and the third was drawing his finger slowly across his throat, pointing at me. They were all overweight and swarthy individuals, each with a murderous look in his eye.

The same thing was happening at the other end of the carriage. We needed to get out of here—and fast.

"Can anyone drive a train?" shouted one of the officers.

I didn't know whether to laugh or cry. "I doubt it," I thought to myself.

More and more people were arriving outside the train, throwing stones, chanting and jeering at us. It felt like being trapped inside a massive coconut shy. Some of the lads were bleeding from the missiles that had been hurled at us, so other soldiers were crouched beside their injured comrades, trying to give first aid.

What a nightmare—and the tour hadn't even started yet.

Suddenly, there was a jolt and the train started going backward, back the way we had come. After two hours, we arrived back at the port where we had started.

"The driver's running away," someone shouted.

Yet again, the small, fat, bald train driver had jumped out and was running off.

"Not again," Ronnie said.

"Let's get him," I shouted, sprinting forward.

Ronnie and I chased after him and rugby-tackled him. He hit the ground like a sack of shit and started babbling. We handed him over to the Greek police before moving down to check on our vehicles, which were in a dreadful state. Sights were smashed, barrels bent; some of the side bins had been broken into and tools stolen. The vehicles had slogans like "killers" and "go home" spray-painted on them. It was a nightmare.

"Welcome back to the Balkans," I thought to myself grimly.

It was May 1999 when we were sent to Macedonia, the first step of a tour that would take us into Kosovo. At that time Kosovo was facing a humanitarian crisis, with Serbian forces from the Federal Republic of Yugoslavia and the rebel Albanian Kosovo Liberation Army embroiled in constant engagements. Kosovan Albanians wanted independence from Yugoslavia; there had been ethnic cleansing and millions of refugees had fled the country. NATO had been bombing the Yugoslav forces in Kosovo since March and it had now been decided that NATO forces would be put on the ground to intervene under the guise of KFOR (Kosovo Force), to try to establish a secure environment. For us, it was the end of two years of waiting and all the training.

The rumors that we would be going had begun toward the later end of 1998, and we had started our usual pre-op build-up package: firing ranges, vehicle skills, fitness and battlecraft. This tour looked like it had more potential for actual combat than the previous dull tour that I had done in the Balkans.

On the day of departure, there were 120 of us on parade. Quite a few of the families came to wave us off. I still didn't have anyone there for me, which on the one hand was sad, but on the other made going away easier.

We were taken by bus to Brize Norton once again—where it turned out there were no normal planes available, so we were flown by C-130 to Macedonia: another shit flight. We arrived in Macedonia safely, only to be told that our vehicles and kit hadn't arrived. Macedonia doesn't have a port, so they were being shipped to Greece and would then be brought in by train.

So, we headed to Greece to wait for them—for three weeks, as it turned out. Finally we watched them being loaded onto flatbed rail trailers, then got on the train to accompany them into Macedonia. It was all starting to feel a bit Mickey Mouse. We had helmets, but no body armor; no weapons and no radios. Not a great way to travel into a combat zone. And then the train was ambushed . . .

We were never debriefed on who our attackers had been but it was obviously a political protest, planned ahead since the camera crew were there. After the ambush, it took us two more weeks to sort out the vehicles. We waited around in a Greek Army base until British Army low loaders arrived with shipping containers on the back. We loaded the vehicles into the containers so that they were out of sight and then headed back into Macedonia once more. This time we got to our base in one piece.

One day, I was tasked with driving the squadron leader to a meeting at HQ. When we met up, he told me I had ten minutes to get some food and then he wanted to leave. I jumped to the front of the scoff queue and was just about to get some food when he stuck his head through the tent window.

"We're off," he shouted at me.

"Fuck me, that was only three minutes," I mumbled to myself, as I headed to the Land Rover, empty-bellied. I started the engine and pulled off in first gear, steering into a corner.

"What the fuck are you doing?" he asked me.

"Steering into a corner," I replied, slightly confused.

"Don't drive like that, you cunt," he suddenly said.

For a moment I was too shocked to react. While I was used to being called names and sworn at, it didn't usually come from the officers. Then I leaned toward him and firmly replied, "Just call me a cunt again . . . sir."

He decided to stay quiet.

"We'll leave it at that then, shall we, sir?" I said and con-tinued driving, eventually pulling up outside HQ.

"You have one hour before I need picking up," he said, starting to climb out of the vehicle. He had one leg in and one leg out before I'd actually come to a stop. I couldn't help myself. As soon as his foot hit the floor, I accelerated. He fell flat on his arse and his paperwork went everywhere.

"Fucking tit," I mumbled to myself, and drove back to our base. When I got back, the second-in-command (2IC) was waiting for me.

"The squadron leader has been trying to get you on the radio. He wants picking up," he said.

I looked at my watch. "I've only been ten minutes."

"Doesn't matter. Let's go," replied the 2IC, climbing into the back of the Land Rover.

We got back to HQ where the squadron leader was waiting, red-faced. He climbed into the vehicle and turned to me.

"You've turned a thirty-minute mission into a two-hour mission . . . you cunt."

I bit my lip but the red rage was starting to descend over me.

Next we drove to see the Italians, who were based on the brow of a hill on the Kosovo border, the squadron leader giving me directions.

"Turn right."

I turned right.

"I said left, you cunt," he snapped.

I drove for another hundred yards, carefully keeping both hands on the steering wheel, looking out of the windscreen, before pulling over.

"I told you, if you called me a cunt again . . ." I said calmly. "Now you've called me it fucking twice!" My voice rose to a roar.

I turned to hit him, but the seatbelt pulled me up short. My flailing punch landed on his shoulder. I tried to hit him again, but the 2IC dived over from the back and grabbed me.

"No, no, no!" he shouted at me, while clinging on.

I got out of the Land Rover and walked around for a bit, taking deep breaths. The squadron leader looked horrified and quickly stomped off to speak to the Italians. A while later, he returned to the vehicle, carrying an ice cream that he'd got from the Italian cookhouse.

"Look, I'm sorry," he said, passing me the ice cream. "I've got a lot on my plate."

I opened the window, dropped the ice cream out and then ignored him for the whole drive back to our base. I found out a day later that he didn't want me as his driver anymore. "What a fucking shame," I thought to myself.

After two months of basic rehearsals and training for the move into Kosovo, the order was finally given that we were going to cross the border on 12 June. "Thank the Lord," was the collective opinion, as there had been enough hurry-up-and-wait. We had been living in mossy woodland under tarpaulins up until now and the ground had turned into a quagmire. Like good soldiers we made it as comfy as we could but we were still delighted to be moving on.

The way into Kosovo was via a mountainous road and a 300-yard-long tunnel. The Gurkhas were guarding the Macedonian side but we knew that once we popped out the other end of the tunnel we would be in Kosovo and into the unknown. The CVR(T) light armored vehicles went through first and I was in the rear, driving a Land Rover. I was just driving spare ammunition and not the squadron leader, thank fuck. Behind us was a massive convoy of NATO troops.

On the Kosovar side of the border was an old checkpoint covered in bullet marks. There was a smell of burning and the unmistakable stench of death. As always seems to be the case in war zones around the world, there was a lone, discarded flip-flop on the ground. It made me want to get out and look around.

We were told on the radio that the Serbian fighters had fled back to the main city of Pristina. At least that meant they shouldn't be in the immediate area to interfere with us.

We drove for hours until I could see Pristina laid out below us, parts wrecked and still smoking. As we approached the city limit and pulled up, I found myself saying out loud, "Fuck me, you have got to be joking."

The squadron leader had got all of the armored vehicles parked up in a petrol station. I didn't know if it was a working station or not—or more importantly if there was fuel in the underground tanks—but we could hear heavy guns firing and there was tracer going up in the air: a special bullet that burns very brightly, making it visible to the naked eye and helping the shooter narrow in on his target. Meanwhile, our CO had got all of the vehicles tucked up next to each other in a nice little car park!

I don't think any of us slept that night. I stayed in my Land Rover, while others lay under their vehicles for protection. The sound of the guns kept us awake and there was a constant smell of burning. Morning couldn't come quickly enough for me but as everyone got up most of the lads had an apprehensive look on their faces. We would be first into Pristina today to flush out the Serbian fighters and that was going to be a job and a half.

The armored troops went in first, patrolling slowly down the streets in single file. Behind each Spartan armored vehicle were six soldiers, jogging along, ready to clear a building if required.

Soon the streets got too narrow for the armored trucks, so they sent in the support troops, of which I was a part. The patrol was eight people strong and, as I was the most senior soldier after the patrol commander, I was made responsible for three of the lads: Ronnie, Woody and Smith. We continued to patrol forward on foot, down a lane, leaving the vehicles behind.

As I came up to an opening, I saw a building with a wire leading to another building a hundred yards away. We had been taught in the build-up training that a wire might lead to an improvised explosive device, so to treat it always with suspicion. The second building had a red tractor and a burned-out car on the front lawn. The car was still smoldering. I took cover behind a wall.

"Have a look round the corner," Dave, my corporal of horse, shouted at me.

I'd just popped my head round the corner of the wall . . . when a shot rang out. It was so close I felt the bullet pass by me, inches from my face.

It was the first time I had ever been properly shot at. For an instant, time slowed down.

Then: "Shit, shit, shit!" I shouted, scrambling backward on my hands and knees.

That was close.

The house behind me had a couple of windows that looked down the lane, so I directed four lads to get in there and provide cover. Once they were inside, I pulled out a smoke grenade and threw it toward the tractor. It was a crap throw and it didn't land exactly where I wanted, but I let the smoke build up and then signaled the support group to provide a burst of fire to keep the enemy's heads down.

I let Dave know that my plan was to take my lads over to the tractor in order to clear the enemy, and he nodded in agreement. I turned to my lads.

"On three we are going to cross the open ground as far as the tractor."

Ronnie stared at me, eyes wide open. Smith took a peek round the corner and Woody just smiled at me, like he always did.

"One, two, three, go!" I shouted.

I charged across the open ground and crashed down next to the tractor. I couldn't see my lads so I assumed they were in my blind spot. I crawled around but they were nowhere to be seen. I ran back across the open ground to where I had started and flopped back down behind the wall. My chest was heaving due to running with 55lb of kit on. The lads hadn't moved.

"What the fuck?" I asked.

"Dave said change of plan just after you ran off," Ronnie explained.

I looked over at Dave.

"Change of plan," he shouted. "The helicopters have eyes on and the enemy have moved off."

"When was someone going to tell me?"

"We thought we would let you do some laps first," he replied, grinning.

All I could do was smile back.

"Let's move back to the vehicles. The squadron leader is trying to find a place to hole up for the night," he continued.

Soon after that, we received orders to patrol to a water plant, where the rest of the squadron were. The plant was at the top of a small hill, with a cobbled road leading up to it and a fence all the way round it, making it easier to guard and a good place to stay.

That night, I was on guard—or "stag," as we call it—at the front gate with another lad called David when a white wreck of a car started driving up the hill toward us. As it got closer, I could see that the occupants had long hair and beards.

"Must be Albanians," I said to David.

The car pulled to a halt in front of us. The driver and passenger were filthy. I then noticed that they had on British Army camouflage trousers and were holding M4 carbines. The guy in the passenger seat wound down his window.

"All right, lads? Got any ammo and food?" he asked in a Liverpudlian accent.

"Fuck me, where have you two come from?" I replied.

"We've been in the woods for the last four months, teaching the Albanians how to fight."

They let me know that they were UK Special Forces and showed me their ID cards, so I directed them toward the ops room and opened the gate for them. They left the car outside.

An hour later, the two refugees strolled back out. "Cheers, mate," said the Scouser, tapping me on the shoulder. They climbed into their car and drove off.

"The things you see, hey?" I said, shrugging.

Once we got off stag, David and I headed off to find somewhere to kip. We'd be back on stag again later that night, so we just wanted to get our heads down for a few hours. We found a boiler room, bare but for a ladder leading up to the huge boiler, laid our kit down and fell asleep.

A couple of hours later I was woken up by a terrible smell; the smell of death. I pulled out my torch and had a look around, trying to identify the source, but I couldn't find anything in the room.

"Can you smell that?"

"Something stinks," replied David. "Like something crawled in a pipe and died."

After a few minutes, I climbed up the ladder and stuck my head over the edge of the big boiler.

"Fuck," I shouted out, almost gagging on the stench as I recoiled.

The boiler was half full of dead bodies.

I forced myself to take a closer look, the beam of the torch showing that the bodies were all men and that they had all been shot. They were probably the guys who used to work here.

I ran round to the ops room, which was in the center of plant, and told them what I'd found. They locked the room and in the morning the boiler was dragged out. I was on the detail to recover the corpses.

"Make sure you treat the bodies with respect," we were told.

A pile of body bags was laid out in front of us and we took it in turns to clamber inside the boiler and try to lift out the bodies. Manhandling the corpses took forever, and was covering us in crap, so in the end we had no real choice but to push the boiler over and tip out the bodies. Once they were out, we put the dead men in the body bags and laid them out in a line: ten bodies in total.

I was tasked with taking them to the morgue; it seemed to be a case of "you found them, you own them." I grabbed one of our four-ton trucks, got the bodies loaded on and headed to Pristina Hospital. There was a para guarding the gate.

"I've got ten bodies for you, mate," I said, gesturing to the back of the truck.

"The morgue's fucked at the moment," he replied. "We're having to use refrigerated shipping containers in the car park."

I drove in, to see fifteen shipping containers lined up. I stopped at the first one and had turned the handle to open the door before the para behind me yelled, "Not that one!"

Too late. Body bags poured out, making me jump back. Behind them, more dead bodies were stacked to the ceiling.

"You could have fucking told me *before* I opened it," I shouted at him.

I managed to squeeze the bodies back in, then drove down to the last container to unload my own consignment, before heading back out the front gate.

What a fucking day.

The Paras had arrived in Pristina at the same time we had; a week later they took over patrolling the whole of the city while we patrolled the border. So, the squadron was tasked with finding a house in Pristina for it to operate out of, and setting up a troop house on the border between Kosovo and Serbia. The troops would take turns rotating between the two. The armored troops headed north, looking for the troop house, while the support troops and the HQ hunted for a suitable squadron house in the city.

It took half a day to find a suitable location for the HQ: an old school on the northern edge of the city. It had classrooms, dormitories, a dinner hall and maintenance rooms. I decided to clear the boiler room of the second building, alongside a lad called Chris, who was from Yorkshire. He was a good bloke and I was glad to have him with me after my previous discovery.

The boiler room was one long space in the basement, with a series of rooms coming off one wall. It was quite eerie moving through it in the dark, with nothing but the crappy light from an Army right-angle flashlight to show the way.

"I've got a bad feeling about this, Craig," said Chris.

"Me too, mate," I muttered.

We looked in the first room. The carpet had been stripped

away to the underlay and the tiles were all covered in mold. We pushed inside. There was a pole in the middle of the room with a rope fixed to it and a mattress on the floor, covered in blood. In the corner was a bucket full of piss and shit. The smell of ammonia made my eyes water and I had to wrap my sweat rag around my nose and mouth.

There were six rooms in all and we moved through each one in turn, not finding any other signs of torture, and hanging a green light stick on the door so that others would know it was clear. Once we had cleared all the rooms down one side, we were left with one more door opposite.

"Chris, come over here and cover me."

I checked the door to see which way it opened. It's easier to booby-trap a door that opens toward you. This door opened inward. I gently opened it, all the while feeling for the resistance of a trip wire. It was really dark inside so I lifted the torch, which cast a dim circle of light.

I saw a leg. It shocked me so much I took a step back.

"You all right, mate?" asked Chris.

"Yes, but I think there's a body inside."

"Fuck, that's all we need."

"We have to check it out."

I opened the door again. In the torchlight I saw the leg again—and then another one. Five women in total: slumped over and pale; covered in blood with dirty hair. They looked like zombies.

Suddenly, they started screaming.

I nearly shat myself and jumped back. It was a fair one: I was there in uniform, carrying a gun, with a rag wrapped round my face, shining a torch at them. I quickly went off to find the female RMP officer who was with us and the female interpreter.

We found out that the basement had been used as rape

rooms. The women had been kept there for weeks. They had been fed like dogs and used as playthings by Serb soldiers.

Using the female RMP to reassure them as much as possible, we gently led the women out of the room. One was so weak that she died as soon as we got her out.

While the medics started treating the women, we did our best to make them feel safe.

The whole incident made me sick and mad for a couple of days. I don't care how hard you are, when you sit and hold the hands of four raped women who don't even speak English, trying to give them hope, it hurts. It stays with you forever. If all men had seen what I have seen, they would always treat women like gold.

We made the school as comfortable as possible but, while it had electricity, we couldn't get the hot water working. The Army—in its infinite wisdom—has a device called a Benghazi burner to heat water with and that's what we were forced to use. It's a metal dustbin with a burner device that drips diesel fuel onto a small fire in the middle to heat up the water. It's lethal. To get it to light is an art form. You have to light a small fire and then gently get the diesel to start dripping on it.

A few weeks after we arrived, it was my turn to sort out the hot water. I headed over to the row of three burners in the playground. I rolled up some newspaper, lit it, and then dropped it down the middle tube.

There was a huge explosion. I was thrown backward into a small tree and the windows around the courtyard all blew out. The lads thought that we were under attack and started manning their emergency positions.

Unbeknown to me, someone had left the diesel dripping

all night, so there was a build-up of vapor. I lost both eye-brows and my hair was gone from the front to the middle. I looked like a right twat. I made a note to check how much diesel was in the bottom of the burner before I lit it the next time. Although the accident hadn't been my fault, as was tra-dition I came in for a huge slagging from the lads.

A few days later, I was standing in the front courtyard of the school when a kid came running down the road, shouting, "Mine, mine!" He pointed at a nearby hill, eyes wide with excitement. The squadron sergeant major, the female interpreter and I followed him back to the hill. Once we got to the bottom, the kid started pointing and shout-ing again.

"Go and have a look," said the sergeant major to me.

I cautiously moved up the narrow rocky path, eyes glued to the ground. There's nothing like the threat of mines to sharpen your attention.

There weren't any mines. Instead, just off the path, two human, female heads lay in the undergrowth, their blue eyes open and lifeless. One had only half its skin on.

"What have you found, a mine?" the SM asked.

Without thinking, I bent down and picked up the heads by their hair and turned around to show him.

"No, just two heads."

Not a good idea. The interpreter screamed and then fainted, landing flat on her face. I realized then that I was no longer shocked by dead bodies. I walked down the hill—with the heads—while the sergeant major sorted out the inter-preter.

We later found out where the heads had come from. It turned out that when one of the women died in the rape rooms, the Serbian soldiers would cut off her head and burn the body. They amused themselves by getting the local stray dogs to fight over the heads. These two must have been dragged up the hill by the dogs.

Following protocol, we bagged the heads and they were taken away by the RMPs as evidence. While I could look at gruesome sights without flinching, I wasn't unaffected by them. Being surrounded by such disregard for human life was starting to grind me down.

After a while, the school started to feel quite claustrophobic and I was glad when our turn to head out to the troop house on the border came around. We loaded up the vehicles and headed off. We'd been tasked to stop at a lake halfway there and question a local fisherman. Every time a patrol went by, they spotted him fishing, so we figured he must spend half his life there and know all about the local area. You can never have too much local information—people, players, useful landmarks—so it was decided that if he was there when we passed by, we would try to have a chat with him.

We pulled up next to the lake and, sure enough, there he was: sitting on a small stool, rod out over the water. The lads pushed out into all-round defense. There was a bad smell in the area. Again: the unmistakable smell of death.

As we approached the guy, it became obvious why he was always there. He had been shot in the head and left in the fishing position, someone's sick joke. He had cigarettes in his pocket and quite a lot of money on him, so he obviously wasn't killed in a robbery. We checked him for booby traps and then gently laid him down.

The RMPs arrived, zipped him into a body bag and took him away. We were just about to leave when Ronnie shouted out, "There's something in the water."

We all went over to look where he was pointing. It was

hard to see anything at first, but then we made out the outline of a body, then another one, then another one. I got a bad feeling about what was coming next.

"Right, who's a good swimmer?" asked Dave, the corporal of horse.

I looked down the line. No one was putting their hand up. Reluctantly, I stuck mine in the air, as did Ronnie.

"Go on, then. Go and get the bodies."

We stripped off, keeping our trousers and T-shirts on, before wading into the lake. Fuck me, it was cold. I swam over to the first body; it was quite a way out. Close up, I could see it was a man who had been shot in the head. He was pasty white, his skin wrinkled like someone who'd spent too long in the bath. He had a rope around his leg, which had obviously been attached to a weight at one point. I put my arm under him and turned to swim back. His skin started to come off, which really shitted me up. I could see fish rising to the surface to nibble at it.

I dragged him to the shore and Ronnie did the same with another body. We just looked at each other, shaking our heads, before wading back in. My next body was a woman. I tried to grab her hair to move her into a better position, but it came away in my hand. This time I expected her skin to come off as I swam back, but being prepared didn't make it any easier.

In total, we retrieved six men and one woman. They had all been shot in the head and it looked like the woman had been raped. By the time we finished, the fish were in a feeding frenzy. They were literally jumping out of the water.

The RMPs came back. This time, they cordoned off the area and made it into a crime scene. We sorted ourselves out and headed on to the troop house. Another crappy day in the Balkans.

*

The troop house was an isolated two-story structure, right next to the one main road that crossed into Serbia. As we settled in, we found it was like running the gauntlet to go for a piss or a wash outside, as the Serbs liked to take potshots with their rifles over the border at us. Annoyingly, we were not allowed to shoot back.

We patrolled up and down the border, both in our vehicles and on foot, sometimes heading north, sometimes heading south. We entered small villages where there were only women. All of the males, even children, had been killed. There were often blood and bullet marks on the walls. Every now and then, the women ran off screaming at the sight of us. They didn't even know the war was over, and one set of uniforms is much like another; they thought we were Serbs. Poor fuckers.

We tried to calm them down and explain the situation through the interpreters. We also tried to get them aid—food, blankets, anything that would make their situation better.

A week after we arrived at the troop house, we were back at the water-pumping factory. I was doing a roving patrol around the perimeter when some Canadians pulled up in their armored reconnaissance vehicles. We had been told to expect them so I wandered over to say hello. A couple of the lads were sitting in the back of the vehicle watching a TV screen. I looked up and saw that the vehicle had a camera on an extendable boom.

"All right? What you watching?" I asked.

"Come on in. Have a look," one of them replied.

On the screen, I saw footage of a village burning and Russians in uniform running around, smashing things up.

"What the fuck? I thought it was the Serbs doing this stuff."

"It is. These *are* Serbs."

"What?"

"Some Russians lent them their uniforms so they looked like KFOR. These villages thought they were safe, but now the Serbs are getting stuck into them."

"Why can't we help them?" I asked.

"Orders: we're not allowed to. The UN just wants us to get evidence for them."

I spent the next two days looking after the Canadians as they searched for more footage. Sadly, it was all too easy to find.

I worked hard to desensitize myself to all of this but the seemingly endless number of bodies, the inhuman atrocities, all the suffering I saw in the villages every day—it all started to take its toll on me. I felt I needed a break before I could head back up north to the troop house.

I got one day to sort myself out—before another grim job came in. Thirty Albanians had been hiding in a treeline when the Serbs brought up a 20mm anti-aircraft cannon and just let rip at them. It was a bloodbath, with body parts, clothes and suitcases flung all over the place. We were tasked with matching limb to body.

When we arrived the gun was still there, albeit now with flat tires and no ammo. Our task was hideous; we had to use clothing color to try to piece people together. The kids were the hardest. Once we had collected as much of one person as possible, we put the parts in an aluminum coffin. At the end of that very long day, the Irish Guards arrived and took all of the coffins away to the morgue.

*

The next time we were at the troop house, resuming our usual patrols, we decided to check out a different route for the vehicles. We stopped in a field—but something did not feel right. Always trust the hairs on the back of your neck, and mine were standing straight up. Phil, one of the lads, needed a piss so he jumped down from the vehicle.

I continued to observe to our front while ignoring the squadron leader on the radio, who was telling us to push on.

"Fuck!" shouted Phil, jumping back.

"What is it?" I shouted back.

"I just looked down and I'm pissing on the torso of a kid. I can see a foot in a boot just over there," he said, pointing at the ground. "Looks like a mine blew the kid up."

The blood drained from my face. We were in a minefield.

"Slowly retrace your steps and get back in the vehicle," I told Phil, reaching for the radio to update the squadron leader.

"I have no trace of a minefield on my map," he replied on the radio.

"Well, that's all right then. What a tit," I thought but managed to stop myself saying. You should always trust the man on the ground.

We backed the vehicles out, careful to follow the route that we'd used driving in. Once we had boxed around the minefield we continued on our original planned route, but we hadn't gone far when we saw a pack of dogs chewing at a hand sticking out of the ground. We marked it and finished the patrol.

A few days later, we were sent back to dig up the hand. We had our chemical protective suits on, which was not really the right kit. The suit was designed for a nuclear, biological or chemical battlefield and was hot and claustrophobic. The respirator was dark black rubber and sweat poured into your eyes when you were zipped up inside.

As we started digging, we were plunged into a vision of hell. There wasn't just one body; this was a mass grave. The dead were all male: some of fighting age, but there were also children and old men. Their bodies were rotten and disintegrated as we lifted them up to put them into body bags. There were entrails everywhere and the stench was hideous.

As we worked, massive dogs circled us, eyeing us and the corpses hungrily. They looked more like werewolves than dogs and we had to put some of the lads on watch, throwing stones to keep them back.

That night, no matter how long I scrubbed, I couldn't wash the smell from my skin. The images were burned into my mind, too. They were there every time I closed my eyes, and every time I opened them. I couldn't believe the horror we were encountering. How could people do this to each other? How could they do this to old people and children? I couldn't understand it.

Toward the end of the tour, Ronnie and I were tasked with picking up another body and taking it to the morgue. It was dusk when we arrived at the scene. It sounds terrible, but we were relieved that the body was fresh and didn't stink. Everything is relative. By now, that was a good day in our books.

We'd loaded up and were driving to the morgue when the Land Rover broke down.

We ground to a halt and the headlights died on us. It was pitch black; we were three miles from base and in the middle of nowhere. We got on the radio and asked for assistance, only to be told that the Royal Electrical and Mechanical Engineers (REME) would get to us, but were on other tasks. We would just have to wait our turn.

"We might as well get some scoff and a brew on," I said to Ronnie.

Our food and brew kit was in the back of the vehicle, so we dragged the body out and put it on the ground. Ronnie jumped in to dig out a cooker.

Suddenly, from behind me, I heard the sound of air escaping and a low moan. Ronnie looked up, thinking it was me mucking about.

"Was that you?" he asked.

"No," I replied, turning to look at the body. "Are you sure he's dead?"

"Of course he's fucking dead; he's been shot in the head."

Suddenly the body inside the bag sat up. We both screamed hysterically and I jumped in the Land Rover too.

"Fuck me, fuck me!" Ronnie was shouting.

I got on the radio and begged for the REME to come and get us. The REME lads arrived soon after, thank God. Ronnie and I couldn't take our eyes off the body bag the whole time we were waiting. I wasn't sure what I would do if it moved again; run away or try to help the poor bloke out of the bag. But I didn't have to find out; it didn't move again after that first time.

We told the REME lads what had happened, but they thought we were pulling their legs. They fixed the vehicle and we got on our way to the morgue.

"No one is going to believe us," said Ronnie.

When we arrived at the morgue, we described what we'd seen to one of the doctors.

"It can happen," he said knowledgeably. "As the gas expands, the body can move and nerves can tighten up. Bet that scared you!"

He had no idea.

*

The tour finished after six months and I ended up in the party escorting the vehicles back to the UK. It was a terrible journey by boat; I have never been so sick in all my life. Three weeks of terrible food, motion sickness and boredom. Fuck being in the Navy.

Back then, coming home from a tour was nothing like it is today. No counseling or psychological help. I was sent into a briefing room in the barracks, where there was a woman sitting behind a desk. I had never seen her before and had no idea who she was. She didn't even introduce herself.

"Are you okay?" she asked.

"Yes, fine," I replied.

"Okay, you can go now."

That was the sum total of my counseling. They kept us in camp for a week and then sent us on leave.

I had terrible nightmares for the next six weeks. I just couldn't get the images out of my mind. The bodies—some just babies—the old men, the fish jumping in the river, the women in the rape rooms. When I went back to work, I asked for a posting to Knightsbridge, hoping that the change would help me forget what I'd seen. Once I got there, they put me in the guardroom and I ended up manning the front gate.

A year later, I was still having nightmares and for the sake of my sanity I signed off and left the Army.

I ended up down in Newquay, doing a lifeguard course. After that finished, I headed up North and moved in with a girl I was seeing. She'd told me that there were lots of jobs up there and I'd have no worries finding work.

Two months later, I still hadn't got a job. Every Sunday,

we'd go round to the girl's mum's house for lunch and every Sunday her mum would ask me the same question. "When am I going to wear a hat?" I never knew what she meant but it turned out that it had something to do with marriage.

Then I heard about a job at a local gym and, just before I left for the interview, my girlfriend turned to me and said, "Will you marry me?"

I was taken aback but managed to answer, "I'll let you know tomorrow."

I got the job at the gym. Just before heading off to work the next day, I explained how I was feeling to my girlfriend. "Look, I'm happy the way things are. No need to get married yet."

She didn't take it well. As I got closer to her house that evening, I saw all of my clothes and things laid out on the grass in the back garden, everything covered in bleach. She'd locked the doors and wouldn't come and talk to me. After shouting "Bitch!" at the house a few times, I gathered up my stuff and headed off. So much for the new job.

Mum bought me a ticket down to Cheltenham and then dropped me at a B & B. She didn't want me moving back home in case I got too comfy. That night, still haunted by all the bodies I'd seen, I had a terrible nightmare. I jerked awake to find myself sitting bolt upright in a single bed, covered in sweat, with no idea where I was. I couldn't work out how my life had ended up going so wrong.

Eventually, I got a job as a fitness instructor at a gym in Oxford. Mark, who owned the gym, was a really good guy and I spent a year working there, only getting into one serious scrape with one of the members. He just needed a slight re-educating but that was done in the car park one night after the gym had shut. But, after a year, I realized that there was no chance of promotion, as Mark was effectively the manager.

At the age of twenty-nine, I decided to rejoin the Army.

6. Invading Iraq

Even though I had been out of the Army for more than a year, my fitness and skills were still there. I'd been doing a bit of military training as I was in the process of joining 23 SAS, a Territorial Army unit, but it's a slow-moving process so I decided to go back to the regulars.

It took about three weeks to rejoin and once I was back in I was sent to D Squadron, the Blues and Royals. They are the squadron attached to 16 Air Assault Brigade, the British Army's premier spearhead brigade, comprising airborne and air-assault personnel. They focus on rapid intervention and always have a squadron of CVR(T) vehicles allocated to them, which are light by design. I was para-trained, like most of D Squadron, which meant we could insert the vehicles by air drop and be in a position to follow them by parachute.

A few days after arriving at the barracks in Windsor, I was still running around getting myself sorted out—kit, documents, medical, dental—when one of the clerks came to find me. It was February 2003.

"Sort your shit out quickly. You're off to invade Iraq," he told me.

After 9/11, the military focus had first moved to Al Qaeda in Afghanistan—and then back to the unfinished business in Iraq. Seen as a destabilizing influence on the region, Iraq's leader Saddam Hussein had been given warning after warning to disarm, in particular his "weapons of mass destruction." He had ignored all of the threats and we were being sent in to make him comply as part of the US-led coalition force. So now 16 Air Assault Brigade, 3 Commando Brigade and 7 Armored Brigade were all assembling in Kuwait, ready for the invasion to topple Saddam Hussein. Altogether it was the largest assembly of British troops since the 1990–91 Gulf War—a force of over 45,000. D Squadron was in a place called Camp Eagle, a pissy little outpost in the middle of the Kuwait desert, which got hit by sandstorms all of the time.

I arrived and my feet didn't touch the ground. Everyone was gearing up for the invasion. While we waited for our vehicles to arrive by sea, we started off with low-level skills and drills. Patrolling, contact drills—that sort of thing. I found it odd that we did all the training without ammunition, even though we were very, very close to the Iraqi border. The reason for this, it transpired, was that there was no ammunition, which meant we were screwed if the Iraqis decided to play with us.

Then the SQMS (squadron quartermaster sergeant) called us all into the briefing tent for an update.

"Well, the ammunition has arrived . . . but it's all blank; no live yet."

Someone had fucked up. At least if the Iraqis had a go at us we could make some loud noises back at them. I ended up as the driver for the squadron sergeant major (SSM), which, from my point of view, turned out to be a very bad decision.

The vehicles, Spartans and Land Rovers, finally arrived. Within a three-man crew there is a commander—in this case the SSM—a gunner, and then, bottom of the ladder, the driver: me. The pressure was on. Myself and the gunner—the other member of the SSM's crew—worked on our Spartan armored vehicle like ants until late into the night, getting it ready for war. Our gunner was a Northener and really down to earth, but he struggled to cope with stress. Once we'd finished, the SSM came over and started stripping things off and moving things around. He moved the radios and we ended up with no room for our personal kit. We spent all night getting the vehicle just how he wanted it. Just in time for him to arrive all fresh for a day's training.

I thought the SSM was turning out to be pretty high maintenance. He never talked to us; he shouted. If his tea wasn't hot enough, he poured it away and made us do it again. Same with his food. At one point he handed me a bunch of laminated cards.

"Place these all around the inside of the vehicle so that they can be read."

I assumed that they were orders cards or SOPs (standard operating procedures). As he walked off, I had a look at them and they turned out to be Bible quotes.

The gunner and I got hammered to do things just how the SSM wanted them. One day, the gunner got his arse chewed out again and I watched as he disappeared round the back of the vehicle, red in the face. After a second, I heard the unmistakable sound of a rifle being cocked. I quickly walked round and bumped straight into him. He was seething.

"Give us that, mate," I told him, taking the rifle off him and unloading it.

The SSM was lucky that day. Our gunner was ready to shoot him.

A few gunners came and went because of the SSM before we got Danny, a short, fit, hard-headed lad.

"I give you a week," I told him.

After another night of unpacking and repacking the wagon, we were finishing up when we heard a woman's voice. She was heading toward our vehicle, dragging a holdall with wheels, a rucksack, a daysack and a laptop. She turned out to be Audrey Gillan, a reporter for the *Guardian*, and she was joining us in the vehicle. I looked at her interpretation of "scaled-down" kit and said, "This isn't a picnic."

"All of this kit was given to me by the MOD."

"Those geniuses in Whitehall have no idea what is going on at the front line."

I went through her kit and stripped out all the things she didn't need; they'd even given her a tent. I let her keep her wash kit and four pairs of knickers. She had loads of sweets with her, which didn't last long.

We quickly warmed to Audrey, who became one of the lads. She had spent a month in rigorous training, getting herself physically and mentally ready for war. The Marines and the Paras said she couldn't go with them, but the Cav said yes. I ran her through the SOPs of the vehicle. We always dig a shell scrape at the front left of the vehicle, which is about four feet wide, six feet long and three feet deep. In a contact with the enemy, I told her she had to get in cover, either in the shell scrape or under the vehicle, or find something else. If she couldn't find anything, she should just lie down. She should never run around out in the open, as that is the easiest way to get hit by something.

"If all else fails," I said, "keep your head down."

"What if I'm not fast enough getting into the shell scrape?" she asked.

"You've got your helmet and body armor, haven't you?"

She pulled out a set of helmet and body armor—with bright blue covers on.

"You're going to stick out like a sore thumb with that lot on."

Her eyes got even wider.

"Just relax—we'll be fine," I reassured her.

The day before D-Day, 19 March 2003, we lined the vehicles up next to the border. The border was a twenty-foot-high sand berm; the engineers would be blowing a gap through it for us to use. Then 16 Air Assault Brigade would flood through this breach and we, the Cavalry's armored vehicles, would head through first to provide reconnaissance for them.

We thought the biggest threat would be chemical weapons; everyone expected Saddam to throw something at us. The pre-agreed code was that if you heard a vehicle horn beeping, you'd know there was a chemical weapon attack inbound—and that you needed to get your chemical suit and gas mask on sharpish. For reasons known only to themselves, the RMPs kept beeping the horn on their Land Rover, and our impressive invasion force started to look like a scene from *Dad's Army* as people flailed around trying to get their kit on and then couldn't communicate with each other through their respirators.

I didn't sleep well the night before the invasion. I had been on so-called operational tours before but this was very different. This was "war," much bigger in scope and with a far bigger chance of violence. In the Balkans, it would have been bad luck to have been killed or injured. This time it was a very real possibility.

We had to sleep in "crew positions," so I tried to catnap in the driver's seat. Just before dawn on 20 March, there was a huge explosion and my head bounced off the side of the vehicle. The explosion was the engineers blowing the breach; it would have been nice if they'd told us before they did it.

It took a long time to get everything moving. The breach wasn't that big and there were a lot of vehicles to go through it. Finally, it was our turn. Once through, I took a good look around before closing my armored hatch down. There were thousands of oil pipes and pieces of drilling equipment everywhere. The Iraqis had knocked the heads off the southern oil wells around Basra and set them on fire. The smoke was turning day to night, the sky was so black. They had filled anti-tank ditches alongside the road with oil and set those on fire as well.

The heat was unbelievable, burning out the night sight on the Spartan and making it feel like the vehicle was melting. I was driving blind and the hideous smoke was almost choking me; the air filters on the vehicle just weren't designed for this amount of smoke. This was what the beginning of the world must have looked like.

After two hours, the SSM told us to stop and I was grateful to get the hatch open. Gulping in fresh air, I looked around: miles and miles of desert with the sky stained gray from all the burning oil. Off in the distance, I could still see the orange glow from the fires. The Iraqis had left quickly and there was stuff lying all over the place: new cars, bikes and kit . . . and two dead bodies, just off to the front—Iraqi soldiers who had been run over.

"Harrison, you need to go and dig a grave for them," the SSM shouted at me.

I stared at the Bible-thumper, unsure if he was serious or not. This invasion was going to take a while if the plan was to bury every dead body we came across.

"Go on, get to it."

I pulled on some rubber gloves and grabbed a shovel to dig a shallow grave. Then I took the first body by the wrist. The smell took me straight back to Kosovo. As I shuffled backward, the heavy pull suddenly went light. Half of the body had come away, and the legs had been left behind. Whatever ran the soldiers over had squished them pretty good. I had to take the shovel and spoon the contents into the hole.

"The bodies need to face east," the SSM shouted.

"What?"

"The bodies need to face east."

I pulled my compass out, checked which way was east and re-orientated the bodies. Then I filled the grave in, washed my gloves and put them on the vehicle to dry. Unsurprisingly, we got told over the radio to get a move on and catch up.

While the armored vehicles' job was to provide reconnaissance, our job in the SSM's gang was to keep everyone resupplied. Once the squadron stopped its advance for the day, we joined Squadron Headquarters (SHQ). We were setting up base for the night in some abandoned buildings and I was just having a nose around, looking at the discarded gas masks and chemical suits, when I heard my name being shouted by the SSM. I found him outside, standing next to an anti-tank ditch full of oil, which the Iraqis had forgotten to light. There was a body floating in the oil. The SSM just looked at me and pointed at the corpse.

I got my shovel, gloves and some poles. I tried to use the poles to hook the body out, but it kept bobbing down. Eventually, it floated over to the edge and I managed to grab a handful of hair and drag it out. I dug a hole, placed the body east and then filled it in.

"I'm not a fucking funeral director," I told the SSM. "That's three bodies in four hours."

He just smiled and walked off.

Danny and I cleared the building that we had been allocated, which had books everywhere and looked like an old school. There was a village just up the road, which was where the Paras had set up. It was an awesome sight to see them patrolling up the road in an arrow formation. They looked like the ultimate professionals.

"I need the toilet. Can you help me with some privacy?" Audrey asked me.

We headed over to a wall and I held up a poncho to shield her. The next thing I knew, there was a loud scream and Audrey ran off, dragging her trousers up. There was a hole in the wall and a platoon of Paras on the other side: five of them had been watching through the hole and one of them was taking pictures with a camera. They were acting like they'd never seen a woman before.

"Come on, lads. Fuck off." I shooed them away.

As we walked back to our vehicle I could see tea and scoff had been thrown on the ground by the usual dissatisfied customer. The SSM was shouting at Danny, who was taking it in his stride. Audrey and I met him round the back of the wagon.

"Can I help?" Audrey asked.

"You could make the SSM his rations," Danny replied. She graciously got on with it and the SSM begrudgingly took it from her.

The squadron was tasked with securing the oil installations, which turned out to be an easier task than expected as most Iraqis in the area were quick to surrender. After a few days we got the order to move on. Then, out of nowhere, our regimental padre appeared. "I'll be joining you for forty-eight hours," he told me, passing me his kit.

"Brilliant," I thought to myself. It took Danny and me a long time to move kit around so that we could squeeze him in. We were both on stag through the night—as we had no idea where the Iraqis were, it made sense to have two of us on guard—and then at first light we all moved out, the Cav leading the advance for 16 Air Assault Brigade, traveling deeper into Iraq.

About mid-morning, we came under heavy artillery fire. The Iraqis were quickly outgunned and a fierce tank battle started up. Our armored Challengers versus their T55s; not much of a contest, really.

SHQ stayed out of the battle in a massive dip. We quickly dug shell scrapes round the edge of the hole and manned positions in case the enemy came our way. At last light, a mist started to descend, which got so thick I could see only thirty feet in front. This made everything even more eerie and my imagination started playing tricks on me. Every shadow was an Iraqi patrol coming toward us.

Once it got dark, the mist turned to rain and the Iraqi artillery gunners regained some confidence. They started bracketing our dip with artillery fire, each round closing in just that little bit more. We could hear the boom of the gun firing in the distance, then the whistle as the round screamed toward us. In that situation, all you can do is sit there, hug your helmet and wonder where the shell will land.

The rounds got so close that we were getting covered in the sand and mud they kicked up, the ground shaking around us, the shock waves rattling our bodies. The noise was unbelievable; like being in the middle of a thundercloud.

"Grab your kit! Let's go, let's go!" screamed the SSM, as he clambered into our wagon.

"Grab Audrey and I'll get the padre," I told Danny.

The SSM was still shouting and getting more and more animated. Danny had got Audrey but I couldn't find the padre. Finally, I spotted him in front of the vehicle, next to the tracks. He was buried under ten inches of sand. I started to uncover him gently, finding that he was zipped up in his sleeping bag. I wiped sand from his face, clearing his nose and mouth.

"Padre?"

I didn't get a reply and I couldn't see whether he was breathing or not. I tried to open the sleeping bag but the zip was stuck.

"Harrison, start this fucking wagon!" the SSM bellowed at me.

I uncovered the padre's mouth a bit more and he gently coughed. Thank fuck for that. I gave up trying to unzip him and just ripped the sleeping bag open. I dragged him out and unceremoniously passed him up to Danny, who pulled him into the vehicle. I jumped in the driver's seat, jammed on my helmet, started the vehicle and drove off.

"We'll be having a word when we stop," the SSM told me over the intercom. That meant a behind-the-wagon "old-school" chat, i.e., a kicking. "Happy with that," I thought to myself. "I'll pull the stupid fucker's head off." In the end though, we never got round to it.

We drove for two hours, the SSM giving me directions. At points, the SSM made Danny get out and walk in front of the vehicle, to make sure that we didn't drive into any ditches or tank tracks.

"Right, stop here," the SSM told us over the intercom.

Danny and I got out and immediately dug a foxhole. The SSM stayed in the cupola while Audrey came over to find me.

"I've left my helmet and body armor behind."

"Go and tell the SSM," I said. "Stay in the wagon for protection."

I was just finishing off the foxhole when the sun started to come up. We all "stood to," which involved manning the firing positions for thirty minutes. After that, I grabbed an hour's sleep.

"Get ready to move out," the SSM shouted.

I started to fill in the foxhole. Looking up, I saw Audrey holding her helmet and body armor.

"I thought you left your kit behind," I said, puzzled.

"I did; I just went back and got it now that the sun is up," she said, pointing behind me. There was a mast about 200 yards away—the remainder of SHQ still in the big dip. The SSM had driven us around in one very big circle.

"Top map reading," I thought to myself.

It took us only minutes to drive back to the rest of SHQ, who hadn't even noticed that we'd gone.

"Where have you lot been?" the squadron leader asked us.

I wanted to tell him. "Driving round in circles all night," but I held my tongue. We set up in our original position and the padre came to find me.

"Thanks for pulling me out last night."

"No worries. I guess God wasn't there last night."

"I guess not," he said and walked off.

Later in the day, the chatter on the radio network really started to increase and we could hear a lot of gunfire off in the distance. One of the troops was in serious contact. We jumped in our wagon and headed toward the location of the battle, in case they needed resupplying. As we got closer we could see a lot of red smoke, the agreed signal for "blue on blue" or a friendly-on-friendly incident—our troops let it off so that friendly planes overhead would know not to fire on them. An American A10 screamed overhead as we approached, only 200 yards off the ground.

"I bet the lads will be happy to see them," I thought to myself. If the lads were in contact, they would be glad for some more fire support.

I couldn't have been more wrong.

It wheeled around and came in for another strafing run; the distinctive buzz-saw sound of the A10 firing its 30mm cannon cut through the air, before pulling up to height.

As we got closer we could see what he had done. On the first run he had engaged *our* recce Scimitar; on the second he had hit our engineers' recce vehicle, which had pulled in front. The vehicles had been practically cut in half; the Scimitar was on fire.

The driver from the Scimitar dragged his commanding officer out of the way and then tried to go back for Matt, the operator. The flames got too much for the driver and he was forced back.

All of us with headsets on could hear Matt. He was screaming down the radio as the flames engulfed him. Rounds started cooking off inside the vehicle and suddenly Matt stopped screaming. I didn't know if the cables had melted or Matt had died, but all of us silently pulled our headsets off. I closed my eyes with an overwhelming feeling of powerlessness.

The A10 lined up for another run, but fortunately the message that he was engaging friendlies finally got through. As he passed over, I could see the shark's mouth painted onto the nose cone and the 30mm cannon barrels spinning. Looking at the damage he had done to the two vehicles, I could see why they called the A10s "tank busters."

SHQ arrived and immediately pushed one of the troops forward. The Iraqis had got some BMP armored personnel carriers and three T55 tanks together, and they were trying to do a cheeky counterattack while we were distracted. They were quickly dealt with. We didn't want to call the A10s back so we used artillery and our own armament.

The vehicles that had been attacked by the A10 burned

for two days, while we guarded them to make sure that they weren't looted. Despite being in the middle of nowhere and nothing but a pile of molten metal, they would still have attracted the locals, who would have tried to sneak in and steal things.

Once the fires in the vehicles had gone out, we put on our chemical suits to protect us from the depleted uranium contained in the shells fired by the A10, and accompanied the doctor to the Scimitar. He went in to retrieve Matt's body, although there wasn't much left.

It turned out that the A10 had had a full load. The pilot had asked if there were any friendlies in the area and some knob had told him no. When the A10 came near to our troops, the lads did the correct drills. They had fluorescent orange marker panels on the front and the rear of the vehicles to identify them as allies from the air, and they let off red smoke after the first attack. The A10 still engaged. It turned out that the pilots were from the National Guard. Part-time, gung-ho fuckwits as far as I'm concerned. It also turned out that a disclaimer had been signed by the coalition, saying that they couldn't get prosecuted for blue-on-blues, so Matt's family never got justice.

It was a grim time for all of us. The padre had to accompany the body back to the airfield for it to be flown home. I think that his near-death experience buried in the sand, and now this, was proving a struggle for him. He drank all of his communion wine—a bottle and a half—to see him through it. Fair enough; I would have drunk my own piss if I'd thought it would make the pain go away.

A few days later we had another incident. One of the troop CVR(T)s had rolled into a drainage ditch and was in serious trouble. We jumped back into our wagon, knocking laminated Bible quotes off in our hurry, and drove forward, escorting an ambulance, which was needed for the troops inside the stricken CVR(T). I could hear the SSM mumbling Bible quotes to himself over the headset.

"If God is our savior, why does He let our lads suffer?" I asked him over the intercom.

He didn't answer.

As we got closer, I could see a rubber track breaking the surface of the water—but the rest of the vehicle was submerged. Corporal of Horse Forster was topless in the ditch, diving under the water. I could see Mick Flynn—one of the regiment's senior sergeants—bobbing up and down as well.

Danny ran off to secure an emergency HLS (helicopter landing site), while I rushed to get our recovery tow ropes out. We managed to get lines attached to the vehicle but our wagon wasn't strong enough to pull it out. Other vehicles were arriving by now and eventually we got lines attached to three and managed to pull the submerged vehicle onto its side, partially out of the water.

I could now see that it was the troop leader's wagon. Chalky, the driver, had managed to get out and was sitting on the bank with his head in his hands. The other two occupants—the troop leader and Karl Shearer, the operator—were still inside and had been under water for five minutes.

Once the vehicle was on its side, Mick Flynn dragged the troop leader out and immediately started giving CPR. The boss's eyes were open, his mouth full of mud.

We took turns giving CPR while the others went back to diving under the vehicle to try to get to Karl. In the end Mick found him by swimming in through the commander's hatch. He dragged him onto the bank and we immediately started giving CPR—until the doctor told us to stop. Karl was dead.

Having only recently joined D Squadron, I didn't know him well, but when someone within the squadron dies, it hits us all hard.

The troop leader was alive, but with every breath he took his entire body lifted. The doctor tried to drain his lungs and we all just hoped that the medical response helicopter got to us quickly.

The Paras arrived and offered to provide all-round defense for us, which was handy as we were just starting to take small-arms fire from an Iraqi patrol about 650 yards away. We hadn't really noticed as there was so much noise. The three vehicles attached to the partially submerged vehicle were on full rev just to stop it rolling back over.

I looked up and saw the SSM pointing at me from our vehicle; he hadn't got out yet. I ran over and jumped in.

"I have been shouting for you for ten minutes," he screamed at me. "When I say you jump, you jump. Do you understand?"

Maybe he had good reason to stay in the wagon (I know he was concerned to secure the area), but I was not in the mood for a lecture.

"With all due respect, *sir*, fuck you," I shouted at him. "I have just watched someone die. I am running around towing rolled-over wagons, giving CPR and trying to help Danny with the HLS. Why don't you get out and take charge instead of sitting in here and praying, because frankly that isn't working."

I jumped off the wagon and walked off.

Two Puma helicopters arrived and hovered above, unwilling to land due to the small-arms fire. Then 7 RHA arrived and quickly set up four 105mm light artillery pieces. They started blasting away and that silenced whoever was shooting at us.

I popped a smoke grenade to give the pilots an idea of wind direction. Once they had landed, we got Karl's body and the troop leader on board. Inside were three Iraqi prisoners, all covered in sand and blood. One of them looked at me and smiled in a "thank you" kind of way. The Pumas lifted off.

We then had to retrieve the rolled-over wagon, which turned into an epic. It took us two hours to get it out. Once it was on the bank, we finally turned the engines off in the towing vehicles. There was deathly silence. Danny and Audrey sat on the bank and just stared at the floor. The smell of spilled diesel was overpowering. None of us spoke; there was nothing to say.

Looking back toward our vehicle, I could see that the SSM had finally got out. I felt sorry for him, because, like others, it seemed as if he was struggling with all that was happening, but then I remembered how he had been treating me and Danny, so that emotion passed pretty quickly.

Not long after, we got another call to push forward and resupply. One of the troops was in contact and the Paras were already securing the area. We drove forward until we came across three pick-up trucks in a line, shot to fuck. Some of the Iraqis had given up but two of them were dead. The SSM just looked at me . . . it was gravedigging time.

Wearily, I pulled my gloves on and dragged the two bullet-riddled bodies out of the second pickup. One of them wasn't too bad but the second body was in bits and the guy's brain oozed out over my boots. The smell was hideous. I maneuvered them both into the hole I had dug and started to fill it in.

"Don't forget to make sure that they're facing east," the SSM reminded me.

One of the guy's arms was sticking straight up with rigor mortis and I couldn't get it into the hole. In the end, I whacked it with the shovel and it folded in on itself. I looked up to see the SSM looking pretty unhappy with me.

"You've got no respect for the dead," he said.

"I have, but not for these fuckers." Karl's death was still fresh in my mind.

Once I'd filled the hole in, the Paras' padre came over and said a few words.

We reassembled as a squadron and pushed forward to Al Amarah, a city in southeast Iraq on the Tigris river, south of Baghdad. The city was divided into two, split down the Sunni–Shia religious divide. We were initially welcomed as liberators, but this view started to fade. Once they heard that we were staying, the atmosphere began to change. We were back to being infidels who had no business being there and the city quickly became a hotbed of insurgency. The battle changed from a conventional fight between armies to one where one side hid among the population and adopted terrorist tactics.

The Battle Group took over Al Amarah football stadium in the city, which made a perfect base as it was massive. We discovered a Scud missile parked in one of the entrance tunnels. It was about forty feet long and seven feet in diameter, with a range of 100–180 miles: a big, sinister thing. Seeing one for myself meant I understood why people were so worried about them. This one had a conventional warhead, not chemical or biological, so we left it alone.

We started patrolling into the city and it was obvious the atmosphere was getting increasingly strained. You could feel the tension in the air and each day more and more people avoided us or glared at us. Patrols started getting shot at. It was hot and dusty work, patrolling in an urban nightmare that provided more rat runs and escape routes for them than it did for us. What started out as reassurance patrols quickly became ones of necessity. If we didn't dominate the local area, it would be all too easy for them to move in and attack us.

After a particularly stressful patrol, which saw us being shot at and having to do a lot of running, I needed to clear my head, so I decided to go for a walk around the stadium. Climbing up the steps, I headed to the roof to see what the view was like up there.

As I got to the top of the stairs, I could see that the stadium was guarded by snipers. There was one just in front of me, staring off toward the city. He looked awesome, very, very professional, like someone who had his shit together. He was fully camouflaged. I could see that he had range cards and data sheets taped to the butt of his L96 sniper rifle. He also had a pistol in a holster and an SA80 assault rifle down by his feet. While his weapons were immaculately clean, his clothing looked like it hadn't been washed in a long time.

"All right," he said with a nod.

"All right," I replied and headed over to him.

He was happy to talk, so I sat down with him and started quizzing him about being a sniper. He let me look through the scope on the rifle and I was amazed at how clear it was and how far you could see.

"How long have you been a sniper?" I asked.

"Ten years."

He had a kind of faraway look in his eyes.

"What does it take to make a good sniper?"

He didn't even glance at me; he just kept staring through the scope on his rifle, constantly scanning, looking for trouble.

"You make a sniper by taking a human being and reengineering him. You go down to the essence of who he really is and then you build him back up from there, except you leave something out. You leave out the bit that says it's not okay to kill another human being. You make him into a weapon and a weapon's job is to kill people. A sniper isn't a man anymore; he is a weapon, a weapon waiting to be fired."

"Fucking hell, that's deep," I said, impressed.

He turned and looked at me. "Well, you did ask."

Over the next couple of days at the stadium, I realized that the snipers got treated like men. Not like little boys, the way the rest of us were treated by the Cav. They were trusted. They worked as teams and as individuals. They were left alone to get on with their job. Even after we were moved from the stadium to an old airfield, I kept thinking about what the sniper on the roof had told me. At this stage, I had had it with the SSM's bullshit, but I knew that I couldn't behave the way I used to. Threatening him or throwing a punch might get me kicked out of the regiment and I couldn't afford that. Instead, I had to suck it up. As a result, I felt he had pretty much broken me, which was in itself quite depressing.

Eventually, I managed to make enough noise to the right people and I was moved to drive the ambulance. What a difference that made. I was working with completely different people and I was treated with respect. After a few weeks, I was moved to Support Troop and we ended up guarding the airfield and the surrounding oilfields. It was not a particularly pleasant task, but at least I was still away from the SSM. It was roasting as if it was July, touching seventy degrees Celsius. The oilfields stank of diesel and natural gas, and there was discarded kit everywhere. It made you really jumpy at night as things were continually blowing around in the shadows.

Toward the end of our six-month tour, we were pulled

back to a holding camp, to wait to go home. The SSMs moved around, asking all of us what courses we would like to go on once we got back.

"Sniper course," I told my SSM when he asked me.

"Fuck off," was his response.

Some people got to go straight home, while others— including me—were held back to help with all of the accounting of ammunition and equipment. There is nothing the Cavalry enjoys more than counting kit.

Part of the regiment was also responsible for providing a Quick Reaction Force (QRF) to the local units. Our armored vehicles allowed us to get to a situation quickly and provide additional firepower. One afternoon, I was humping and dumping ammunition crates when I heard a helicopter approaching. Wiping sweat from my eyes, I saw that it was a Chinook with smoke pouring out of it. It had been shot to fuck.

As soon as it landed just outside of camp, our medics ran toward it. It turned out that the Chinook had dropped off a platoon from 1 PARA for a patrol in a village south of Al Amarah and, on taking off, came under fire.

I was still watching what was going on when Sergeant Simpson from 3 Troop shouted over to me. Simo, as he was known, was a tall, fit guy and really affable. He called everyone by their first names. "Craig, are you a gunner?"

"Yes, mate." As part of the build-up training, I had qualified as a gunner.

"Good. You're coming with us."

It turned out that the Paras were under heavy fire and had got themselves pinned down in some buildings. They had called for the QRF, which was currently 2 Troop, but when they arrived on the scene they got pinned down as well.

It had been decided that we would send a hastily put-together troop of reinforcements.

We had a fifteen-mile drive ahead of us but the wagons couldn't be pushed due to the danger of overheating; the engines would blow up if they went over 4,000rpm. We threw crates of ammunition in the back and headed off; we could use the journey to sort ourselves out. Listening to our comrades on the radio, our position sounded grim. The Chinook had injured lads onboard, the QRF had taken casualties and the Paras were now running out of ammunition and were in danger of being overrun.

The village of Majar al-Kabir was a ragtag collection of single-story stone and brick buildings, with dusty streets crisscrossing in various directions. There were battered old cars and litter everywhere. As we pulled up to the outskirts, it was like a scene from the film *Black Hawk Down*. I could see the streaks from rocket-propelled grenades (RPGs) flying all over the place and there were locals with AK47s running along rooftops, firing wildly down into the streets.

We stopped next to a 2 Troop wagon; it was Mick Flynn's. I watched as he traversed the turret and opened fire with the 30mm cannon. The rounds hit one of the gunmen, launching him backward and shattering him against a wall.

I spotted a sniper in a window and started traversing my cannon but Mick got there first, blasting the window and surrounding wall, vaporizing the sniper.

I could hear rounds pinging off our wagon. I could also see something to my front, but couldn't quite work out what it was through my observation window. I opened the hatch and realized that it was a para in a shell hole. Rounds were splashing along the lip of the hole. Sand was getting kicked all over him. As a minimum, the Paras work as a section, which is eight men, so I had no idea how he had ended up on his own.

"You okay, mate?" I shouted.

"What the fuck do you think?"

"How much ammo have you got?"

"About half a magazine left."

"Okay, then," I said and closed my hatch.

He stared in disbelief at the vehicle. I popped the hatch open.

"Only joking, mate. Bet you thought I'd gone," I told him.

"Fucking funny; now get me out of here."

At that point a stripped-down Land Rover pulled up, a Para sergeant with a big handlebar mustache on the back, blasting away with a .50 caliber machine gun.

"Let's get my man out of trouble," he shouted over.

"Roger that. On my call, rapid fire," I told him.

"Now!" I shouted, and he started blasting away again. "Jump up and grab hold of one of the storage bins, and hang on," I called to the para in the shell hole.

He ran around the vehicle, jumped up and grabbed on. As soon as he had a hold, I told the driver to floor it and we started reversing at speed, as did the Land Rover. I was staring through my periscope when it shattered. The small-arms rounds were really slamming into the vehicle—although armored, it can't take too many hits—so I pressed the button for the smoke dischargers. Nothing happened, so I frantically started pressing harder. Then I remembered that all of the smoke grenades had been taken out, ready to go home.

We were coming under even more fire and I started firing bursts of ammunition toward an enemy RPG team I could see. Looking out of one of the other periscopes, I saw flames close by. Fuck. My webbing, which was in one of the side bins, was on fire. I had ammunition and grenades in there, which wouldn't do much harm to the vehicle if they went off—but would hurt the para on the back. I flipped open my hatch.

"Throw the webbing," I shouted. The para couldn't hear me over all the noise so I reached over and tossed my webbing myself. As I straightened up, an RPG streaked by my face.

"Fuck, that was close," shouted Sergeant Simpson. "Fuck this."

He started blasting away with the 30mm cannon.

We pulled up next to a resupply wagon and the para rolled off the back. We gave him a wave and then pushed forward again. As we came to a halt back in the village, the fighting just stopped; I mean absolutely stopped. It was now deathly quiet. All I could hear was the sound of the vehicle ticking over and my heavy breathing.

Then a dog limped across the deserted street.

"They must be getting ready for a last big push," I thought. "The silence must be them regrouping."

I was right. The calm was suddenly shattered by gunfire from all directions. The vehicle was ringing to the sound of rounds hitting it.

I started blasting away with the 7.62mm machine gun while Sergeant Simpson fired the 30mm cannon. I watched two gunmen run for a building on the other side of the street. I cut the first one down out in the open. The other made it to a corner. I waited for him to reappear. Giving him a slight lead as soon as he took off, I cut him down as well.

It fell silent again.

"What the fuck triggered all of that?" I asked Simo.

It turned out that the Paras were in the right place at the wrong time. Six RMPs had been helping the local Iraqi police in the village of Majar al-Kabir when the locals took offense and started rioting. This turned ugly quickly and soon the mob was after blood. The RMPs ended up retreating to the police station and fighting for their lives. Sadly, they were overrun and all killed. The Paras were trying to fight their way in to help them.

The next day, we escorted the investigation team back into the village. The presence of armored vehicles seemed to keep the hostile locals away. Either that or they were all dead.

The sight that met us at the police station was horrible; poor fuckers. All of the RMPs were shot to ribbons. One of the SA80 assault rifles was missing and that snapped something in the brigade commander. He sent in the heavy tanks and they started firing huge barrages of artillery in order to allow troops to search for and clear any enemy from the remainder of the village.

Unsurprisingly, with the amount of firepower going down, the rifle was quickly found in someone's house and handed over. But what is one rifle when six lives have been lost?

We headed back to the holding camp, recounted the ammunition and then flew home.

After six months on tour, I was physically and mentally exhausted. The SSM had come close to breaking me—but one man had saved me: the sniper on the roof. He had allowed me to see something that I didn't know existed. Soldiering at the ultimate level. Man as weapon. I had thought of those snipers every day since. I had also made up my mind.

I wanted to be one.

7. Becoming a Sniper

I soon found out that my regiment was stuck in the Stone Age. Frankly, it was surprising we didn't still use muskets. I pissed off so many people by trying to get on the sniper course. I asked everyone—my officers, the training wing. All they kept saying was that we were Household Calvary and there was no need for snipers.

"Why?" I kept asking. "Because we ride fucking horses? And look like toys and bring thousands of pounds of tourism into the country and drive round in little tanks that were built in the sixties? Wake up—the Army is moving on."

I decided that a war of attrition was the best option. I just kept asking—literally for years—until I ground them down. They gave up and finally I was booked on to the course.

The only trouble was that there was no one to give me a precourse workup. Before attending a course, there is always preparation that you have to do. I felt it was important because I didn't want to look a complete dick—but no one in my regiment could help me prepare and, worse than that, we didn't even have the kit I needed. Little things like a fucking rifle and a spotting scope. I was literally going on the course blind.

I got my physical fitness up to a high level, but, as for the rest of it, I really did not know what to expect. I begged and borrowed as much kit as I could and on 12 February 2006 I reported to the training camp in Pirbright, Surrey, where the course was going to be held. I knew it would be a long nine weeks.

I was met at the guardroom by a lad called Bradders, a Scots Guards private who was the course store-man. He led me to the block that would be my home for the next nine weeks. What a shithole. The block was a dilapidated Second World War Nissen hut. I could piss faster than the showers and my bed had no springs, so when I lay on it, my arse was on the floor and my knees were by my head. I had to take my locker door off and shove that under the mattress to give it some support.

There were some lads there already but, as on all courses that you go on, no one talked on the first day. Now and again, one of us would give a quick glance around the room, just to eye up the other lads, but that was it.

It didn't take me long to unpack. I then sat on my bed, watching the other lads pulling out all this kit, and I turned my head to look at my stash. "Fucking hell, I've got fuck-all," I thought to myself.

I checked the timetable that was pinned to the wall, which told me that we had an eight-mile speed march carrying 60lb of kit first thing the next day. As I listened to some of the other lads talking, self-doubt started to creep in. Most of them had been in a sniper platoon for a year, or at least a couple of months, and it sounded like they knew their shit.

"Better to start as a clean canvas than to have bad habits," I told myself, then started to shove kit into my rucksack to bring it up to the correct weight. As soon as my admin was done, I got my head down.

I didn't sleep well, as more people kept arriving through the night. It felt like as soon as I closed my eyes it was time to get up. We were all still ignoring each other in the morning. I decided to skip breakfast because I had been taking carbohydrate supplements through the night and since I'd got up. Instead, I lifted my kit onto my shoulders and headed for the course offices.

As soon as I turned the corner, my mouth opened. There must have been a hundred blokes in a line, all wearing their kit. "Fucking hell, I hope these aren't all on this course," I thought.

Now I was *really* doubting myself—but it turned out that the speed march was for a number of different courses, including ours. I had my kit weighed by one of the instructors and started to mill around.

"Snipers to the rear," someone shouted, and I headed to the back of the group.

That was when I met our instructors: Daz, a Royal Marine and the chief instructor; Frank, from 2 PARA; and a Welsh Guard, called Jap. I was shocked straight away because they just talked to us; there was no shouting. The lads on the other courses were getting bellowed at by their instructors. It felt good to be treated like an adult.

Daz introduced all of the instructors, then surveyed the carnage at the front.

"You're all supposed to be A1 soldiers so we aren't going to scream and shout at you," he said. "Plus, there is so much to take in that we really don't have time."

"Kit on. Form up in three ranks," the physical training instructor shouted from the front. "If you drop back more than a hundred yards from the main pack, that's a fail—and you're binned from whatever course you're on."

A fail before you had even started.

"Quick march!"

And we were off. He set off like a rocket. Gaps immediately opened up and people started running, even though we were supposed to be speed marching. The pace was relentless and it didn't get any easier. It became obvious quite quickly that this march was designed to separate the men from the boys. People started to fall back and peel off immediately. I pushed round those dropping back and concentrated on staying with the pack.

We stopped for our first water break and people were strung out all down the track. Some had dropped out already. I'd only managed a sip when we were off again. Most of the next section was uphill—and the hills were covered in snow. It was grim but I pushed on, forcing my way to the front so that I could be near the instructors.

One hour and fifty-five minutes later we were back where we started. Eight very fast, very painful miles done.

The people who never made it were sent packing: no second chances on this course. I got back to the room, sat on my bed and smiled. "Not bad for a donkey walloper," I said to myself. I beat all of the Guards and some of the Paras. My feet were a bit sore and I had some hot spots, but apart from that I felt fine.

I fucked the shower off; there were only eight of them so there were big queues already. I washed my face and my balls in the sink and then headed straight to the classroom. We had more tests to do: map reading and general knowledge. I was fine with map reading—but general knowledge! It brought back memories of the careers office: me sitting there looking at the clock and out of the window at Tom. I ended up guessing quite a few of the answers.

The results were posted on the office wall later that afternoon. If your name was in red, you had failed; that's you gone. If your name was in blue, you had passed.

"Fuck, at this rate there's going to be no one left and I still haven't spoken to anyone . . ."

I approached the board. There was my name in blue—I had only gone and passed. If only I had done the lottery that day! The rejects headed off and, after scoff, we had to lay our kit out in front of us for the instructors to see. I watched as the other lads laid every single bit of their kit out—it looked quite impressive. I felt a bit of a dick as I had a rucksack, some webbing, and an assault rifle. I hadn't even got a sniper rifle. The instructors told me not to worry, and I was issued all the kit that I needed.

That same night, we had a night navigation exercise. This course was full-on. Before the night nav, I walked to the office to look at my results again. I felt like a little school kid, a smile from ear to ear. I wanted to do a little dance.

Back at the accommodation, Bradders walked in. "Still here?" he asked.

I just smiled at him.

"The instructors had a bet that you wouldn't make it through the opening tests," he told me.

My smile got even bigger. "Well, I'm full of surprises," I said, as I grabbed my rucksack and headed out the door.

The night nav started off in an office, where we were given ten minutes to write down the grid references of the eight checkpoints. We were sent off at five-minute intervals and I was the third to leave. I took my time setting off as I didn't want to burn myself out. Once out of camp, I started running through the woods, my sniper rifle in my rucksack sticking straight across horizontally, and my assault rifle pointing forward in my hands. It was how we were told to carry them and it formed an annoying crucifix. It was mental; the sniper rifle kept hitting the trees and making me fall over, throwing me backward. It was four steps forward and two back, and when I did fall over I lost vital seconds getting up.

I found the first checkpoint. You had to be spot on with

your compass bearing and distance as the marker was a small light stick, dug into the ground so that you could only see it when you were five yards away. I made a note of the reference, and the time I got there, and set off again.

Before I knew it I had five checkpoints under my belt and three more to go. I felt fucked and I could feel myself slowing down. It had been a long day. I was soaked with sweat, my feet were sore and my rucksack was hanging off my shoulders. I told myself to get a grip and pushed on.

The cut-off time was two and a half hours to complete the nav. I finished in two. I was bent over, sucking breath, when Frank, the instructor, came over and gave me some water.

"Not bad for a donkey shagger," he said.

I smiled at him—praise indeed—and then shuffled off back to the block. What a first day . . . but I was on the course properly now.

I handed my weapons back in to the armory and then enjoyed the luxury of a cold shower as there was no hot water. By the time I climbed into bed it was 0100 and we had to be up at 0530. I had learned my lesson on other courses—shared accommodation is a nightmare for noise and movement—so I'd brought an eye mask and ear plugs with me. I was asleep before my head hit the pillow.

Day two and there were only ten of us left on the course. We'd lost twenty on the first day. It was funny, but lads started talking to each other now. I guess once they knew they were definitely on the course they could relax a bit. There was one officer on the course: a young captain from the Coldstream Guards. He turned out to be a top bloke, for a Rupert. I quickly became friends with a lad called Gaz. He was from the Pathfinders, and had just failed Special Forces selection. He'd got malaria in the jungle, poor fucker, and he was still yellow.

The week progressed quickly and we learned all of the characteristics, safety details, stripping and assembly of the sniper rifle, plus positions that you can fire from. Some of them you'd have to be like Houdini to get into.

On the Wednesday night, we did another night nav; this time at a place called Ash Ranges in Surrey. The ground was flat, but marshy and hard-going. We were split into two groups, starting from opposite ends of the course. We had to carry the same weight as before and the crucifix on our backs. Luckily, this time there were no woods.

I made good time as I was not being knocked over by trees and before long I hit a wire fence to cross. I underestimated how much weight I had on my back and slipped on the fence as I was crossing, so that I was straddling it. It was only at that point that I realized the fence was electric. I could feel my bollocks burning, the pain going up into my throat. I rolled off the fence and collapsed on my back. I lay breathless with pain on the ground, looking up at the sky and holding my bollocks, hoping the agony would subside soon.

I had just decided to pour water on my poor burned balls when I heard a scream. It was Gaz—who had done exactly the same as me, just a few yards away. Now there were two of us lying on the ground hugging our bollocks. I had to take my kit off to stand up; it's just too heavy to stand up from a lying-down position with it on your back. Once I'd sorted myself out, I started laughing at how ridiculous we must look.

"Try pouring water on them," I told Gaz as I jogged on by. Seconds later, I heard a high-pitched sigh of relief as he took my advice.

The night navs were hard. You had to be absolutely spot-on with your navigation. What I did love, though, was being on my own. There was no one else to blame but yourself if you fucked up. I also enjoyed being pushed and having to push myself; the instructors pushed me harder in those nav exercises than the Cavalry had ever done. Before long, this one was over and I was in the back of the minibus. Warm, dry, fresh kit on, dozing while waiting for the others to arrive. It was a good feeling.

The whole of week one was all about the rifle: safety, firing, movement and carriage. It was only on the Friday that we got to fire it. We made our way to the local range and sorted ourselves out. I had never fired the L96—as the sniper rifle is known—before.

I moved into position behind my rifle and loaded the first round. As I started to lie down, I placed my finger on the trigger and *bang*! The rifle went off. The trigger was way more sensitive than I'd thought it was going to be. I knew I shouldn't have put my finger on it until I was ready—and now I'd shot a hole through the corrugated iron roof above us. Fortunately, some of the other lads had started firing so no one noticed my shot. I waited for one of the instructors to run over and kick me, which was the treatment I expected after all my years in the Army, but nothing happened. I shook my head at my error. "Whoops," I thought.

The aim of this shoot was to get all of your rounds into as tight a group as possible. We shot at distances of 100 and 200 yards. Once I was getting all of my rounds into a group that was 15mm in diameter, I was happy. I adjusted the settings on my scope and called it a day, happy that my rifle was zeroed—meaning the rifle sights were aligned properly and I could fire it accurately. Week one done.

I headed home for the weekend. Back in summer 2003, I had met a wonderful woman. I was in a pub in Bedford, nursing a pint and waiting for a mate to show up, when out of the corner of my eye I saw her legs. I jerked my head up in time to see they belonged to a beautiful young woman with long brown hair, wearing a very short dress. Moments later she disappeared. I tracked her down to the pub next door, where she was watching her friend play on a slot machine.

"Gambling's addictive, you know," I said. She smiled and we spent the rest of the night talking. I found out Tanya managed an Early Learning shop, was newly single and had a nine-year-old daughter called Dani. She was also warm and funny, and I knew straight away she was the one for me. After grabbing a few hours kip on my mate's sofa, I surprised her by turning up at the shop.

"You're a scruffy bastard, aren't you?" she said. Maybe I should have shaved and changed my T-shirt. Suddenly I felt like a twat standing there, a hulking tattooed squaddie surrounded by toddlers and their mums. There was a little kid picking his nose who took one look at me and started crying. It was a relief when she agreed to see me again and I could escape. We got married eighteen months later, and now I couldn't wait to see her. Before the sniper course I had been on a twelve-week Cavalry crew commanders course in Warminster, so I had already been away a lot. Tanya was pleased to see me—but not so pleased when I told her I had homework.

"It's always Army first, me second," she told me.

"I've got to give a hundred and ten percent. I don't want to look like some Cavalry knobber."

I'm not sure that was what she wanted to hear. The homework was time-consuming: we had to make our ghillie suit over the weekend. The ghillie suit is the sniper's primary means of camouflage. It's a jacket and trousers covered in hessian, burlap and other scraps of material; when done properly, it should look like a bush.

I'd organized with the tailor in camp to use his office and sewing machine and spent most of the weekend making the suit; on Sunday, Tanya decided to join me in the tailor's office so that we could be together. The effort was worth it, though, and I had my ghillie suit built by the end of the weekend. Some of the other lads hadn't finished theirs and had to keep working on it each night during the week while I used the time for dry training.

Dry training is all about practicing the fundamentals without any ammunition. That way you can do it anywhere. For me, it was all about lying still for an hour or so, holding my position, then opening and closing the bolt. For the sniper the ability to lie undetected is crucial. Each night I got my DVD player, put it at the end of the corridor and watched a film, while lying in a firing position behind my rifle. Once I had mastered the stillness, I started balancing a ten-pence piece on the end of the barrel, just to really hold myself to account.

We spent the whole of week two at Stony Castle Ranges. On Monday, we collected firing data from 100 to 650 yards, basically learning what happens to a bullet at different ranges and the implications of different firing positions. That week, I also learned that firing in a ghillie suit is hard. It is hot, restrictive and uncomfortable.

On Thursday we had our first qualification exam, the results of which went toward our earning the sniper-shooting badge. For those who failed, there would be a retest on Friday. It's funny, but those who fail on the test mostly do so at the short and mid ranges, and not the long-range shooting; fuck knows why.

The pressure was bad on test day. I hadn't dry-fired the night before, wanting maximum rest. I stayed as calm as I could throughout the exam and just did what was asked of me. I passed. As each day went on, I loved the course more and more. Each night, I sat at the end of my bed and stared at my kit, thinking about how I could improve it: trying to work out how to make my rucksack more comfortable, or how I could make my observation post notebook more waterproof—anything I could do to make life a little easier.

The next weekend, I was back in the tailor's shop, modifying and improving my kit; poor Tanya. I felt bad that I was not spending more time with her, but she was starting to realize how much this course meant to me.

On week three we headed to Bisley Ranges to start doing longer-range shooting: 750 to 1,000 yards. "Fuck me," I said to myself, as I climbed out of the minibus and saw the range for the first time. There were flags everywhere—every hundred yards on both sides of the range and up the middle. To make matters worse, a lot of them were fluttering in slightly different directions, meaning that the wind was fluctuating over the distance I'd be shooting.

It looked utterly baffling but the instructors made us lie on the firing point for an hour and just take everything in: the sounds, the wind, the flags, the trees and grass—anything that moved. After that hour the environment started to make sense. Some people just have a knack for tuning into their surroundings and some don't. I am one of the lucky ones, helped by my childhood out in the countryside.

We got the opportunity to dry train and I focused on maintaining my firing position and my trigger control. I then moved onto the firing line. To take in all of the range flags, you would need a head like a fish—eyes on either side of your skull—and I quickly found it easier to focus on the furthest flag. That was where the bullet would start to slow down and therefore be most influenced by the wind.

I loaded my rifle and got myself into position, concentrating on the rhythm of my breathing—in and out—and trying to lower my heart rate. I wanted to make myself as still and as relaxed as possible. I waited for that furthest-range flag to drop and when it did I squeezed the trigger and felt the reassuring recoil of the rifle in my shoulder.

After each shot, the target frame was lowered. An orange disk about the size of a saucer was placed on the hole that your bullet had just made and then raised to indicate where you had hit.

The first shot is known as the cold bore shot. As the rifle bore and barrel warm up with each shot, the bullet will behave slightly differently each time you fire. What you really need to know is where your round is going to land when the rifle is cold, as this is the position you will be in as a sniper. You never adjust your position based on the cold bore. As the barrel is cold, the first shot will always be slightly low or high. Once the rifle has warmed up with the first round, it becomes a lot more accurate.

I fired again. If I had mucked this one up, then I could make an adjustment.

We continued like this every day.

On Thursday we had another shooting test, this time at the longer ranges. They stopped telling us the results and just posted them outside the office. There was a retest on Friday, as before—but if you failed that, you were off the course. As I was driving the minibus back to the office, I had a bit of fun, driving straight past the building so people couldn't see their results. Made me laugh—but nearly caused a drama, as people were jumping out of the bus before it had stopped.

We crowded round the bit of paper and it turned out that we had all passed the shooting phase. What a result.

Next week, the sniper phase would begin. That was the bit of the course I had really been looking forward to, as I loved being out in the field.

Monday was all classroom work, learning about the

sniper skills. We knew how to shoot on the range, but now we needed to learn how to shoot as a sniper. We learned about judging distance, observation, map reading, camouflage and concealment—and finally stalking. All of these skills would be examined and you had to pass them all to earn the right to wear the sniper badge. It was going to be another challenging week ahead.

The first stalk we did was hard as it was cold and raining. On a stalk, you get dropped off at a distance back from where you will fire. The aim is to move forward cross-country, undetected, and get into a position where you can make the shot. This can involve crawling for hundreds of yards in your ghillie suit, all the while trying not to attract the attention of the watchful instructors, i.e., at a snail's pace. This means that you are crawling for hours.

Of course, as this was the first stalk, we all got found.

The exercise started with camouflage and concealment. We all lined up facing a large gorse bush and were then given an area that we must stay within and fifteen minutes to blend ourselves into the environment as best we could. Once the fifteen minutes were up, we all had to come back and critique each other.

"Veg is the edge," the instructors kept saying.

It's true. Local vegetation blends you in far better than anything man-made. I was proud of my ghillie suit but it was so thick I looked like a walking sasquatch. Looking like Bigfoot may sound fun, but the suit was heavy—and doubled in weight when it was wet. Plus, it never seemed to quite match the surroundings. Some lads had a few plants and bushes shoved into their suits; some had loads. Lots of people hadn't covered their heads and shoulders, which is an obvious "human" shape; others had made the mistake of shoving plants in so that the white roots were showing.

Once all of these points had been made, we had five minutes to rectify the faults and then twenty minutes to find an area that would be our FFP: final firing position.

"Go!" shouted Daz.

I hared off into the bush and found a brilliant position. I had good eyes on the target, there was a good backdrop and I knew I blended in with the surrounding vegetation. Then I heard a voice hissing, "Pssst."

"Fuck off, I'm here," I whispered. I looked around but couldn't see anyone else. This was *my* spot.

"Pssst."

I looked around again . . . then up.

"No way."

The officer had climbed up the tree above me. He must have been twenty feet up.

"People tend to look down not up," he said smugly.

"Nuts," I replied, and ran off to find another spot.

"Time's up," shouted Daz five minutes later, and the instructors all turned around and started trying to spot us.

It must have taken them all of ten minutes to find us. All of us except the tree-dwelling officer. The rest of us had joined the instructors at the target when the wind picked up and there was a scream, followed by the shape of a person falling out of a tree, followed by his sniper rifle and a crash. We all fell about laughing.

"That makes all of them," said Frank to Daz.

For the next three weeks we continued to develop our sniper skills. We were out every day doing some form of activity relevant to our trade. It was hard work and the weight started to fall off me. It was great to watch our development, though: from being spotted within ten minutes and falling out of trees to becoming a well-formed team—stealthy, professional and capable. These weeks were designed to prepare us for the final exercise, when we would be assessed on everything we had learned. Exercise Precise Eye was held in Wales—and was designed to be our toughest challenge yet. It would be conducted in "hard routine," so no cooking, no brewing up, no light, minimum noise. We wouldn't even be allowed to brush our teeth, which I hate.

The week-long exercise would begin immediately after a final two-day block of instruction. Frank took us out on to the area to do hides training: our last lesson. A hide is a lying-up position from which the sniper operates. Frank took us through the different types.

"First there is the expedient position. This hasty position ensures the sniper's silhouette is as low to the ground as possible, yet still allows him to fire and observe effectively. It requires little construction and conceals most of the body and kit, but you get little freedom, little protection overhead and weapons and optics might be exposed. Effectively you are relying on heavy camouflage, so this might be nothing more than a gorse bush. This should take between one and three hours to construct and you should occupy it for anything between six and twelve hours.

"Next is the belly hide. It's like the expedient position, but it's got a roof. It requires extra construction time, extra materials, and it takes four to six hours to build. It can be occupied for anything between twelve and forty-eight hours. This position can be built under trees, rocks or any available object. The darkened area allows the sniper more freedom and the ability to move freely.

"Finally, there is the semi-permanent hide. With this one you have total freedom of movement inside. You can stand, sit and lie down. Complete construction is four to six hours but you will need up to four people to construct it. You can live in it for up to forty-eight hours."

Once Frank finished the lesson, he briefed us on the evening's activities.

"You are to head out in two-man teams to a grid reference I will give you and construct a semi-permanent hide by first light."

They issued us with axes, picks, shovels and sandbags. Once this was added to the kit we had already, it weighed an absolute ton. I was paired up with Gaz; once we got the nod, we headed off into the woods. We had to move tactically, as the instructors were out and about trying to find us. We got to the right place and sorted ourselves out, finding a small depression in which to hide our bulky kit so we could just keep the essentials with us.

"I'll dig first," I told Gaz, once we were good to go.

I rammed the spade into the ground and the vibrations rattled up my arm into my head; it was like hitting concrete. The ground was frozen and felt rock solid.

"This should be a fun night," I thought to myself.

I plowed on and once I was through the frost, the going got a bit easier. Once we'd filled the sandbags with soil, the rest had to be moved away from the hide area so as not to compromise it. We used my rucksack to move loads of earth 200 yards away, all the while trying not to leave too much sign of our presence.

"We'll need some local vegetation for camouflage, and some logs to reinforce the side of the hide," I whispered to Gaz.

"Right-o," he replied and moved off into the darkness.

Suddenly, there was a noise like fucking thunder. Gaz had felled a forty-foot tree and the crash was unbelievable. He appeared out of the gloom.

"Was that a bit loud?" he asked.

"I don't know; could you have picked something bigger?"

We waited tensely to see if the noise had attracted the instructors. Once we thought we were all right, Gaz headed back to the Canadian redwood he had just felled to saw it up, and I went back to digging. After a while, we swapped over and I headed off to finish cutting up the tree.

"You can't miss it," Gaz told me.

He wasn't joking. It was massive; I had to remind him that we were trying to build a sniper hide, not a log cabin. A semi-permanent hide is supposed to take four men four to six hours to build, so we had to work like Trojans all night to achieve the same thing. At first light the instructors would sit 400 yards away and try to spot our hides.

In my mind, we were going to build the best sniper hide ever—but, stepping back and looking at it, I wasn't sure we were there. It looked like a hole surrounded by logs. It had a log roof but we couldn't stand in it; in fact, we couldn't even kneel in it. We could both just about squeeze in with our kit. Top tip, though: if you want to dig a semi-permanent hide, you have to put a loophole in—somewhere to fire from—otherwise all you have dug is a grave. At that moment, we had a grave. A few alterations later, it was pretty much as good as it was going to get.

The hardest part of constructing a hide is making sure you can actually see the objective, or get "eyes on," as we call it. Often you are so low to the ground you can't actually see the target. This hide was a bit low, but just about workable.

Just before dawn, we stopped work and dragged all of our kit in. At dawn, I crawled out and did the first-light checks, making some hasty improvements to the camouflage. I then crawled back in and waited for the instructors to arrive. We were both hot and sweaty from the labor, but the chill soon crept in. They seemed to take ages. And the longer they took, the more I needed a shit.

"Please, mate, just hold it," Gaz begged me, but I couldn't; the pain was too much.

I laid out a square of cling film, rolled myself just above it and did the deed. Not good in such an enclosed space. Gaz was gagging and I was worried about the instructors smelling us before they saw us. I got Gaz to roll it up as I couldn't reach back in the position I was in.

"Come on, mate. Teamwork," I reminded him.

Once he had wrapped it, I put it in a Tupperware container and popped it in a pouch in my webbing. I had just sorted myself out when the instructors arrived. They immediately started trying to spot the hides. Once they thought they knew where one was, they would run over and jump on the roof and try to collapse it. If you have built it properly, the enemy should be able to walk right over it.

One by one, the hides were found. We were the last one, but we were spotted in the end. Nothing is black in nature and our loophole gave us away. We were debriefed about our individual hides and then given time to fill them in. Once that was done, the training was over. Now, our final exercise began: immediately. This was what we'd been building up to throughout the course. It was make-or-break time.

It was hard right from the outset. The instructors didn't let up. We went straight into contact drills: a fighting withdrawal as our hides had been compromised. After that, the pressure was constant. We dug another hide—this time with five of us to do it. We rotated through the construction in four hours; four people working, one resting. We were like zombies, making small mistakes, but we pulled it out of the bag; we worked hard as a team.

As soon as the hide was complete, we were forced to

move. We secured a helicopter landing site and were then picked up and flown to Wales for the urban phase. The flight was an hour and a wonderful chance to get my head down. After what felt like minutes, we were woken up. The back tail ramp of the helicopter was down. The RAF loadie woke up a lad called Phil and gave him a thumbs-up to check if he was okay. Phil interpreted the thumbs-up as "we are here," undid his safety belt and stepped straight off the ramp. We watched wordlessly as Phil disappeared into the darkness and then all fell about laughing. It turned out that we weren't on the ground yet. We were actually in a hover fifteen feet up in the air. Fortunately, he only broke his leg. These things happen when you are tired.

Urban sniping is no picnic. It looks like it will be easy—basically hiding in a building—but it is actually a nightmare. The environment constantly changes, so you have to change your camouflage all the time. The weekend before the exercise, I had made myself an urban ghillie suit from an old set of desert-pattern combats that I painted brick patterns onto. I was going to need it.

The exercise area was an old American Cold War base, covered in hangars, warehouses, accommodation blocks and even a disused railway station, although the tracks were still in use. At one point I was on a stalk next to the railway line and a train packed with civi commuters passed by; it was surreal.

We had only days left now and I was running on pure adrenaline. On the last stalk, we were briefed that we would be doing a coordinated shoot on the train station. I was given arcs that I must be able to observe and engage—and three hours to get into position before first light. I started off by climbing into a disused train carriage. It is amazing how high they are when you aren't standing on the platform. I found a good position, but also realized it was an obvious position. In the sniper world, anyone trying to spot you will look at the obvious first, so I moved on to a big, empty warehouse; I needed to pass through it to get to the missile silo that I wanted to use as a firing point. I found a small door and cracked some infrared light sticks. I tossed them into the building and then looked through my night-vision goggles, just about seeing where to go. The place was massive and I soon got lost. I felt like Hansel and Gretel, leaving light sticks rather than breadcrumbs.

All I could hear was the sound of dripping water and the echo of my footsteps. I tripped over and hit the ground hard. The ground stank, and with all of my kit on it was a struggle getting up. My hand pushed into something soft and I realized it was a decomposing sheep. Poor fucker must have starved to death. Eventually, I found an old wooden door out and dashed across thirty yards of open ground to get to the silo. I made it without anyone spotting me.

Once inside the silo, I spotted a platform that would be perfect. I had to make a jump of about four yards to get onto it. That doesn't sound like much—but it might as well have been fifty yards. I had no idea how far down the drop was.

I checked my watch; I had been going two hours and was running out of time. A leap of faith was required. I stripped off my kit and tied a rope round my waist. I tied the other end to the padded case containing my rifle, also known as a drag bag. I ran, made the jump and then pulled my rifle over. The ledge was good, but there wasn't actually a loophole to fire from. I rummaged around in the drag bag and pulled out a metal stake. I started to scrape away at the mortar around a brick, praying that this part of the building was only one layer thick. Fortunately, it was. As I got the first brick out of the way, I could see that I had perfect eyes on the objective.

I slipped with the second brick and it dropped with a clang off the ledge. I quickly looked over at the rail platform as there were now "enemy" on it. Fortunately, no one looked over.

Once the hole was big enough, I got myself set up and listened in to my radio. We were all given separate targets to engage and then there was a countdown. "Three . . . Two . . . One . . ." The nine of us all fired simultaneously. Although we were only firing blanks and the enemy were role-playing, it was satisfying to watch my target drop, simulating that he had been hit. The most important part was that we were all in a position to fire and fired together.

Over the radio, we were told to extract, and then came the words we had all been waiting for. "Endex": military slang for end of exercise. Job done.

But our exam wasn't over yet—not by a long way. We were picked up by helicopter and flown on to another large range complex in Wales. We were dropped off next to a barn and, after our admin was sorted, given a full night of sleep. In the morning, we started the next assessment: the unknown distance shoot.

This was very similar to a stalk, but we would actually fire our rifles using live ammunition. The directing staff (DS) sat with the target and tried to spot us as we approached. If they didn't spot us, we would fire a blank round. If they still couldn't spot us, they would move out of the way and we would be given two live rounds. We had to hit the target with one of the rounds.

We were dropped off an unknown distance from the target. On the command "go," everyone started to head right, so I went left. I took my time and started to crawl forward painfully slowly, trying to stay as low as possible, until I reached a large gorse bush, where I gently raised myself up to try to spot the DS. I could see sheep to my front, moving in and out of the gorse, so I slowed down even more so as not to scare them. It is easy to give yourself away with wildlife. As they wandered off, I realized that the sheep had created natural tunnels through the gorse, which was a gift. I could now move more freely and make up some time.

I crawled forward and hit an old wall. I checked my watch; I had half an hour left. Blank shots off to my right meant others were in a firing position already. One thing you can never do is panic, so I kept calm and slowly looked over the wall. I could clearly see the instructors. I assessed my position: I had the gorse behind me, making a good backdrop, and the wall in front of me, making a good frontdrop. I needed only minimal natural camouflage—just my head, shoulders and the barrel of my rifle.

It took me fifteen minutes to sort myself out and build up my position. The instructors were scanning in my direction, but I would have had to really fuck up to be seen. I fired my blank round, and waited for my live ammo to be delivered.

"Sniper?" I heard from behind me. It was one of the instructors, known as "walkers" when they are walking around a stalk.

"Walker," I answered.

Daz came over and handed me two live rounds. I saw the DS move away from the target and I started to work out my firing data—range, elevation, deflection—and dial the adjustments into my scope.

I took up the slack in the trigger and squeezed. *Bang.* Miss. I saw my bullet strike just to the right of the target, so I dialed in three clicks left.

"Take your time," I reminded myself as I exhaled.

Bang. Hit.

It was the best feeling in the world—but there was no time for high-fives. I had to extract without being seen as well. Most of the lads got caught on the extraction. Fortune favored me that day as I made it back without being seen. But I had used up nearly all of my time getting into my FFP—I made it back to the barn with only minutes to spare.

Out of the nine of us, only three hit our targets. I felt extremely proud to be one of them.

The last week of the course was also based in Wales, at a hideous exercise area called Sennybridge. No matter what the weather in the remainder of the UK, it is always raining in Sennybridge. We lived in a small wooded copse for the week and worked through a series of tests: the last hurdles we had to cross to qualify for our sniper badge. Once the badge tests were out of the way, all of which had gone okay for me, as far as I could tell—the instructors were giving nothing away—we had one final night nav. It was in the Black Mountains and I was well up for this one. There were eight checkpoints—eight buried light sticks to find.

I set off, but I had only gone less than a mile when I fell down a hole. It was the size of a manhole and it was only the crucifix of the sniper rifle on my rucksack that stopped me from disappearing into the water below. I'm sure I would have drowned with all the weight I had on.

I threw my assault rifle forward, gave a huge kick and crawled out. As I lay on the ground getting my breath, I felt something stabbing in my nose. It was a stick as thick as a pencil and the same length. If I had fallen on it as I was crashing into the hole it could have driven into my brain. It shitted me up big time and I felt like throwing the towel in. I was cold, wet, beyond tired and I hadn't even made it to the first checkpoint yet. "Fuck it; it's the last test," I said to myself. "Keep moving; keep warm."

I banged through the checkpoints with plenty of time to spare and ended up being the first one in. Once we were all finished, we drove straight back to Pirbright, to wait to hear how we had done. We spent a day sorting out all of our kit and then we were lined up outside the offices. They weren't going to pin the results to the board this time—they were going to call them out.

Daz started to shout out our names. Lads marched forward once their name was called out and collected their sniper badge: an embroidered set of crossed rifles.

"Harrison . . . top student," he shouted.

It took a moment for it to sink in, and for me to move. I marched forward and collected my badge. I was about to march back when Daz told me to stay where I was.

"The lads have also voted you the best character on the course for help and friendship."

I felt on top of the world.

Just before I left Pirbright, Daz grabbed me. "If all of the lads from your regiment set such high standards, there will always be two places on the course for them."

I shook his hand and headed off. "Not bad," I thought to myself as I drove out the gate. "Fuck-all precourse, no knowledge of sniping and no one in the regiment to help me. Not too bad at all."

Now, I needed to spread the word in the regiment.

Now, I was a sniper.

8. Insurgency in Iraq

In May 2007, I was back for another tour in the shithole that was Iraq, where the situation had deteriorated massively since my last visit. After the initial invasion, the Iraqi Army had been disbanded, making thousands of qualified soldiers redundant . . . and disgruntled. They soon took up arms and the insurgency—a war among the people—had continued to grow. Senior officers talked about "reconstruction" and "development," but really it was survival mode now. It was my first tour away from Tanya and I hoped that she was going to be all right, but I knew she was mentally strong, plus she had a good family behind her. For me, the tour was a dream come true. Ever since my last trip to Iraq, where I'd met that sniper in the football stadium, all I had wanted to do was to deploy on operations as a sniper. Well, here I was.

I had an L96 sniper rifle. This is the Army's 7.62mm sniper rifle, capable out to 1,000 yards. There was a new .338 caliber rifle coming into service that put it to shame, though. That thing could shoot way past 1,600 yards, or so we had been told. It sounded awesome.

Basra was the main British Army operating base in Iraq, but we were heading to the Maysan province, which was northwest of Basra. Everywhere in Iraq was dangerous for a Western soldier, so it didn't really matter where we went. The regiment had formed a Mobile Operations Group (MOG), intended to find the enemy and "shoot and scoot"—that is, engage and then pull back. But of course they could see us coming from miles away, so they could choose whether to engage us or simply melt away. We basically drove around the desert all day, moving from spot to spot, getting sunburned. My sole source of entertainment was watching the lads putting the camouflage netting up over the vehicles.

We were attached to the King's Royal Hussars (KRH) Battlegroup, which was proving frustrating. We were a reconnaissance regiment, but the KRH already had its own recce troop. At each orders meeting—or O group, as we call it—you could bet on who would be leading the next battlegroup move: recce troop, not us.

There came a point where I couldn't contain my frustration and I felt I had to say something at the next O group.

"Any questions?" the CO asked at the end of his orders.

I put my hand up.

"Yes."

"What are we doing here? I mean, what is *our* purpose here?"

There was deathly silence; you could have heard a pin drop. Cavalry officers don't like being questioned.

"Any real questions?" someone shouted from the back, and people started giggling.

The officer didn't reply and just walked off.

We spent most of our time operating out in the desert. Our food and water were dropped off at night on makeshift drop zones. For each resupply, we circled the wagons on the outside of the drop zone and placed an infrared strobe in the middle. The RAF flew over and pushed out ten pallets of supplies. Each time there was terrible waste as you could guarantee that three or four parachutes wouldn't open and the pallets would smash into the ground. For some depressing reason, the pallets of fresh food always seemed to be the ones that creamed in.

It was Russian roulette for us as well. If one of the pallets with an unopened parachute landed on one of the vehicles, we would be toast. There was also the risk of it landing on locals. No matter how far and how deep we got into the desert, people always seemed to find us. Who knows what the locals were doing there. It's quite unnerving to be forty miles out in the desert, having a piss behind a sand dune, when some kid pops out of nowhere and asks you for a sweet.

The whole thing also seemed ruthlessly inefficient, as we had to burn the parachutes once we had collected the supplies. Eventually, they stopped doing air drops and we had to carry more supplies with us—or move to logistical nodes for resupply.

At least being in the desert, with its relative lack of people, meant it was easy to spot dickers. A "dicker" is anyone who watches us and passes information on to the enemy, and is a clear threat to a patrol. If he is coordinating activity or relaying information to the enemy that could threaten the patrol, then he can be legitimately engaged. Plus the desert makes it really easy to spot people moving around on motorbikes, which was the dickers' preferred mode of transport.

There were two snipers in the MOG: myself and Eddy, who was really fit—in spite of being a bit on the tubby side—and had a dry sense of humor. I'd trained Eddy up and he'd done really well on the sniper course; he'd also got top student. So that was two Cavalry lads beating the Guards and the Paras at their own game. But do you think that the regiment was interested in sniping? "No" was the short answer.

We received orders on a Monday that the following week we were to move from our current location out in the desert back to Basra airport. I noticed that day that we seemed to have picked up a dicker. Every time we moved, the same guy was on our tail, following us on a motorbike.

On Tuesday, our friend was still out there. Always hanging back about half a mile, but always there.

When we stopped for a break that day, one of the lads grabbed a shovel off a vehicle and walked out into the desert for a dump, or "shovel recce" as it was known. He had just dug his little hole and was squatting over it when we started to receive incoming artillery. A round landed quite close to him and he made a great sight trying to run back to the vehicle: trousers round his ankles, loo roll in one hand and weapon in the other. We all started laughing at him.

I'd dug my foxhole properly when we'd stopped—I like digging and it gave me a bit of a workout—so I felt reassured when I jumped into it. Some of the lads had been getting sloppy, though, and hadn't dug theirs very deep. Now they could see why you shouldn't cut corners. The rounds were fucking close. I crossed my arms over the top of my body armor and sank into the hole, mud and sand splattering over me. The lads with the rubbish holes were taking cover under their vehicles.

The rounds stopped and then someone yelled, "Incoming!"

The second wave was inbound.

In the lull, one of the young lads had climbed out from under his vehicle. As the rounds exploded, he stood out in the open, paralyzed for a second, before running around like a headless chicken. Everyone was yelling at him to get under a vehicle. I sprinted out and grabbed him, pushing him under the nearest wagon.

"Get your head down," I told him.

"I've never seen incoming before," he stammered.

"That was almost your first and last time."

I don't know why but I sprinted back to my hole. A round landed twenty yards away from me as I was running. I felt the sand hit me and the shock wave drive me into my hole. I ended up face down, looking at sand and my boots, praying that the next round wasn't on target.

You would have thought that we would move on, as the enemy artillery had now bracketed us, but the CO gave the order to stay. He was concerned that this might be a trick to lure us into moving on to something even more deadly. As you could see for miles in all directions, I was not convinced about his logic. At that precise moment in time, the plot of land we were on seemed to be the most dangerous.

The rounds stopped landing and after twenty minutes we all started to crawl out from our various shelter positions. Some of the vehicles had had their tracks knocked off so we quickly got them back on in case we did have to move.

On Wednesday morning, I slid my sniper rifle out from its case and built up a firing position behind it. Sniping is a perishable skill and it needs maintaining; dry firing is a good option for keeping up to speed. After thirty minutes of dry firing, a shout went up.

"Dicker."

One of the lads pointed me in the right direction and I got myself set up on a sand pile. I quickly located the dicker: it was the same guy we had been seeing for the last few days. It was probably the same guy who called in the rocket attack. I loaded a live round into the chamber of my rifle and started to observe our friend. The heat shimmer in the scope was pretty bad, plus there was some wind. I estimated him to be 500 yards away and made the necessary adjustments to my scope.

My heart was beating like mad. I could actually see my heartbeat in my cross hairs as each beat rippled through my chest. This was my first real shot as a sniper and emotions were getting the better of me. "Slow down. Breathe," I told myself.

I took a deep breath and slowly exhaled, bringing myself under control. I kept taking longer breaths until my heart settled. All I was waiting for was the order to fire; I was praying that the CO had some balls and would let me shoot.

I could see the glint coming off the dicker's antenna. He clearly had a radio.

Eddy ran over. He had been off speaking to the CO, asking for permission for me to engage.

"Green light," he said and lay down next to me.

I settled the cross hairs onto the target—the base of his neck—and then aimed slightly lower, just so there was more target mass. The heat shimmer was really not helping, making the image swirl round my scope. I took up the slack in the trigger and held. This was it.

Bang.

I watched the round as it swirled through the heat shimmer. I reloaded and fired again, not even adjusting from the first round. I could see that I had hit him with the second round as the heat shimmer died off at just the right moment.

I cycled another round into the chamber and ran for my vehicle.

"Get us down there," I told Seamus, the driver. He stopped the vehicle about forty yards from the motorbike. We both got out with our weapons and cautiously moved forward, ensuring that we were covering each other.

The motorbike was still running, an AK47 strapped to its side. I reached over and turned the engine off. Then I saw the dicker.

I had shot him through the throat. He was gasping for air and trying to reach out for his radio, which had flown out of his hand. There were voices on the radio. I pushed it away from his fingertips and knelt down next to him. I placed my hand gently on his chest. He bled out seconds later, taking a last, rasping gasp.

"I bet you never told people how much you loved them and how much you care," I told him. "It doesn't matter how much you shout and cry; they won't hear you. When you're dead, you're dead."

I reached over and closed his eyes. He went so quickly there was nothing anyone could do.

It was only then that the implications of my first kill with a sniper rifle hit me. Due to the magnification of the scope, you do tend to see the person you are about to shoot. Of course, in this case, I had been right next to him when he died. I knew he was a clear threat to the troop and that I had done my job. Yet I wasn't totally prepared for the intimacy of the whole experience.

At the end of the week, we headed back to Basra. The kill was on my mind over those few days. I kept replaying the shot and seeing the final moments when the dicker bled out. I just wanted to be left alone but people kept asking me if I was all right. Once we were back at Basra, I called Tanya; she told me that I didn't sound happy. I lied to her and said that I was fine.

Later in the tour, the squadron leader sent for me. Naturally I assumed that I was in trouble, but it turned out that there were some problems at the Iranian border, revolving around a local police chief. The squadron leader had been told to head over and try to sort things out. He wanted to take six people with him and—just my luck—he had picked me to tag along. To add real insult to injury, there was a ban on vehicle movement, so he wanted to walk. We all looked at each other with amazement.

After we had sorted our kit out, we headed off. We were taking our webbing and daysacks plus a lot of water; I mean shitloads of water. The heat of the day was hideous; it felt like we were on a Foreign Legion death march. For five hours we trekked across the desert in an arrowhead formation. It was lucky the boss picked fit lads, as no one really did long-range foot patrols out there.

As we got close to our objective, we saw a massive building on the border that I assumed must be the police station. I put the lads in all-round defense and Eddy and myself walked forward with the squadron leader so he could have a chat with the police chief. The issue was quickly resolved. By then, fortunately for us, the vehicle ban had been lifted. The lads came and picked us up—which was great, as I felt like my feet had been pressure-cooked.

Once back at Basra, we were told that the whole squadron was on standby to help Special Forces conduct strike ops. Basically, we would provide cordons and cut-off groups to allow them to go in and do their strikes. The rest of the regiment was in the process of leaving; vehicles were being moved by low loaders and the lads were being airlifted out. Fortunately, Eddy and I weren't on the initial move as we had been out on the death march. Instead we were in the cookhouse, getting some scoff, when one of the troop leaders came to find us. The squadron leader wanted us again.

"There's an enemy mortar team that have been going round the perimeter of Basra station testing our defenses," he told us. "We want you guys to neutralize them."

"What the fuck is the RAF regiment doing?" I asked. "Isn't that their job and don't they have snipers?"

He couldn't answer that question. I answered for him. "Those wankers are more concerned with how they look than with doing their job properly."

Either way, Eddy and I were tasked with finding the mortar team. We ended up lying on top of a shipping container that overlooked the fence where the enemy had last been seen. We headed out mid-afternoon, which meant that the container was fucking hot to lie on, though this becomes a godsend at night when the temperature drops.

Sniping is actually more about surveillance and observation than shooting. The hard part is keeping your mind active while lying there. I counted, as did Eddy, as I had taught him. I also scanned right to left, just to do something out of the ordinary. We are taught to read left to right, so scanning right to left is slower and the brain takes in more information. Plus I tried to speed things up or slow them down to break the monotony. Rapid scan, rest, slow scan. I rested my eyes periodically for twenty seconds to give them a break too.

Nothing happened until 0300 hours. At that time, I picked up some movement near a pylon through my night sight. It was only about fifty yards away. There was a person clearly trying to stay in cover. They had identified a blind spot in the camera coverage along the fence and were trying to get to it without being seen. Eddy picked him up as well.

"He can't be alone," Eddy whispered to me.

He was right: five minutes later two more people arrived. They approached the fence and placed their hands on it. I was relaying all of the information to the headquarters on my radio, just waiting for the green light to engage.

The next thing we knew, vehicles were racing up with their lights on full beam. It was like a bad *A-Team* episode, starring the RAF regiment.

They screeched to a halt and soldiers started to clamber out. Of course, by this point the three suspicious people had run off. I knelt up.

"What the fuck are you cunts doing?" I shouted at them.

It was clear by the look on their faces that they had had no idea that we were out there.

"Sorry," they sheepishly replied, before getting back in their vehicles.

Eddy and I climbed off the container and walked back to base. The squadron leader complained to higher HQ about the cock-up and for the next three days we commanded the operation—but of course our little friends didn't come back.

Then the KRH were told that they were being short toured: sent home early. It didn't take long for the Chinese whispers to start and the rumor spread that they were being sent back because they were so shit. They needed more training. From what I'd seen of them, I could only agree. The squadron leader called the entire squadron together for a meeting. One hundred of us soldiers were crammed into a tent designed for twenty. It was boiling with all of us in there. Of course, we were all assuming that he was going to tell us that we were being short-toured along with the KRH.

Instead, he told us that the whole squadron was being re-located to Umm Qasr port to conduct operations around there. Umm Qasr is the key port in southern Iraq, vital as a logistical hub, so it has to be secure. Fortunately I was scheduled to head home for two weeks' R&R just before we relocated. Not only did I get to see Tanya and Dani, but I also missed the move. The Cav are very anal about packing and repacking kit.

As soon as I got back, I went straight to work building a sniper hide on the roof of one of the main port buildings. All the lads had to do was patrol around the port, the docks, the lorry park and the HLS. I made sure we could provide over-watch.

This task soon got very, very boring; there wasn't much going on and certainly not much enemy activity. They made us move camp and, in traditional Cav fashion, we completely tore down the old camp and then rebuilt a new one. It felt like they were inventing stuff to keep us occupied. I started going out on the patrols simply for something to do.

Just as the boredom was becoming unbearable, Eddy and I were called to see the squadron leader again. He told us that we were to go to Basra Palace, the main British HQ in Iraq, and report to the PJOC: the Permanent Joint Operations Center. We were at the HLS at 0300 hours to be picked up by Lynx helicopter. It was safer flying at night as the enemy enjoyed taking potshots at military helicopters during daylight hours. The flight was only twenty minutes long and we got a good view of the palace, which was situated on the outskirts of the city next to the Tigris, as it was so well illuminated.

It was a nightmare getting into the HQ due to all the security, but fortunately there was a Cav officer there to meet us. He took us out to a place called the penthouse, which was where Saddam's servants used to live. We were given a room that had a bed, a sink and a shower next door. Eddy and I did rock, paper, scissors for the bed and I won.

It turned out that we were close to the fighting. There were rocket attacks on the base and the only thing separating Eddy and me from the outside world was a forty-foot-high wall. I slept like a log on the first night, despite the incoming fire. On the second, I didn't sleep so well. It was like Guy Fawkes Night with all the explosions going off.

In the morning I put on my helmet and body armor to move around. There was a proper siege mentality—people hunkering down to stay out of the rocket attacks.

Heading for breakfast in the cookhouse, you had to cover a fifty-yard gap between the blast walls. You needed to run like the wind—because people would take potshots at you as you crossed the gap, firing from the surrounding buildings. Eddy and I ran together and immediately the sand splashed and we heard the loud *crack* and *thump* of rifle fire as someone started shooting at us. We skipped and danced over the rounds like two dads at a disco. We must have looked like right twats. We got to the other side and, as ever, started laughing. It's all you can do.

Eddy and I were the only sniper pair at the palace. We hung around waiting for tasking. On the third day, we were told that the Special Forces wanted us to support an operation they were doing. They were going into Basra city and conducting a snatch operation: lifting a high-ranking bad guy.

We were picked up at 2300 hours and driven into the city. The SF had already inserted, so Eddy and I were to be dropped off near the objective and left to sort ourselves out. We had been told we could put our observation post where we liked. Our job was to stay in a position where we could observe for up to an hour after the SF had left, to gather intelligence and see what effect the SF op had.

We were being dropped off by Bulldog armored vehicles and they would be our support if we needed any. I agreed the extraction plan with the officer and was not reassured when he told us that in case of a problem we should "run like fuck."

Eddy and I had studied some aerial photos of the area before the op and had identified a six-story building that we thought we could use.

The journey in was hideous. The wagons got pummeled with fire as soon as we approached the city. Eddy and I were scrunched up in the back of one of the Warrior armored personnel carriers, basically an armored taxi. Its crew had left the top hatches open; one of the lads was manning the machine gun on the turret and providing top cover.

"I'm not happy with the roof being open. Anyone can throw something in," I told the vehicle commander.

"Don't worry, lads. They never shoot down," he replied, trying to reassure me.

There was an explosion as an RPG hit the vehicle and dust and sand poured in the open top hatch. My ears were ringing and Eddy and I started nervously laughing. Then there was another explosion as we got hit again. "At least these vehicles can take the knocks," I thought. The Warrior lurched to a halt and the commander turned back to me.

"Lads, we can't get all the way through to the drop-off point," he said. "It's about fifty yards away and you'll have to run the rest. I'll fire smoke grenades; let the smoke build for three minutes, then go for it."

I heard the smoke grenades discharge and climbed out the back door of the vehicle, tucking myself into the bar armor while I waited for Eddy to get out. I looked up to see an RPG warhead sizzling away, stuck in the bar armor. It was nice to see something the Army had bought actually working but we needed to get out of there. Eddy joined me.

"On three," I told him. "One . . . Two . . ." I started running.

"Wanker," he shouted after me and ran to catch up.

We stopped by a small wall and waited, just to get our bearings and take stock of the situation. Looking back, we could see the Warrior was still there. It should have pulled back as soon as we'd run off. I tried calling them on the radio, but there was no reply.

"Something's wrong," I told Eddy. "We need to go back."

The smoke was dying down now, but we managed to sprint safely back to the vehicle. Once at the back door, we looked in. The officer had climbed forward into the driver's cab and was desperately trying to help the driver, who had been shot through the throat. In Warriors the driver has a small slit to look through while he is driving; the round had passed straight through this slit and hit him.

"Throw more smoke," I told Eddy, as I climbed into the vehicle.

I held the lad's throat to try to stop the bleeding, but there was blood everywhere, oozing through my fingers. One of the other crew members clambered into the driver's seat. With such a serious casualty, they had to get him out of there and back for medical treatment fast. Eddy threw some more smoke grenades.

"Come on, Craig. We've got to go," he yelled.

The commander took over from me and I climbed out. Immediately tracer fire started slamming into the vehicle, inches away from me. Eddy and I sprinted back to the wall and watched as the vehicle reversed off.

Suddenly, there was silence—and it was very, very eerie.

"We need to move off," I whispered to Eddy.

"Roger that, mate."

All of the commotion had eaten into our time. We had only thirty minutes to get into position. We started running in a crouch, moving from building to building. We got to an open square; opposite the side we were on was the building that the SF were going to hit.

I looked at the aerial photo and then up at the building we were next to.

"Shit."

"What's wrong?" Eddy asked.

The aerial photo hadn't shown that the building I wanted to use was actually open-sided: a multi-story car park. It had a low wire fence all the way round it and a spiral staircase up the middle.

Eddy and I started to patrol forward cautiously. I stepped onto the top strand of the wire fence and the whole thing collapsed. We made it to the staircase and then headed up to the fifth floor. It gave us good observation, but we had to be really careful moving around: the floor was riddled with holes where rockets had slammed through.

We found a decent firing position and got ourselves set up. Twenty minutes to go. I took my sniper rifle out of its padded case on my back and put my SA80 assault rifle in it. I got set up behind the rifle while Eddy sorted himself out behind the spotting scope.

Suddenly, there were two huge explosions off to the right. The shock waves rippled through our building and masonry poured down on us. I had my helmet on but Eddy didn't. Swearing, he rapidly slapped it on.

The explosions were two car bombs going off outside a mosque, just down the road. It was the end of prayers so lots of people were coming out. There were dead and dying everywhere. I relayed all of this to HQ on my radio. It looked like a vision of hell down there, but we were told that the op was still going down.

We switched our arcs back onto the target building and saw the SF lads stacked up along the wall. The SF were very, very slick. In the blink of an eye, the op was done. One minute they were stacked up; the next they were streaming into the building, appearing only minutes later, dragging a fat fuck with them. They tied the guy up, threw him in the back of a white pickup truck and raced off. Now we had to watch for one hour and see what happened next. Only after that could we extract.

Within minutes, I heard some noise beneath us. It sounded like someone was on the second floor. There was only one way in and out of the building and that was the staircase; if we got stuck on this level we would be fucked. I flipped down the night-vision goggles on my helmet and pulled out my pistol. I crawled back to the staircase and looked over the edge. I couldn't see anything, but I could still hear noise—like someone tiptoeing across the floor below.

I let Eddy know what I was up to and then I set up a trip-wire across the stairs, attaching one end to a smoke grenade. If someone came upstairs, the distraction of the smoke grenade going off should allow us to get into a fighting position.

I was just tying the wire to the pin on the grenade when I heard movement again. I froze. This time it sounded like it was on the third floor. Someone was clearing the building.

I crawled back to Eddy and grabbed my radio. "We need an evacuation *now*," I whispered into my handset.

"Roger that. We are five minutes out," replied the vehicle commander.

We grabbed our kit and came up with a hasty plan—to drop smoke grenades down the stairwell and throw them onto each floor as we ran down the stairs.

"One minute out," I heard over my radio.

We started throwing the grenades, pounding down the stairs. Just as we cleared the building, I saw the Bulldog reversing down the road and then smashing through the perimeter fence. It was also discharging smoke grenades so the smoke was everywhere. It got to a point where we couldn't even see the vehicle; we just plowed on in the direction that we had last seen it, until we bumped into it. We felt our way round to the back door and clambered in, dragging our kit after us as the vehicle tore off. I hadn't seen anyone as we'd run down the stairs—but if there had been anyone else in that building, they'd stood a good chance of dying of smoke inhalation.

The journey back was without incident. But as we pulled back into base, we had to get out and unload our weapons. The driver of the Bulldog started unloading his .50 caliber machine gun . . . and accidentally discharged the weapon. The round hit the ground behind me and Eddy, making us jump. Typical: we'd run the gauntlet out there—and then almost got killed by our own people back in camp.

After a quick debrief in the ops room, we headed back to our room. I had never been so happy to see my bed.

Days turned into weeks, and once again the monotony and boredom started to become a killer. We did a few small ops with the SF lads but nothing big. Eddy and I decided that we should hit the gym—we might as well do something to keep us entertained.

The first challenge was getting there. You had to run over a small bridge and people tended to shoot at you from both sides. Once there, though, my jaw dropped. I had heard of spit and sawdust, but this really took the piss. The punchbag had bullet holes in it. The spinning bike's front wheel was buckled. Eddy sat down at the rowing machine and took a pull; the bar came off and he flew off the back, still sitting on the seat. I think we actually burned more calories running over the bridge. We gave up.

Eventually, we were told that we'd be moving to another operating base, hitching a ride on one of the constant convoys moving troops and supplies from location to location. We would be traveling down a road nicknamed Champagne Glass due to its shape. In normal circumstances, it would take about twenty minutes to walk down this road, but it would take us about two hours to drive it, due to all the contacts with the enemy.

We headed off in a Warrior and, yet again, the top hatches were open. At least this time it cooled us down. An hour into the journey, we hit an IED. We were really lucky to survive.

There was an explosion and the vehicle rocked with the blast, which was so loud it left us with ringing ears. Fortunately, the only damage we'd suffered—as far as we could tell, at least—was a lost track. Thinking fast, the crew in the vehicle behind drove into the back of us and then pushed us out of the danger zone.

Within minutes, though, I felt a jolt as an RPG round slammed into the side of us. I could smell smoke and then see flames as they curled over the top of the open hatches. Looking out of the top hatch, I saw that a box of rations on one of the outside storage bins had caught fire. I pried it free with a shovel before clambering back in.

We had to be shoved all the way to the base, the machine guns on the turrets firing pretty much the whole way. It was a nightmare urban environment, with buildings everywhere for the enemy to hide in.

Once inside the base, a large walled compound, we tried to get out—but the rear door of our vehicle was now fucked. We had to clamber out of the hatches. Outside, we could see that two road wheels were gone and the sprockets had been ripped out. The vehicle that pushed us was peppered with bullet strike marks.

These lads did this move every month. Fuck that.

We headed into the ops room for a briefing, meeting up with some lads from B Squadron and a sniper pair from the Guards. It was good to see everyone. The base was only 160 yards square, with a main building in the middle and then tents and a cookhouse. The ops room was on the second floor of the main building. There was a poster of Winston Churchill on the wall, giving his famous victory salute—and a hole where an RPG round had detonated.

"There is a sniper hide on the roof," we were told. "Your job will be to man it between 2300 hours and 0500 hours each night. During that time, there should be no movement so you have free rein to engage targets of opportunity."

Eddy and I headed up to the hide and took in the view during daylight. The first thing we noticed was that the hide stuck out like a bulldog's bollocks. It was made of sandbags, wood and hessian sacking, and riddled with bullet holes. The enemy clearly knew what it was. There were a lot of enemy firing points in the local town that looked on to the sniper hide.

To the front there was a long wall with a seventy-foot hole in it that gave a lot of firing points for the enemy. This was known as RPG alley. To the right was a wheat factory, which now looked like something out of Stalingrad, and to the left was a half-finished house. A river ran off to the front and we were told that insurgents would come down by boat to shoot at the base or pay local drunk lads to take potshots. We had heard the horror stories about this base—it got attacked all the time and they were constantly taking casualties. Eddy and I headed off to get some rest before our first shift.

Well, the horror stories were true. The first night it was like the gates of hell had opened up. Every man and his dog shot at the base.

The base itself was on full manning. Lads manned the corner positions and poured machine-gun fire out at enemy firing points. I watched as tracer fire poured from the wheat factory and landed in the base. I could see the shooter just back from the window, but he had silhouetted himself. I lined him up in my cross hairs and fired. I missed.

I realized that we hadn't prepared ourselves properly so Eddy and I pulled out a map and worked out the ranges to all of the prominent landmarks. When you know the range, you can make much more accurate adjustments to your scope. Once we had done that, I started to have more success.

"RPG alley," Eddy told me.

Rounds slammed into the sandbags behind us as I swung my rifle around, picked up the gunman, gave him a slight lead by moving the cross hairs just off center of mass and then fired.

Hit. The guy dropped like a sack of shit.

"This hide is crap," I shouted at Eddy, struggling to be heard over all of the machine-gun fire.

"I agree. Let's head on to another part of the roof."

As we ducked down and ran out of the hide, an RPG streaked by. We found the other sniper pair who, like us, had sought a different FFP.

"That hide's shit," one of them told us smugly. "It's like a bullet magnet."

I resisted the temptation to punch him in the face.

The night passed quickly as there was so much action. At first light I was about to head off the roof when I noticed a market setting up in the town. I watched as the local people went about their daily business, stepping casually over all of the bloodstains on the floor.

We headed into the ops room and filed our kill reports before going to bed. The base continued to be attacked by rockets during the day, but we were fairly safe if we stayed in bed behind the blast walls.

On the fourth day the ops room sent out a Warrior armored vehicle to knock down the wall at RPG alley. All this did was create rubble for the enemy snipers to hide in.

That night we were back on the roof and it was worse than ever; rounds slammed into us from every direction.

A new rocket system then arrived, the Javelin, which costs £65,000 per rocket. Designed as an anti-tank rocket, it has its own tracking system, so it is "fire and forget." Once it has acquired its target, all you do is press the button and the rocket will do the rest. We were told that its tracking system was so good it could locate a person just as easily as a tank. We all watched in awe as the first one was fired. It dropped down, climbed up, shimmied a bit and then fucked off into the distance, completely missing the building it was being aimed at. No one knew where it went.

After the first night on the roof, I'd quickly realized that the enemy worked like we did: in pairs. If you shot one, the other would appear fairly quickly; you just had to be patient. I told the GPMG (general purpose machine gun) gunners not to fire, as I didn't want the enemy's attention to be drawn onto the roof.

One night, I saw an enemy sniper at the bottom floor window of the wheat factory. I rushed my shot and hit the guy in the stomach. He writhed around for a bit before—as expected—his partner in crime dragged him back and picked up the sniper rifle. As soon as he pointed it toward us, I nailed him, too.

The action was so intense that Eddy had his rifle out and couldn't spot for me. It was draining having to take in so many details myself. It also seemed fairly futile, as we weren't really achieving anything. Every night we were on the roof and, despite moving positions, the enemy knew we would be up there somewhere. You could never relax; it was too hot to have a decent sleep during the day, and then we would be fighting all night. By the end, I was utterly exhausted. There was a real camaraderie among everyone, though: a sort of Rorke's Drift spirit.

On our last day at the base, we were almost overrun. There were so many enemy, coming from all directions, that everyone within the base had to man a weapon. Even the chefs were manning the battlements. The GPMG gunners were firing so many rounds that they were pissing on their barrels to cool them down. At one point, I thought of ringing Tanya just to hear her voice; I was that convinced that this was the end.

Once the sun went down, the craziness got worse. They fired RPGs at the vehicle park, trying to hit the fuel truck, but were so close to us that the RPGs didn't even have time to arm. That was lucky—because if the fuel truck had gone up, we would all have been toast.

It was an entire night of killing people. I lost count of how many people I shot. I just acquired targets, shot, reloaded. Come morning, there were bodies and blood trails everywhere.

The next day, I was recalled back to Basra airport. Eddy was ordered to stay and I felt like shit leaving him, as he was my wingman. Once again, I ran the crazy gauntlet back down Champagne Glass. It was actually quite light this time—mostly just rifle fire—only one RPG hitting the vehicle.

A few days later, Eddy arrived. They were closing the base down—it was just too dangerous. It was impossible to extract all the nonessential kit so they just left it. Tents, TV, gym kit, even an armored shipping container, were all left behind.

Just before we headed home, I was told that I had been awarded a General Officer Commanding Commendation for sniper support to the SF, command in the Maysan desert, the Iranian border patrol and the sniper support to the crazy base. The commendation was great—but what really meant a lot to me was a letter that the commander of the base wrote to me. In it, he said that Eddy and I "define what the word sniper means."

For me, there was no greater compliment.

9. First Afghan Tour

The squadron was lined up in the ports at Umm Qasr, waiting to head home from Iraq.

"Squadron . . . Squadron . . . 'Shun!" bellowed the sergeant major, and we all stood to attention.

The squadron leader took the salute from the sergeant major and then turned to face us. "Lads, I'm sorry to do this to you but I need a volunteer."

One thing everyone knows in the Army is never, ever volunteer for anything. Out of 120 lads, not a single hand went up. Then one arm shot up—belonging to a young lad who had only been with the squadron a week and didn't know any better. His arm was straight as a die and he looked really pleased with himself for volunteering.

"Good lad," said the squadron leader. "You're off to the Caribbean for three weeks on a sailing expedition."

There was a collective groan from the rest of us.

"Right, for the remainder, we have been put on standby to deploy to Afghanistan later this year."

He filled in some more details but I couldn't take them in. I couldn't believe it. We hadn't even finished in Iraq yet and already we were chalked up for something else. Afghanistan wasn't as crazy as Iraq, but it was a completely different environment—much more rural than urban, with far bigger areas to cover. The US and its allies, including Britain, had removed the Taliban from power in 2001 but they were far from defeated and years later they continued to wage guerrilla warfare. The Taliban were very influential in the rural areas in the south and east of the country, particularly in Helmand province, where the British Army was stationed.

As soon as we got back from our post-tour leave, it was straight into training. The IED threat that had been pretty much limited to Iraq had now morphed to Afghanistan too, so there was much more emphasis on counter-IED training. We spent a lot of time learning how to spot them, what to do about them and, most importantly, how to deal with a casualty situation involving them.

Coming back from a tour and then going straight into training, which often takes you away from home, was really hard for all of the families—and us. There was one bright spot, though, for Eddy and me. One day we were called into the armory.

"Here you are, lads," said the armorer. "The new .338 sniper rifle is in."

He laid a rifle and all of the accessories out on a counter for us to look at.

Simplistically, the .338 rifle is a bigger, heavier version of the L96, shooting the larger .338 bullet. The L96 has an effective range of 1,000 yards and can harass out to 1,200 yards, whereas this bad boy can be comfortably used at 1,600 yards plus. It has a more powerful scope and a much more powerful round. It was like Christmas for Eddy and me. We just couldn't stop playing with it.

"You aren't allowed to cover them in camouflage tape or spray-paint them," the armorer told us firmly.

I'm not a fan of spray-painting rifles as it can block the moving parts, but we normally covered our rifles in subdued canvas tape to break up the colors. Apparently, the Cavalry didn't want us making their nice, neat, new rifles dirty. But you can't be a sniper with a glowing new rifle.

The next day, we got to fire the rifle on the range. The Paras were there as well and had already taped up and spray-painted their rifles, making them pretty cool or "ali," as the Paras call it. Meanwhile, our rifles stood out like bulldogs' bollocks with their new paint.

"It's not the tool but the man behind it," I reminded myself.

I set myself up behind the rifle and very quickly I was dropping targets. What a piece of kit! It was just awesome. A bit heavy for snap shooting, but apart from that it was brilliant. It shot well, the new scope was impressive and you could feel the power of the round just by the force of the recoil.

We had two weeks' leave and then, before I knew it, I was back in camp, saying goodbye to Tanya. As I held her in my arms, she started crying. She worried about me, especially since I'd become a sniper.

"It's okay. Six months isn't that long," I told her, giving her a cuddle. Though I suppose it is when you are waiting at home for news.

I gave her a kiss goodbye and then found a seat on the bus. Just as we started to pull off, she looked up and gave me a little wave. I had a lump in my throat as she disappeared from sight.

We got to Afghanistan after the usual appalling journey that always goes hand in hand with traveling with the RAF. We then had a few days of low-level training at Bastion, which was the main British Army base in Helmand province. It was pretty much the same training we had done in the UK—but now in the sweltering heat.

Eddy and I spent the entire time pestering people to let us go on the ranges with our new rifles. We really needed to see how they performed in the higher temperatures of Afghanistan. The rifles have "fluted barrels," which means they have grooves machined into them. This is to increase the surface area, which allows the barrel to cool quicker—but we needed to find out what kind of difference they made to the rifles' ballistics.

We got onto the range eventually: an open piece of desert with sand berms bulldozed to create backstops. There were no fences and the locals tended to wander around it at night to collect the brass cases. We tested our pistols, our SA80 assault rifles and, finally, our .338 sniper rifles, firing them at 100 and then 200 yards. They were spot on. The heat wasn't making a difference and the rifle scopes hadn't been knocked during their long journey here.

The last part of our training was a lecture on the Rules of Engagement (ROE), which dictate when force can and can't be used. Just as there had been in Iraq, there was talk about "winning hearts and minds" so the locals wouldn't get so sick of us they'd support the insurgents. Overall, the ROE were slightly different for this tour, but still restrictive. The challenge that the sniper has is that most officers don't understand how to employ snipers and often don't understand the basics of marksmanship. They want to tell us where to go instead of letting us pick the best position. We will see threats at much longer distances, but the ROE often won't let us engage unless someone is in direct threat. It makes our job a struggle. If an officer doesn't know how to use us, doesn't understand the challenges of shooting at long distances, and then gives us too-restrictive ROE, our job becomes a nightmare.

Once our training was finished, we got our first tasking.

I was in my tent sorting my kit out when I was told that Eddy and I would be deploying to support a patrol base (PB) on the edge of the green zone, the fertile agricultural region that follows the River Helmand. I wasn't sure why we were being sent to the PB—as we were supposed to be in vehicles and this task was to be on foot—but before I knew it I was in the back of a Chinook flying over the desolate and barren landscape of Afghanistan. It's just miles of desert and the odd isolated compound before the green zone comes into view: a lush, green belt stretching for a mile or two along the banks of the river before the desert starts again.

The Chinook came in low and landed next to the PB, and we all dashed into the base.

The guys in the PB gave us a day to sort ourselves out so, after some briefs on the local terrain and likely Taliban firing points, we tried to get some rest. The PB was small and I didn't sleep well. I couldn't help thinking about my first patrol the next day and the IED threat our training had focused so heavily on.

The next morning, Eddy and I joined the patrol of twenty soldiers as it stacked up against the blast wall, ready to leave the base. This was my second tour as a sniper and I was glad Eddy was with me. We'd hit a point now where we both knew how the other thought.

The PB was set two hundred yards back from the edge of the green zone, out in the open. The drill was to leave the base gate, run twenty to thirty yards while zigzagging, and then break into a walk and start patrolling. The idea was to make yourself a hard target while you were vulnerable in the base doorway. All of the lads manning the sangars—guard posts fortified with sandbags—were on maximum alert and everyone was scanning, looking for a threat.

I watched as the guy in front of me at the gate dashed out.

Once he had finished his run, I looked back at Eddy to let him know I was going and, as soon as he had acknowledged me, I ran out. The PB was set back and uphill from the green zone, so the initial run was a nightmare. The ground was pitted and rutted and it was only by luck that I didn't twist my ankle. Plus, it's no fun knowing that you are a very slow-moving target.

Entering the green zone felt like entering the lion's den. I suppose it was, really; this was the enemy's home turf, and they usually knew we were coming. It was also eerie: a warren of tracks, streams and dense jungle-like foliage. We pushed deeper into the "zone," our movement slow and deliberate. Every now and then the patrol halted to make sure we weren't being flanked or followed. Each time we stopped, I knelt down and checked that I had some form of solid background behind me, so that I didn't stand out.

Ten minutes into the patrol, sweat was already pouring into my eyes as the temperature climbed to over one hundred degrees. The sniper bag they had given us wasn't helping. When on patrol, we carried our SA80 rifles and hid our sniper rifles in the drag bag—supposedly so that we didn't identify ourselves as snipers, but you would have to have been blind and stupid not to realize what the guys with the big rifle cases on their backs did in the Army. The new drag bag was rubbish. The straps were too close together so that when you knelt down, the butt of the rifle hit the floor and the top of the barrel jabbed your helmet, forcing it down into your eyes.

We kept pushing on and, before long, we found a compound. The walls were about ten feet high and made of compacted earth, with large metal gates allowing access. Surrounded by dense undergrowth, it just appeared out of nowhere.

Again, as we paused, I dropped to one knee. Things now felt really eerie. There was no one around. In the distance, I could hear odd noises and a dog bark, but apart from that . . . nothing.

I looked back at Eddy, who grinned at me. The remainder of the patrol would deal with any compound clearances, while we stayed outside and provided cover if needed. I took my helmet off and wiped my eyes with the sweat rag that was tied loosely round my neck.

I'd only just put my helmet back on when a burst of fire shattered the silence.

"Contact right!" screamed Pete, the patrol commander.

We all switched right and the lads immediately started firing in the direction of the enemy threat. I couldn't see the enemy, so I held off. An RPG whooshed overhead and exploded behind us.

"Fuck," I cursed, as I hunched down and then immediately popped back up, trying to locate the insurgents. I couldn't see anything conclusive but the RPG had left a white trail of smoke, which would be leading back to the location of the firer.

For some of the lads, this was their first tour and their first contact, so they were pouring fire down the flank. Eddy and I had experience with all of this so we started giving them a bit of direction. Then we crawled off to the flank and moved into the compound, looking for a spot with some elevation so that we could start doing our job. This seemed to be a "shoot and scoot," though, as no sooner had we started to climb onto the roof of the compound than it all went quiet.

We waited twenty minutes. Eddy and I stayed on the roof, scanning our arcs, but nothing happened. We climbed down and the patrol continued. As we headed out of the compound there were a couple of locals hugging their children and watching us; their stares went right through me.

After fifty yards, I looked back over my shoulder to see that the green zone had swallowed the compound already; it was just so easy to get sucked into an ambush in there.

There was a ditch off to my left, full of water and turds. A sudden burst of automatic fire sent us all scrambling for cover, and before I knew it I was in the ditch up to my chest.

"Man down," was shouted from a flank. The words everyone dreads—someone had been injured.

"Let's get these fuckers," Eddy said, while dragging my .338 rifle out of its case. He handed it to me.

"You're right. Let's fucking do this."

We stayed in the water and used the ditch for cover, while starting to push forward toward the enemy firing points.

"I'm moving forward on the left flank in the ditch," I told Pete on my radio.

"Roger. We're dealing with a casualty," replied the patrol commander.

Once we had pushed forward, though, we still couldn't see anything. Eddy rested his SA80 on the bank and started scanning through its scope. You have to look through cover, not at it, and it was his job as my spotter to find me the targets.

"Two hundred yards away there is a compound wall, and I think I can make out a man's silhouette next to it," he said at last.

I scanned through my more powerful scope and agreed he might be on to something. I called one of the other patrol members over, a man nicknamed Tank.

"I need you to start putting fire down at that wall when I tell you to," I said to him, pointing. I then told Pete that we were about to start firing.

"Right," I then said quietly to Tank and Eddy. "On my call. One . . . Two . . . Three . . . Fire."

Tank started firing at the wall. I saw movement, but it was hard to get a lock on it. My scope kept steaming up and my helmet was pushing down into it.

"Fuck this," I said, and took my helmet off, while Eddy kept scanning through his binoculars.

I cranked the settings down on my scope—we were so close I didn't need much magnification—and then wiped the lenses down. It was only then that I noticed the overpowering stench coming from the ditch. It was like the smell of ammonia and it was making my eyes water.

I got myself back behind the rifle and started scanning again. Suddenly, I caught a guy popping his head round the end of the wall that Tank was firing at. He had a rifle and he was firing bursts at the patrol. I placed my cross hairs onto the empty space where his head had just been and waited, all the while weeping at the stench of stale piss. I was so low to the ground that my round was going to pass through the undergrowth. Not ideal as a round is very vulnerable in flight, and even a blade of grass can knock it off course.

His head popped round the wall and I fired.

"Miss," said Eddy calmly from behind his binoculars. "You hit the wall to his right."

I fired again.

"Miss."

I could hear the round cracking as it passed through the undergrowth. I knew my zero was correct, so the foliage must be affecting the trajectory. I aimed off slightly, moving my cross hairs just off the target, and fired again.

"Miss."

"Fuck."

I fired again.

"Hit."

I watched as the guy tumbled out from behind the wall. He wasn't moving.

"He's dead," said Eddy. "Solid hit."

I quickly chambered another round and continued to scan the area; these guys never worked alone.

"Close in on the emergency HLS and give us some cover," Pete ordered us over the radio. We had to move.

"Watch and shoot," I said to Tank, who kept scanning to the front while Eddy got my sniper rifle back in its case on my back. Before he put it away, I reset the scope to its battle setting, which for me was twelve clicks of elevation.

We clambered out of the stinking ditch, which was a relief to say the least, and headed back 300 yards to the HLS. The casualty was duly picked up by helicopter without further contact, and then the remainder of us patrolled back to the PB. Once back in the base, the troop leader of the PB came to find us.

"Thanks for the support you provided out there," he told us, which was good of him.

First patrol and first kill of the tour—so I was pretty pleased as well. Once I had cleaned my rifles, I stripped off my stinking uniform. Somehow, I didn't think it would be possible to clean it.

"We've got spare uniforms; let's burn these," I suggested to Eddy.

"Good idea."

We washed ourselves down with big bowls of water. The PB was small and sparse, and water was at a premium; we only shaved once a week and only ever washed in bowls so we never got properly clean. As we took the stinking uniforms to the burn pit just outside the gate, I could still detect a faint waft of shit on me.

We chucked our clothes in the pit. With all the methane, they went up like old Christmas trees. All of the PB's rubbish was thrown in the pit and then periodically burned. The burn pit was in view of the sangars so it was pretty safe to go out there. Usually . . .

I was relaxing on my camp bed when there was a huge explosion from within the PB.

"Stand to!" someone yelled and I tumbled out of bed, grabbing my webbing and rifle.

"Come on, mate. Let's get to a sangar," I said to Eddy.

As we were sprinting across the open space in the middle of the PB, the gate opened and a lad called Scotty staggered in, covered in red.

"Medic," I shouted and we both veered off toward Scotty.

Quite quickly, it became clear that we didn't need a medic—but a chef. Scotty had gone outside to the burn pit with a load of rubbish and set fire to it. Unbeknown to him, the rubbish included foil ration bags with baked beans in them. Still sealed, as they heated up they exploded and he got covered in red tomato sauce. He was all right apart from a few minor burns and the fright of his life.

"Stand down . . . breakfast is served," the ops room told everyone.

Our plan was to head out on every other patrol, so there was a thirty-six-hour lull before we left the PB again. In the interim, it was attacked multiple times: mortars, rockets, rifle fire—whatever the enemy could throw at it. The PB was like a sitting duck, but at least it was secure, so we could hunker down inside and wait it out.

There were sixteen of us on our second patrol of the tour.

Apart from me and Eddy, the rest were Paras. We zigzagged out as usual and hit the green zone. Locals spotted us straight away and we knew we were being dicked. It wouldn't be long before the enemy showed up.

We ended up back at the eerie compound where the contact had happened before. I looked down and saw blood on the floor, along with bits of medical kit. It made me feel sick. I squeezed the hand grip on my rifle hard and, through gritted teeth, whispered, "Fuckers."

This was supposed to be a "reassurance" patrol for the locals—but a fat lot of good it would do. The locals didn't care and meanwhile the Taliban would have laid IEDs or set up ambushes for us.

We kept moving forward, and then Eddy called me over.

"This is the same route that was taken last time and has been continually used."

He pulled out a map.

"Where did you get that?" I asked him. He had what is known as a patrol trace, a map with all of the previous patrol routes and ambushes marked on it. It stops you setting patterns by using the same routes all the time.

"One of the outgoing snipers gave it to me."

The patrol stop-started as some of the lads talked to village elders. Each time we stopped, Eddy and I faced in different directions and covered our arcs. We ended up halting for a while, so I positioned myself to look into the green zone. I had a bad feeling so I started to scan right to left. I saw movement and brought up my SA80 to look through its scope.

"Eddy, I've got movement about two hundred yards to my front. I'm getting my rifle out."

I lay down, shrugged the case off my back and swapped the two rifles over. I had the .338 rifle with me that day; sometimes I took the 7:62mm rifle. It all depended on the ranges I thought I would be engaging at.

Once I was happy, I started to crawl forward into the vegetation while Eddy radioed the patrol commander to let him know what I was up to. The patrol commander was forward in the green zone, so he stood up to pull back to the patrol.

All hell then broke loose. A burst of automatic fire poured down at the commander and he started running. The remainder of the patrol started pushing back into the compound and the patrol commander was sprinting, trying to join them.

"Cover him," I shouted to Eddy.

Eddy fired a burst from his assault rifle and I got back behind my scope. I saw an insurgent with an AK47 running, trying to get into a position to fire into the compound. I gave him a 2mm (two-mil-dot) lead in my scope and smoothly squeezed the trigger. The .338 has a boom to it but I stayed focused and watched as the fighter crashed to the ground and slid forward, face first, into the dust.

"RPG!" someone screamed.

A vapor trail streaked across the ground in front of me. The rocket went straight through the compound entrance and exploded on the back wall. The patrol was in there.

"Let's go!" I shouted to Eddy.

I slung the rifle onto my back and started sprinting. I could hear rounds buzzing past my ears and thwacking into the trees and walls around me. Eddy was firing controlled bursts to cover me.

"Magazine," he shouted. This was his way of letting me know that he was out of ammo and needed to change magazines.

I swung back round to see Eddy trying to get a fresh mag

in his rifle. My SA80 was in the rifle case and the sniper rifle was slung on my back so I pulled out my Glock pistol and started firing in the direction of the enemy. Using a pistol at that range wasn't great but it was better than nothing.

"Back in," Eddy called out when he was sorted. I heard him fire a burst and I continued running. I'd nearly made it to the compound when there was a massive explosion.

"Man down," someone shouted.

The enemy knew our drills. They knew that in a contact we would try to push forward and to do that we would use cover. One of the Paras had jumped into a ditch and the enemy, predicting someone would do that, had put a pressure-plate IED in there. As I got closer, I could see the para in the ditch had lost his left leg. There was blood everywhere. It looked like a couple of other lads had been caught with shrapnel as well.

I reached down, grabbed the injured lad and pulled him back into cover behind an earth mound. The medic arrived and got to work on the injured lads. "You crack on," he told me.

The patrol was split between a few lads outside and the remainder inside the compound.

"Everyone all right?" Eddy shouted to those in the compound. He got a thumbs-up as a response.

We sprinted into the compound and rejoined the patrol commander.

"Why don't we try to get everyone into the compound?" I suggested.

"Good idea," he replied. He barked some orders to his lads and then sent a message on his radio to the remainder. "Throw green smoke behind the ditch and then, on my order, run back into the compound," he told those outside.

The FAC (forward air controller) threw a smoke grenade and Tank started a countdown.

"Three . . . Two . . ."

That's as far as he got; the lads just started running while the medic dragged the casualty. Everyone made it inside.

"What the fuck happened to 'one'?" Tank asked one of the lads.

"Fuck that; the ditch was filling with water."

An Apache helicopter arrived overhead and the FAC started talking to the pilot, vectoring him in on the enemy positions. It was awesome to watch the pilot turning his head and the gun barrels turning with him. Once he was happy, he started firing. The noise was deafening and brass cases started to rain down on us. Of course the Apaches always work in pairs; we hadn't seen the other one, but we could hear it hammering away as well.

After a short time, they stopped. You could have heard a pin drop: absolute silence, broken only by a dog barking, far off in the distance.

"Right, let's get him out of here," Tank said, referring to our injured comrade. "We can't get a medevac in here, so we'll have to carry him out."

The medic pulled a collapsible stretcher out of his pack and the casualty was loaded onto it. Tank got four guys to cover off around the stretcher. He pushed some lads forward to cover front and then got Eddy and me to cover the rear.

"Let's go," he said, and we all started running out of the compound.

In the heat, with all of our kit on, it was an epic challenge. The track was thin and the guys to the front were trying to clear it, but there was not much they could do. The lads carrying the stretcher were really feeling it. We took turns either providing cover or carrying the stretcher. Pretty soon we were all fucked. Fortunately, the PB sent out their quad bike, which came bombing down the track to meet us halfway.

We call it the "golden hour." If you can get a casualty back to the field hospital within one hour, they stand the best possible chance of surviving. We were all determined to get the lad back. He was loaded onto the quad and one of the medics jumped on with him. It turned around and raced off. The remainder of us kept jogging down the track until we popped out on the edge of the green zone.

A Chinook raced overhead with its back ramp down, the loadmaster peering out. Eddy and I stopped on the trail and faced back, in order to cover the direction we had just come, protecting the helicopter as it came in to land. Sweat was pouring down into my eyes and Eddy tapped my shoulder and passed me a sweat rag.

"Cheers, mate."

Once the helicopter was safely away, we jogged the remaining distance back to the base and both collapsed in sweaty heaps.

That turned out to be our last patrol out of that base—as there were orders waiting for us when we got back, moving us to a new location: Musa Qala. "That place has seen its share of fighting, so this could be interesting," I thought. In some ways I was quite pleased to be going. I couldn't really see the point of what we were doing round here. We'd been out twice—and not made it past the first fucking village!

The next morning, six of us stacked up behind the back wall of the patrol base. A Chinook shot overhead, wheeled round and touched down, just out the back of the base. At the same time, the mortars started firing smoke bombs to obscure things. The loadmaster on the back ramp gave us the thumbs-up and we all started sprinting for the helicopter. The quad bike brought our kit and soon the big green behemoth was lifting us up to the safety of 3,000 feet.

The flight to Bastion was thirty minutes, so I shut my eyes and got some much-needed sleep. It was good to have a hot shower and a tasty meal in the cookhouse. We ended up being given a day of downtime to do our admin. I spoke to Tanya, which was fantastic, and sorted out all of my kit. It was nice to go to bed that night and not have to sleep with one eye open.

The next day it was back to Cavalry work—sorting vehicles out. We would be using Spartan armored vehicles for the remainder of the tour and we had two days to get them ready to head out. This was no mean feat, as the vehicles were in a terrible state, like they had been in the Dakar Rally. Lord knows what the lads on the previous tour had done to them. The plan was for us to drive north up to Musa Qala and then stay there for the remainder of the tour. Once we headed off, we wouldn't see the luxuries of Bastion again until we were either on R&R or heading home.

I was not that comfortable with the drive north. So many Afghans work in Bastion that it's pretty easy for one of them to tip the Taliban that there are nineteen vehicles looking like they are getting ready to leave. We wouldn't even be leaving at night, which was normal practice, but for some reason would be departing in daylight. The dust cloud we would create would make it pretty obvious where we were. Eddy and I went out to the range to check that our weapons were zeroed, which went some way toward putting my mind at rest about the drive, although I still had a bad feeling.

We headed off the next morning. I was in the back of the vehicle and it was hideous. There was no air conditioning so it was like being in a sweatbox. Every time the vehicle stopped I opened the back door to let in some air. I also climbed out to get my bearings; I like to know where I am. My .338 sniper rifle was in its hard transit case strapped to the roof, so I also wanted to check it was all right. Six bumpy, sweaty hours later the vehicle suddenly lurched to a halt.

"Contact . . . IED!" someone shouted.

"Shit, shit, shit."

I opened the back door. It was midday and the heat hit me like a furnace. I carefully stepped out onto the track that the vehicle had just made: the one area guaranteed to be free of mines. I climbed up onto the roof of the wagon to see what was going on, Eddy following me. One of the vehicles to the front was in a dust cloud.

"I'll go and see how bad it is," Eddy volunteered.

He climbed down off the front of the vehicle, into the next set of vehicle tracks, and sprinted forward. As he opened the rear door of the blasted wagon, smoke bellowed out. One of the lads in the back was dead. He didn't have his helmet on, so his bare head had smashed into the side of the vehicle. It was obvious he had gone; at least it would have been quick. Eddy just hung his head. The medic arrived and took over, and people were tasked with securing an HLS. Eddy headed back to our vehicle.

I kept scanning the surrounding area; we were in a vulnerable position and it would be easy for someone to shoot and scoot at us. As I looked around, I saw it: a wire leading away from the ambush site. This IED was detonated by a person with a battery, not a pressure plate. It meant that they might still be around.

I hastily undid the clips on the transit case and pulled out my sniper rifle. I rested the rifle on top of a bergen—an Army rucksack—that was lashed to the roof of the vehicle and then got down behind it. Once I was looking through the scope, I could trace the direction of the wire as far as a nearby hill. I started scanning right to left on the hill. "No fucking way,"

I said to myself. There was a man on the hill, peering round rocks, exactly where the wire led.

"Eddy, there's someone on the hill in the direction of the firing point. Let people know that the HLS is not secure."

"Roger." He got on his radio.

Through my scope, I could see that this person had something in his hands, which looked like a walkie-talkie or a black box. This constituted a direct threat to us and the heli, so he needed taking out.

"Let people know I'm firing," I told Eddy.

I got out my laser range finder and zapped the distance: 200 yards. Not far, but I had to factor in that I was firing uphill—and that changes the point of impact. I made some adjustments to my scope and settled the cross hairs.

"Fate, don't fail me now," I thought to myself, and then started the trigger pull.

Due to my improvised position on top of the vehicle, the recoil knocked me left slightly. I looked back through the scope. I could see that I had hit the man through the calf. He'd moved when he was shot, so I could see him much more clearly now.

I cycled a new round into the chamber, readjusted my position and placed the cross hairs on his neck. I wanted to sever his spine so he couldn't press any buttons and detonate anything else. I fired—and again the recoil knocked me off my unstable position. I looked back through the scope, seeing blood all over the rock that he had been sheltering behind. There was also what looked like bits of skull and brain. I tracked forward and saw him in a heap with his head thrown back. I just stared through the scope.

Eddy broke me out of my trance. "Talk to me, Craig."

"He's dead."

"Roger that." He let everyone know on his radio.

A patrol was put together to go out and clear the area, but I stayed with my vehicle. When they got back in, one of the lads came over to find me.

"Craig, you should have seen the bloke you shot. His face is literally gone. No eyes, nose or mouth; it looked like mincemeat."

I just pushed sand around with my boot and stared at the patterns I was making.

"Cheers, mate," I mumbled. The way I saw it, I'd taken a threat out of the equation. After that, I needed to move on. I didn't want to talk about it.

The helicopter came in and picked up our dead body. The Taliban corpse was loaded in as well. It didn't seem right to me; the two of them being laid side by side.

Two hours later, we got moving again. Come dusk, we circled the wagons and made a "ring of steel." I got myself a brew and found a quiet spot, wanting to be alone with my thoughts. I pushed the image of the Taliban man with his face shot off out of my mind.

We spent the next few months traveling the length and breadth of Helmand province. We traveled from Patrol Base (PB) to Forward Operating Base (FOB) to desert lie-up. The bases varied in size but all had a common theme. Large walls to stop fire, a mixture of sandbagged buildings and shelters—and toilets that were just a trench in the ground. There wasn't much logic or background explained to us. We were like "rent-a-muscle": we just went where they needed us and the support that our vehicles could provide to an operation.

It was a strange existence; we were like military nomads. We ended up with big beards and long hair due to having to conserve water when we were moving. Some of the lads had a go at cutting each other's hair; most ended up looking like they were recovering from an operation. One of the best bits was when we headed up to the Kajaki Dam. We got to swim in the crystal, freezing water and scrape the dust out of the cracks. Real life only rarely caught up with us: mail and spares for the vehicles were dropped at whatever base we were heading toward, ready for us to receive only after we had completed whatever job we had just been given.

One week, we were tasked to go to FOB Edinburgh, which was off to the east of Musa Qala. It was in the middle of nowhere and looked like something out of a Foreign Legion film. As we approached, we could see that the gates were closed. We pushed forward, expecting someone to come out and greet us—but nothing happened. Simon, one of the corporal of horses, debussed and walked up to the gate.

"Hello," he shouted.

He kept shouting, but nothing happened. He peered through some cracks in the gate, picked up a rock and threw it over the gate toward an office.

"Oi, you fucker, open the pissing gate," he bellowed.

The sentry was asleep.

There was some Welsh infantry regiment manning the fort—and they turned out to be an absolute bunch of tossers. The sleeping sentry was just the start of it. Simon chatted to the officer in charge and after being told the 101 rules of the FOB—including commandments on shaving, haircuts, clean uniforms and correct parking—he made an executive decision.

"Fuck this shit. We'll stay outside," he told us.

We pulled back from the FOB and made the ring of steel . . . and then camped there for the whole duration of our stay: the lepers of the desert.

It seemed that we and our vehicles had been brought to

this place to "expand the footprint" or "increase the presence." The CVR(T)s certainly added a quick and very visible presence to the locals. Our squadron's main task was to man vehicle checkpoints that were positioned on the road that passed in front of the base. Two small hills to the north of the base created a natural bottleneck that the locals had no choice but to go through.

Eddy and I decided to put ourselves on another hill off to the left, which gave us good views of the surrounding area and provided overwatch to the squadron. We sorted ourselves out and both took sniper rifles. Normally Eddy, as the spotter, would just take his assault rifle, but we decided to take an assault rifle and a sniper rifle each, just so we had enough firepower for any situation. We moved out while it was still dark and got ourselves set up on the hill before dawn.

I found us a small depression to get into, which gave us good observation yet also meant that people couldn't sneak up on us. I allocated arcs for the pair of us and then we waited until first light. At dawn, we put up a shelter to keep the sun off. The hide wasn't supposed to be covert; we wanted people to see us so that they didn't flee.

We both placed our sniper rifles on top of our daysacks and started to scan our arcs. The first thing we noticed was two small compounds off to our right. There was movement in one of the courtyards, which drew our attention. There were a few people milling around—and a car. It looked like the compounds were in a position where they couldn't be seen from the FOB, so it was something to be aware of. We marked it on the range card and kept scanning.

Over the next couple of hours, we watched as cars and one colorful delivery truck, jingling from all the decorations attached, passed through the checkpoint. It became obvious that word had got out that the squadron was manning the road as traffic started to become lighter and remained light for the rest of the day. Then, at 1600 hours, a white car approached from the south and stopped.

"Two hundred and seventy yards," said Eddy.

He had broken the half-mile stretch of road that we could see into fifty-yard sections on the range card. This made it easy for us to work out our firing range.

The car stayed still for five minutes, moved forward at a crawl—and then stopped again.

The residual heat from the ground was causing a lot of heat shimmer, making observation harder, but I could nonetheless make out three people in the car. The rear wheels also looked quite tucked into the wheel arches, as though there was a lot of weight in the boot. The car started to turn around. All of this was very, very suspicious.

"I'm going to shoot," I told Eddy.

"Roger that."

He got on his radio and gave an update to the guys on the checkpoint and the ops room in the FOB.

"Okay, mate. You're clear to fire."

I placed the cross hairs at the top of the front wheel, so that I would hit either the tire or the engine block. The heat shimmer was still causing me a problem with my sight picture, so I gave myself some leeway. I slowed my breathing and took up the slack in the trigger. I paused, exhaled and then squeezed the trigger. The rifle recoiled solidly into my shoulder and I watched as a burst of steam shot from the bonnet—I'd hit the engine. The car instantly stopped.

Lads from the checkpoint raced down the road and dragged out the occupants of the car. It turned out that they were Taliban and a search of the car revealed six artillery shells in the boot. We didn't have time to celebrate, though. Just as we were watching the guys being pulled from the car, there was a large explosion off to our right.

"What the fuck?"

"Compounds," replied Eddy.

I swung my rifle round and looked through my scope at the two compounds we had spotted earlier. There was a big plume of smoke coming out of one of the courtyards and a huge crater where the car had been earlier. I focused my scope and tried to see what was going on.

Suddenly, a man carrying an artillery shell started sprinting across the courtyard. I had to act quickly. I placed the cross hairs on his head and then swung through him to give him a bit of a lead. Once the cross hairs were in front of him by one-mil-dot I fired. He cartwheeled forward and slid to a halt. The artillery shell rolled away. He wasn't getting up; the .338 round had taken the top of his head off.

I winced from the noise as Eddy fired next to me.

"What have you got?" I asked him.

"Opening at the far end of the house," he replied. "I saw somebody with a weapon."

I swung the scope round and looked. There was a man lying half in the doorway with an AK47 by his right arm. We continued to scan, but nothing else happened.

A clearance patrol was sent out from the base and we provided overwatch. It was a grim scene. There were bits of bodies dotted around from the explosion, as well as the two guys that we had shot.

It turned out that it was a bomb-making factory, right near the base. The patrol found artillery shells, detonators and all the components needed to make bombs. Something must have gone wrong and one of their devices had detonated in the car. It's always nice when a bomb-maker scores an own goal.

We stayed at FOB Edinburgh—well, outside it—for a few more weeks but nothing else interesting happened. We then moved on to Musa Qala and conducted patrols in the local villages.

I left my R&R to the very last opportunity and it was just wonderful to come home and spend ten days with Tanya and Dani. I'd missed them both so much and Tanya's warmth and beauty offset all of the horror I'd witnessed.

Once I got back to Bastion, we had only four weeks of the tour left. Those four weeks were taken up with preparing the vehicles for handover to the next unit. The time passed pretty painlessly—and before I knew it I was back in the UK, with another tour under my belt.

10. My Own Troop

After that first Afghan tour I was promoted to corporal of horse. This gave me a decent level of responsibility and men under my command. I finally had my own troop.

Only six months after returning from Helmand, the whole regiment was got out on parade—and told that we were going straight back again. It didn't come as a shock. Everyone already knew another tour was in the cards, as the Chinese whispers had been rife for weeks.

The problem we had at this stage was numbers of men. We were nowhere near up to our full complement. The squadron was severely depleted; my troop had only four blokes in it—instead of what should have been nearly thirty. We were told that our squadron would be going down south, while the rest of the regiment would be operating further north. There would have to be a big shuffle around of manpower to get all the right people in the right place.

It took about a week, while people were moved around and extras brought in from the Household Cavalry, but after that we were up to our full complement of lads. We would be spending the next six months training to get ready to go, which meant we would be busy and away a lot. I winced a bit at the news, thinking, "Tanya's going to love this."

I had a lad called Cliff in my troop, who seemed a good guy, so I started to use him to help me. A South African, Cliff had their usual stoicism and was down to earth, despite coming from a wealthy family. He displayed a maturity and intelligence beyond his years; I had him in mind as a new spotter for me, since Eddy had been posted outside of the regiment.

"Can you call the guys together so we can start to get to know each other?" I asked him.

While he was away, gathering everyone together, I had a look at the list of names I had been given. It read like the Dirty Dozen; I'd been given just about every criminal in the regiment. I went straight to see the squadron commander.

"Sir, how come I've been given this lot?" I asked him. "This lot are a fucking nightmare."

"Well, you take no shit and you're highly motivated. Plus, you are going to be Support Troop, so you'll spend more time on your feet doing infantry work. You have the best background in that."

I couldn't really argue with that, unfortunately, so I headed off to find my band of pirates. Cliff had got the troop assembled behind the HQ block: they looked a right ragtag lot. I realized I needed to make my mark quickly, so I strode straight up to them.

"Get your physical training kit on and be back here in ten minutes!" I bellowed at them. "Every minute that you are late back, I add fifteen minutes to what we're doing."

They scattered and ran off to get changed. It was twenty minutes before they were all back.

"Right, we're going for a little jog," I told them. They would soon come to learn that my definition of "little" and theirs were violently different.

We headed off as a squad, with me at the front: out the front gate and left toward Windsor Great Park. They were still laughing and joking around so I upped the pace. We hit every hill I could find, sprinting for ten repetitions up and down. Soon they were spread out all over the place. After an hour and a half of running and hill reps, we headed back to camp. I slowed the pace down so that people could catch up and we could reform as a squad. As we got close to the gate, I asked them a question.

"Can anyone tell me what I said would happen if you were late?"

There was a pause before a lone, labored voice responded: "That for every minute we were late, you would add fifteen minutes to what we are doing."

"Very good," I replied—and kept running straight past the front gate. Behind me came a chorus of groans and muttered curses.

I didn't do the full punishment, I just added another mile and a half, but it served its purpose. After a few more of my "little" runs, the lads changed our name from "Support Troop" to "Assault Troop" and I could see a light at the end of the tunnel. They had started bonding, pulling together, and they were taking some pride in themselves and acting like professionals. Our role in Afghanistan would be to get out of the vehicles and clear enemy positions using infantry tactics. As we trained, they started to realize the ramifications of that job. Things are different when there isn't a nice armored vehicle around you.

The squadron got a bunch of young officers fresh from Sandhurst and for training purposes they were all allocated to my troop. They quickly came to realize how I worked. I punished everyone. If one person was late we all went into the push-up position and waited for them. It sounds harsh but the crucial word was "we"—and that included me. I'm a big believer in the mantra "If you can't do it yourself, don't dish it out."

The training started at troop and squadron level, and then built from there in complexity. We went away for week-long exercises to test all that we were learning. The first exercise gave me a chance to see my lads in action. I needed to see how well they could shoot, so that I could decide who would be a gunner and stay with the vehicle and who would be a dismount—that is, get out and fight. I pushed them to their limits, broke them down until they were empty, and then filled them back up with soldiering skills and the instinct to kill. I made sure they were under no illusion as to what we do: we kill the enemy.

After the first exercise, we really came together as a troop. We trained constantly. While other troops were playing Xbox, we were out running. While other soldiers were sorting out wagons, we were practicing infantry skills. We did casualty evacuation after casualty evacuation. I simulated me being taken out, so one of them had to take over and coordinate things. We became a team: there was Jim, who I'd served with in Iraq, Cliff, Lucky Malone, Ridge, Wardy—the troop clown who swore so much he sounded like he had Tourette's syndrome—Jones, Clark, Groom, Wit, Mark, DB and the Rat.

I pushed them hard because I knew that their safety was my responsibility. Mistakes are paid for in blood in combat—and I didn't want that to happen on my watch.

I also got a new troop leader: one of the young officers. He became the boss of the troop and I became his right-hand man. I try never to judge a book by its cover but my initial impression of the lieutenant was "Fuck me, he is posh and as rigid as a broom handle." Andy turned out to be a very good man, though, and we quickly became friends. He was keen and he was fit, and that would do for me.

We all headed up to Castlemartin to conduct live firing, as we all had to qualify on certain shooting tests. We had to fire rifles and machine guns, and vehicle commanders had to qualify on the vehicle-mounted machine gun too. Once that was all out of the way, I decided to put myself through the sniper qualification shoot again—it's a tough test and I wanted to maintain my own high standards. Castlemartin is a really good range complex. On one of the ranges, you shoot out toward a little island, which is really cool; you can see the rounds hit the rocks and watch as they slam through waves.

Range 10 is the sniper range and it has an elevated platform to shoot from and targets out to 1,300 yards. It's a really good one to stretch yourself on. I managed to convince the regimental second-in-command and the colonel to come and watch me shoot. I wanted to show them how effective a single rifle can be and how a sniper can have an effect without having to level whole villages with artillery.

I had a chat with the guys in the range control tower and decided to put myself under a bit of pressure. They wouldn't tell me where the targets were going to be. I'd have five minutes to set up behind my rifle and make my range card before they started popping targets up at random distances.

I lay down at the firing point behind my rifle, pulled out my binos and a map, and constructed a hasty range card, trying to identify easy-to-spot features and then work out the range from my map. I glanced at my watch. Seconds to go. After a quick look at the grass to work out wind speed and direction, I was ready.

I could feel the colonel's eyes boring into the back of my skull but I tuned that out and started scanning and controlling my breathing. I needed to nail this. The first target appeared. It was fairly close; I glanced at my range card: 400 yards. I dialed in the corrections, took up the slack in the trigger, exhaled and squeezed. Hit: the target dropped down. I smoothly chambered the next round.

The next target appeared at 1,000 yards. I dialed in the corrections and fired. Hit.

Two targets appeared at slightly different ranges, but still at roughly 1,000 yards. I used the mil-dots in my reticule to "hold off" and dropped the first target.

I switched on to the second target, fired—and missed.

"Fucking wind," I said to myself.

I chambered a fresh round, held off one more mil-dot and fired. This time, the target dropped. Once the rifle was unloaded, I stood up. I could see that the colonel was impressed because he was smiling.

"Thank you, Corporal of Horse," he said, before walking off.

My troop worked through a variety of ranges. We all got very used to the obstacle course in camp; I made us all go over it every night. I only gave the lads one night off—and regretted it. One of them ended up getting arrested and Wardy smashed a pool cue over someone's head! We all need to blow off steam and, to be fair, they behaved exactly as I used to when I was their age.

The next day I drove the troop out to the local beach and for two hours we thrashed ourselves: sprinting up and down the sand dunes, wading into the surf, rolling around and crawling. I noticed that DB was drifting away from the group; he was a bit of a loner. The troop leader noticed as well.

"What are we going to do about DB?" he asked me.

"Not sure. All we can do is keep an eye on him and try to bring him back into the group."

We continued to notice erratic behavior from DB over the next few days. On one of the runs he took his boots off and ran barefoot with them tied round his neck. He missed a few parades. The final straw came at the end of the week. I drove the troop out to another training area for a two-hour run in boots. As soon as we got there, we lost DB. It took the whole troop an hour to find him—he was hiding in a bush with his boots tied round his neck again.

"What the fuck are you doing?" I asked him.

"I am Jesus," he confidently told me.

We set things in motion with the doctor and the regiment, and a week later he was off to the nuthouse. Andy went to visit him and was met by DB in a bathrobe and sandals, still claiming to be Jesus. Poor lad.

Over the next four months of training, the troop got tighter and tighter, and my relationship with Andy just kept getting better. We actually started to get people from within the regiment asking to join our troop, as our reputation was spreading. Of course, there are always unintended consequences when making a high-performance team . . .

One morning at Windsor, there was a squadron parade. Out of the whole troop, only Cliff and Wardy reported for duty. I walked over to Cliff.

"Where's the rest of the troop?" I whispered urgently in his ear.

"They got into a huge fight in town last night," he replied. "They ended up doing a big section attack down the high street—and they were all arrested."

Andy then rocked up, so I took him to one side and explained what was going on. We just looked at each other. I had already been accused of making the lads too gung-ho; we were both going to get a bollocking for this. Together, we headed to Slough police station.

"Come through," the custody sergeant said.

One by one, they opened the cell doors and the lads sheepishly appeared.

"What happened?" I asked the sergeant.

"Once the fight started, they split into half sections: one

half went forward into the fight while the other half flanked them. It was all very impressive," he said, with a smile on his face. "Look, no harm was really done and I know that you're off to Afghanistan, so I'm going to give them all a caution and we will leave it at that. Let it be a warning, though."

"Thanks. That's really good of you," I told him.

It's a bit annoying when you have to take a *minibus* to pick up your lads from a police station . . .

Once back at camp, the troop leader and I got our bollockings, as expected. I then took our little darlings for a run, just to bleed off some of the surplus energy they clearly had. It was cold and steam was pouring off their bodies by the time we headed back to camp after an hour and a half in training. I couldn't tell them, but deep down I was actually very proud of them. They'd worked as a team, they'd used tactics to defeat the enemy—and they'd won. Not much more you can ask for . . . apart from don't get caught; they clearly failed at that one.

The troop was as good as gold after that and the lads were still on their best behavior when we headed off as a regiment to Norfolk, for another exercise. The training area was dotted with different forward operating bases and there was a mock Afghan village and real Afghans to interact with. The squadron got set up in its FOB and I decided that our troop would leave the vehicles in the base and patrol on foot. That would offer better practice for our infantry skills.

One of our first tests as a troop was to defend the FOB against a simulated attack. We stalled their initial attack by being calm and thinking through the problem. In another exercise, the Directing Staff, or DS, wandered around and nominated casualties in our troop, as well as simply telling us what the injury was, such as "a gunshot wound to the leg" or "shrapnel to the head." We then had to "treat" them. I really hated it, as understandably it didn't prepare the lads at all for what they would see if and when we took a casualty for real.

The next training serial was to flush some Taliban out of a village. The troop split into two assault elements and the troop leader told me to take my lot round to the right and conduct a recce, which quickly turned into an epic as we had to wade through a swamp. It took us three hours to get through and all I could do was lead us, trusting my compass bearing. We ended up being late for the RV (rendezvous). When we finally caught up with the troop leader—just as it was getting dark—Andy and his element were all clean and dry. We looked like we had been down a mine and then rolled in shit. But shit or no shit, now the crux of the exercise was on us.

I pulled out my sniper rifle and attached the night sight, pushing forward to conduct the recce. I quickly identified the targets. I always feel the butterflies as I place the cross hairs on someone—even when it's not for real—and tonight was no different. Once I had the info, I crawled back and briefed the troop leader. I stressed that we had to hit the objective fast and then push on, otherwise the enemy would have the chance to escape. He disagreed over how the attack should be done; however, ultimately it was his ballgame, so we went with his plan. He wanted us to focus on securing the house where the Taliban were, rather than pushing on and cutting them off.

The attack went pretty well. We secured the objective, but the enemy had the chance to let off some smoke grenades and it nearly choked some of the lads. A couple of them threw up; because the smoke was colored green, they looked like the Incredible Hulk after a long night downing Jägerbombs.

We were told to push on to the next village. As we started moving, we were informed that a neighboring unit had pushed too far forward, stormed the village and taken a significant number of casualties. The remainder were pinned down. We approached the village with caution—clearly something the Coldstream Guards didn't do—and avoided anything that could be booby-trapped. Once inside, I found the company commander and then pushed on, flushing the Taliban out as we went. After we had cleared the village, the DS called a halt. I gathered my troop together.

"Well done, lads. That was a cracking job," I told them.

We talked through what went well and what didn't, and, once we were all happy, there was then the little matter of a serial called the "river run." This was a hideous attack lane that followed a river for about a mile. The troop leader suggested that we just stayed in the river and this worked. The whole thing took about three hours and we spent the entire time in a series of rolling contacts. It was a nightmare trying to evacuate casualties up and down the river, but by staying in the water we didn't expose ourselves as much and therefore took less of them.

Then we heard the words that can cheer the coldest heart. "Endex."

At the debrief, the DS were very complimentary; apparently no one had got that far down the river in that quick a time before.

We had two weeks to sort ourselves out before we faced the final exercise. This would be the big one: three weeks long. The two-week interlude allowed me to spend some time with Tanya, who was finding this all quite hard. I had promised her before going to Afghanistan last year that it would be my "last tour," but here I was again, getting ready for another one. The problem was that I loved this shit. And it wasn't just about me this time. I had a responsibility to the lads now, to my troop. I had to make sure that we were at the top of our game. I knew that they had changed from the ragtag troop I'd first seen lined up before me. They were ready now. They loved the challenges; they loved being the "beasts" of the regiment.

The week before the final exercise, we all headed down to Devon to learn to drive the vehicle we would be using in Afghanistan. The Jackal is an awesome bit of kit. It looks like something out of *Mad Max* and can pretty much go over any terrain. It can absorb IEDs and mine strikes, but there is no real protection for the crew if you get shot at: the vehicle is a chassis, engine, seats and then roll bars.

The good thing about the final exercise was that it used laser-tagging equipment. Every weapon was fitted with a laser, and vehicles and people were fitted with sensors. The tech meant you actually knew if you hit someone or were hit. It taught you much better lessons than exercises without it— such as when you were actually in cover and when you weren't.

The "enemy" for this exercise were the Royal Fusiliers. I had my sniper rifle and it was fitted with a laser; I was determined to wreak havoc.

Over the final week we left the troop vehicles hidden and spent a lot of time on foot. We probed the enemy camps and got a lot of information. At a briefing before the last week, the colonel in charge of the Fusiliers came in and said, "I am offering a bottle of champagne to anyone who can capture the enemy leader. In ten years, this has never happened."

I hadn't had the chance to really use my sniping skills yet and I wanted that champagne. I spent some time studying the map, trying to work out where the enemy might be, and then had a chat with our squadron commander, who, after a bit of convincing, agreed to let me go where I wanted. I thought I'd identified an enemy supply route and I wanted to ambush it. The troop and I got to the area late that night and I got the vehicles hidden, but positioned in a blocking formation. At about 0200 hours, I saw some headlights approaching on the track we were monitoring. Once the enemy vehicles were in the area, our Jackals popped out of their hides and forced them to stop. We surrounded their four-by-fours, shoved weapons in people's faces and generally convinced them not to move. No shots were fired. It turned out that this was an enemy convoy. Plus, in a real coup, the enemy commander was there.

We dropped the prisoners off at a makeshift detention center and then headed back to the main camp for a debrief. After the debrief, I was in the cookhouse having a brew when the colonel from the Fusiliers strode in. He plonked a bottle of champagne down in front of me.

"Well done, Harrison," he said. "Have a drink on me."

"Thank you, sir."

I took the bottle over to where my troop was sitting.

"Well done, lads. This is for you. Plus, as an extra treat, you can stand down for the evening." Usually, we would have to work late into the night, sorting out the vehicles, but they had earned a night off.

The next day, we did a move from hell: from one end of the training area to the other. It would take twenty-four hours and would be particularly hard on the drivers, who would have to use night-vision goggles for the night phase. I saw my job as keeping Cliff awake while he drove, so we spent hours talking crap. By the middle of the night, we were both struggling.

"Stop!" I called out.

"What?" Cliff stamped on the brakes.

"There's a cow in the road."

"What? Where?"

"Over there, a cow," I said, pointing. Then I blinked at the empty road; I was hallucinating.

It was a grim night. We were told that it was to simulate a major move in Afghanistan, but it seemed like most people practiced getting lost, hallucinating or falling asleep at the wheel.

The next day, we were informed that the enemy was approaching in vehicles. My troop was told to halt until the battlegroup could get into a position to attack. We found a nice wood to hide in and then worked out a plan. The troop would set up to engage the approaching enemy with anti-tank weapons, and I would take out the enemy commander. I got my ghillie suit on and decided to take Cliff with me—I needed a spotter. I put some elastic bands on him and then stuffed grass into those, and this worked quite well to break up his outline.

We set up on the opposite side of the valley from the rest of the troop. Before long, we heard the noise of the vehicles approaching. I started scanning the wagons. Once I was happy, I got comms with the troop leader on the radio: "Fire."

They immediately fired simulated anti-tank weapons at the vehicles. The sensors started flashing on the enemy front and rear vehicles, signaling "hits." I watched through my scope as someone jumped out of the commander's seat in one of the enemy vehicles and started giving directions. "That must be the enemy commander," I thought. I placed my cross hairs on him and squeezed the trigger. The blank round still went *bang*, but instead of a round leaving the barrel, a laser beam shot forward.

I watched as the commander's vest started beeping. He was slapping at the vest, unable to believe what had happened.

Enemy then started jumping out of the vehicles; I cycled

the bolt and shot them one by one. I was back in the zone—
the mechanical sniper—controlled breathing, low heart rate,
minimal movement. Cross hairs on target, fire, move on.
Soon, all I could hear was beeping as their sensors went
off. Things started to blur as I looked through the scope and
suddenly I was back in Iraq, bodies dropping after I'd placed
the cross hairs on them and squeezed the trigger. I froze,
time slowed down and my hearing went. I felt myself sinking
into the ground as if it was treacle.

"Craig, are you all right?" Cliff asked.

There was a pause before I snapped back. I looked down
at my rifle. "Yes, mate; out of ammo."

The DS halted the exercise not long after and turned off
all of the beeping sensors. All the enemy were milling around,
not knowing where the shots had come from, until Cliff and
I stood up.

"This is what being a sniper is all about," I told Cliff. "The
element of surprise."

One of the enemy walked over and shook my hand. "Fucking hell, we had no idea what was going on," he told me.

I just laughed.

We were all exhausted by the end of the exercise. I knew
it would take a few days to sort out our kit for the tour, but I
was now confident that, as a troop, we were at the top of our
game. Everyone had worked hard and we had done well, so I
wanted to make sure the troop knew it. Once we were back
at camp and all the admin was sorted, I got the lads together
in one of the communal rooms.

"What is the difference between a war and a conflict?"
one of them asked.

"What?" I replied, taken aback.

"When I went in the cookhouse earlier, the regimental

corporal major was in there and told me that I was going to a conflict, not a war. What's the difference?"

The squadron leader had explained this to us so I could answer this one. I opened my mouth to speak.

"A conflict is a disagreement between two parties, whereas a war is an arms contest between two hostile powers," Wit jumped in, before I could say anything. "That term suggests that actual armed hostility is acted out. A conflict can end up as more political due to international law, although there has been some deliberation about what constitutes a war due to the rise of non-state actors."

We all just stared at Wit.

"Fucking hell," I managed. "The answer is what he said."

I then got back to the reason I'd called them all together. "Right, lads: training is done," I said. "It's been a long, hard six months—but we are ready.

"I won't lie to you. On ops there are going to be good days and shit days, but you are ready to face what is coming. The head shed might screw up, your girlfriend might dump you, the enemy might hurt you . . . but we have a shared commitment to each other now. A commitment to protect each other—and that is nonnegotiable."

I looked round the room and saw they were all listening intently.

"Our feelings for each other will only get stronger and deeper over time. The willingness to die for each other is a form of love that even religion can fail to inspire. The experiences we will have will change us forever, but the bond to each other can never be broken."

You could have heard a pin drop.

*

There was paperwork to do before we could all go on leave. We had to write "final letters" and hand in a nice picture to be remembered by. I would hang on to them—and send them to the lads' parents if the worst happened. As I collected their photos, the responsibility for their lives sat heavily on my shoulders. I had never had this many people relying on me before.

Our troop had a week off before the RAF had available flights and we were recalled to camp. I decided to have a party at my house before we left, inviting the whole troop as well as some mates. About fifty people came and each person brought a crate of beer and a bottle of wine. It turned into an epic drinking session.

Some of the guys brought their families to meet me. Each parent said something similar to me: "Oh, you're the one we've been hearing all about." And: "Please look after my son."

"Of course," I replied to them all, but I could feel the pressure mounting. Tanya understood, and smiled at me, squeezing my hand.

By the time the party had finished, there was only one bottle of wine and a can of Guinness left, so we'd got through a fair bit of booze. Apparently, there was food, but I have no recollection of making any. I woke up the next morning wearing my stepdad's T-shirt and a pair of underpants. To this day, I have no idea what went on.

11. Sniper Sense

The RAF remained true to form and fucked us about as much as humanly possible: flight delays, cancelations and changes to routes; all part of the service. We ended up flying from the UK to Kuwait, Kuwait to Kandahar and then finally down to Camp Bastion in October 2009. During the week of in-theater training and acclimatization, it was so hot that I had to keep reminding the lads to drink plenty of water and the air conditioning in the tents became a real treat.

At the end of the week, we found out that we weren't going south anymore. The colonel wanted his own recce troop and had picked us, so we would be heading north toward Musa Qala to locate Taliban hot spots. A few days later, we were flown forward to the base in Talajan, just outside Musa Qala.

After a quick tour and an explanation of the dos and don'ts, we started the handover/takeover. We had five days before we had to be ready to start conducting operations. A short, fat Royal Anglian who didn't look much like a soldier came up to me.

"Follow me," he said, throwing me a bunch of keys and taking me round to two shipping containers.

"Everything in these two containers you are accountable for," he told me. "Your vehicles are round the back."

"Right, have you got paperwork for it all?" I asked him. I could hear a helicopter approaching in the distance.

"Let me just go and get it," he said, smiling at me. He picked up his daysack and jogged off. I watched him run down to the HLS, pick up his kit and get in the back of the helicopter. What an unprofessional little turd.

I unlocked the containers and just stared in shock. There were claymore mines and hand grenades all over the place, mixed in with piles of kit. With a bad feeling, I walked around the containers to check the vehicles: five Jackals. I pulled the cover off each one and, as I'd feared, they were in a shit state. This was going to take longer than five days to sort out.

I called the lads together and we got going. It was a nightmare as all of the paperwork had to be sorted out and the vehicles had to be readied.

While sorting out all of our kit, we still had to mount local security patrols too. One afternoon we were patrolling through the local village when the troop leader spotted a local sitting behind a wall. He looked a bit older and we thought he might be a village elder so the boss was keen to strike up a conversation.

"I want to talk to this local," he told me over the radio.

"Roger that," I replied and got the lads shaken out so that they could provide defense. As the troop leader got closer, we all noticed that the local had a strange look on his face, like he was straining. It turned out he was squatting, having a dump. Before the boss could work out what his opening line should be, the local stood up, put a stone on top of his pile of poo and walked off.

Welcome to Afghanistan.

After a few weeks at our first base, the troop leader headed off on his R&R, leaving me to take command of the troop while he was away. We were still in Talajan, waiting for the next operation, when we received new orders over the radio from the squadron leader, telling us that we were to support the Afghan National Army (ANA) and the Yorkshire Regiment (known as the Yorks). They were moving east to clear a town called Karza and we were to provide support.

Once the squadron leader had finished, I pulled out my map and summoned the commanders, Paul, Rocky and my second-in-command Jim, to give them a heads-up. We studied the map, looking for a decent route. Our job would be to support the patrol by dominating the high ground.

The next day, prior to the op starting, we linked up with the Yorks and I had a chance to chat with their commander. I'd studied the map again and the ground looked shit, really hard-going. It was undulating, with numerous gullies and ditches, which would prove challenging for our vehicles—and provide good cover for the enemy. I wanted to set off before the Yorks patrol, so that I would be in a good position by the time they left their base. If I set off behind them, I wasn't convinced I could maneuver quickly enough to help them if they got into a contact.

They agreed with my plan so we left first. Our base was on the outskirts of a village, so as soon as we set off there were kids all around us and youths on motorbikes. We had an interpreter in the back of my vehicle, listening to the enemy radio, and it wasn't long before he heard someone say, "there is a patrol on the ground." One of the youths must be a dicker. The Yorks and the ANA hadn't left their base yet, so we knew they were talking about us.

I had four vehicles and wanted the lead wagon to clear the way and keep about half a mile in front of the Yorks. This meant that the rear wagon would be about 650 yards in front of their patrol. That way my wagon, in the middle, could see both the front and rear vehicles.

As the Yorks started their patrol and we pushed on, I could hear a rolling commentary on our progress over the enemy's radio. Clearly there were dickers everywhere. The ground was a nightmare for the vehicles, just as I'd suspected it would be, with ditches everywhere. Some of them we just couldn't cross, so we wasted a lot of time searching for alternate crossing points.

We were stuck trying to cross a river when the Yorks and ANA overtook us, quite early in the patrol. There was a compound with a low wall on the far bank, off to our right. Right by the river's edge, it would offer us cover from the Taliban while we crossed.

Jim came over to my wagon. "Looks like we can cross here," he said.

"Yeah, roger that. You wade across and the wagon will follow. Clear the route."

"Okay," he said and headed off into the river. The first wagon followed him slowly in a low gear. We all crossed safely, but we weren't much help to the patrol at that moment. We were behind them, we couldn't see them and we were in low ground. Pretty useless really, but we pushed on and finally got onto some high ground.

"Dicker, one thousand yards away in a blue dishdash," said Wit, pointing off at two sandhills.

I looked through my binos and saw the man, as well as a glint that looked to be coming off his radio antenna. I grabbed my spotting scope. With x40 magnification it is much better for positively identifying enemy, and I confirmed that he was holding a radio.

"Wit, keep an eye on him," I said, then directed Jim to push a bit further forward in his vehicle, so that he could maintain a visual with the Yorks. The chatter on the enemy radio was getting more and more threatening. We could hear that they were ready and in a position to attack. It was time to remove the dicker.

"Wit, pass my rifle."

He passed my rifle forward from the back of the vehicle and I walked over to a low sandbank on the edge of the hill we were on.

I lay behind my rifle and started going through my pre-shot routine. I got comfortable, positioning the stock firmly in my shoulder, and then looked through the scope. There was a lot of heat mirage but in fact I could actually use this to estimate wind direction, so it wasn't all bad. I turned my scope until the mirage appeared to "boil" in a certain direction. Where it is "boiling" from is also the direction that the wind is coming from. I did some quick mental calculations and estimated the wind to be about 4–5mph. I made the necessary adjustments to my scope.

"Wit, tell the patrol I'm going to fire."

There was a pause while Wit got on the radio to the Yorks.

"All clear," he replied.

I took up the slack in the trigger, exhaled, paused and then fired.

The dicker was blasted back into the sand dune. I saw the round strike him—but it was only a leg wound. "Shit," I said to myself. I was taught to be bold with my corrections on the scope, so I should have put more elevation in. Saying that, I would rather miss "low" and hit him in the leg than miss "high" and have the round pass over his head. At least this way he would bleed out.

I dialed some elevation into the scope and continued to scan where he went down. I couldn't see him, but we could hear him on his radio and he sounded in a shit state.

"Must be our guy," I thought to myself, and fired again at the ground where he went down. More babbling on their radio—it was definitely him.

I started to scan the area and saw a compound off to my left with a green door. Previous patrol reports had mentioned this very compound—and that dickers had been spotted and killed there before on more than one occasion. It seemed amazing that they insisted on using the same place over and over again.

While I'd been taking out the babbling dicker, the Yorks and the ANA had achieved what they wanted to on this patrol, so we got the order to start heading back. There was hard ground to cover and the patrol was pretty much moving faster than us, so I needed to think quickly about our options. I had identified a withdrawal route on the way in, but it would probably force us to bunch up and slow down as we crossed the river. This meant that the crossing was a "choke point"—a point that made the patrol unavoidably vulnerable. Even so, it was still the best route to take. I'd planned to leave Jim and his vehicle on the high ground while we pushed through first, but I changed my mind when I saw that we were in a slightly better position to cover him and sent him on ahead.

Once he was through the vulnerable point, we would push up to him and then he could move on again—and we would continue this leapfrog motion until we were safely back in the base. The fourth wagon would continue to cover my rear and push up to me as necessary. We had pretty good observation in most directions and we could still see the patrol, so this seemed like the best plan.

Jim's vehicle pushed off, followed by Wardy's, and I lost sight of them as they drove behind a compound.

Then the silence was shattered by a huge explosion.

"Contact, IED, wait out," shouted Jim over the radio.

The Yorks and the ANA went to ground. "No, no, no," I was thinking to myself.

"They are laughing," the interpreter said to me, as we heard jubilant voices on the enemy radio.

I pushed forward and got to within eighty yards of the IED strike. As I'd feared, the crossing point had caused us to bunch up and both vehicles had been struck. One of the Jackals had been blown up on the driver's side. The front right wheel was 200 meters up the hill and the vehicle itself was on its side, embedded in the compound wall. The other wasn't as bad but it had clearly still been struck.

The Yorks started coordinating the casevac (evacuation of casualties by air), their medics pushing their way forward, clearing for mines. That was what I should have been doing—checking my route for mines—but emotion got the better of me. These were my friends, these were my soldiers, I needed to get to them. I started running to the vehicles. People were shouting at me to stop but I ignored them. It was a silly thing to do, but I had to get forward to help.

As I got close I saw that Wardy, the driver of the second vehicle, had been blown into the back of the wagon and his arm was on fire. Steve, the gunner, had been thrown out of the wagon entirely—he thought they had just hit a bump. Jones, the commander, had been blown out of the front left seat and had landed on a huge pile of dried opium in the compound.

Steve ran forward as soon as he realized what had happened. Wardy turned to him. "Mate, could you put my arm out please?" he casually asked.

Ever since I'd met Wardy, every sentence I'd heard him say had had the word "fuck" in it. Now that he had been blown up and set on fire, he had gone all polite!

At first, I thought that there must be someone underneath Wardy, as there was a leg sticking out at an odd angle. Then I realized it was his. Leaving him to Steve, I pushed over to Jones and held his hand. He was as white as a ghost.

"I need to check you over, mate," I said to him. "I'm going to remove your body armor. Okay?"

"It's my legs," he mumbled.

"I'll give you some morphine." I found his morphine injector and was just about to stab him with it when he grabbed my hand.

"Other way round," he said. I was about to inject my thumb.

"Fuck it. Steve, come and do this!"

Steve ran over and smashed the morphine into Jones's leg and then checked him over. At this point, a Yorks medic arrived and started to help with Wardy, moving his legs back in the direction they should be pointing. Wardy let out the most incredible scream of pain.

I started to wrap up Jones's leg. He was lucky that he had landed on the pile of opium. It looked like he had only broken his ankle.

"It'll be okay, mate. Just relax," I told him.

I started hunting for a marker pen. The SOP is to write details of medical treatment on a casualty's forehead so that the medics back at the hospital know what has been done in the field. I couldn't find a pen anywhere.

"Jim, have you got a marker pen?" I shouted out to the other vehicle.

Jim sent Chris over with a bag of pens that his mum had sent him. They were all ballpoints and not one of them worked. "For fuck's sake," I cursed. In the end, I found a marker in my daysack and wrote the details of the morphine administration on Jones's forehead.

The intelligence network was alive with chatter from the Taliban. They were all laughing and one guy described how he had laid a mine in the field and the vehicle had only just missed it.

Suddenly there was the crack of small-arms fire passing overhead.

"Contact!" I shouted out. "Jim, move south, and Rocky, move east, but maintain a visual on Jim."

The lads ran to their assigned sectors and started returning fire.

This was just a fucking nightmare. We had Chinooks inbound to pick up the casualties and we were still in contact. Wardy and Jones were loaded onto stretchers and carried back over the river to the HLS that the Yorks were securing for us. The river was waist deep and freezing, and we had to lift the stretchers up to stop the lads going under.

"Two minutes," the Yorks officer shouted to me. The Chinook was nearly there. Thank God, the lads were going home.

The Yorks popped a green smoke grenade and the Chinook clattered into view. It churned up the smoke and the dust until no one could see a thing. Wardy and Jones were rushed onboard and I went with them. I shook each one's hand and looked them in the eye. They both nodded, but each seemed lost in his own world. I had a lump in my throat and was fighting back tears. My lads: injured, but at least they were going home.

I ran off the back ramp and watched as the Chinook lifted off and pulled away. I could see that the rest of the lads were looking lost, turning to me for an answer. I got the Yorks to take over from Rocky and Jim as I needed them back.

"Right, lads. Strip out the radios, ammunition and weapons from the damaged vehicle," I told them.

As we were taking out all of the essential kit and loading it into my wagon, I saw a piece of Wardy's ankle bone in the blown-up vehicle. It looked like a smashed chicken bone. I picked it up and put it in my map pocket, as I didn't want the lads to see it. Unfortunately, Steve saw me do it. There was an awkward silence before he turned away and carried on as if nothing had happened.

I'd just tasked a couple of lads to go into the compound and check there was nothing in there when I was called over to my wagon for a radio message. The Quick Reaction Force (QRF) was on its way and we were to hold the ground and wait until an incident exploitation team could get to me and ascertain what had happened. The Yorks were to head back in. I argued against this—I just wanted to get my lads out of there—but I was told to stay where I was.

We started taking fire again, so I got the wagons to spread out, keeping Jim on the other side of the river and pushing Rocky east. Then I grabbed my sniper rifle and radio and told Cliff to come with me. We jogged about a hundred yards downhill to a small pump house and clambered onto the roof. I set up my rifle while Cliff started scanning the area with his spotting scope.

There was that compound with the green door that we'd seen earlier—and we could see movement. I grabbed my radio handset and asked how long the QRF were going to be. I was told twenty minutes.

"Fuck this," I muttered, pushing the radio away. We hadn't got twenty minutes.

I fired a warning shot straight through the green door. All I could see were the lads' faces in the back of the Chinook as I said goodbye to them. I still had a bit of leg bone in my pocket. In truth, I just wanted to kill these people—but a sniper keeps his composure.

Next, I heard Jim opening up with the .50 cal. I wasn't sure what he was shooting at but I was sure he was feeling the same as me. I looked back through my scope toward the green door and saw a head poke round the corner. I fired another round into the compound.

Eventually, the fire we were taking stopped, just as the QRF arrived. They took over the sentry positions from us and the American inspection team got to work. They figured out what had happened quite quickly: forty pounds of home-made explosive had detonated on the driver's side.

Just as we were getting ready to leave, I walked over to the river and took the bit of bone out of my pocket. Checking that no one was watching, I placed it into the water and watched as it floated away downstream. We then drove back to Talajan, towing the damaged wagon. It made for a miserable, forlorn sight, this battered, wrecked shell being dragged behind one of the good vehicles.

There was an officer waiting for me when we pulled into the FOB.

"Tell your lads to rebomb; the next op is tomorrow morning," he said.

I had to shake my head; they couldn't even give us some time to come to terms with our mates being seriously injured. I told the lads to sort themselves out and once they'd moved off the officer continued.

"I'm afraid that Wardy has lost one leg and they are fighting to save the other. Jones's ankle is broken but he will be all right."

I felt so guilty, and I didn't know what to do. We were back out again tomorrow and I needed the lads to keep their head in the fight. Should I tell them about Wardy now, or wait until we were back in? I found the lads gathered round a fire they had made, cooking some food. They were all quietly chatting to each other and fell silent as I approached.

"We're back out again tomorrow and then, when that has finished, we head back to the district central."

They nodded. I took Jim to one side, gave him a hug and then told him the news. The remainder of the lads just looked on. They could hear what I was saying, but they stayed out of it.

"It's not your fault," I told him. I knew as my 2IC he'd feel that he'd let the lads down. I felt it myself. Jim also knew he'd been lucky—his own vehicle had somehow missed the IED.

The next day the op went well. The enemy were quickly pushed back and we ended up not having a huge amount to do. Once released, we headed back to our main operating base in Musa Qala. We had to strip the remainder of the kit out of the blown-up wagon, but as ever the rats had done some of the job for us. All the rations were gone.

"Hopefully we might get a break," I thought to myself as I prepared for sleep that night. Before I lay down on my camp cot, I taped a piece of sponge to the stock on my sniper rifle. I needed something to absorb the sweat so that my cheek didn't slip on the stock as I was firing. I wanted to make sure I could fire as accurately as possible. I wanted to make sure that I had done everything possible to prepare myself and my kit for the battles I knew were coming.

12. The Longest Kills

The shithole of a compound we were living in, right next to the Afghan police station, was beginning to get on everyone's nerves. The compound was only about the size of a football pitch, with high blast walls, so it was easy to get claustrophobic. We did the best we could, making the compound as habitable as possible, but it was still crap. Frankly, it stank permanently of shit. The only saving grace was that we could get all of the Jackal vehicles in and it was secure. We fortified the place with sandbags and made sure that the Afghan police couldn't come and go as they pleased; there was no way you could trust those fuckers.

I made myself a brew on one of our disposable cookers and wandered into our makeshift operations room. One of the lads was always monitoring the radio networks and I'd got my timing just right. We had just received an operations order for today's activities.

I scanned through the text and it looked fairly straightforward. The Yorks and the ANA were to mount a clearance patrol into an area two and a half miles south of Talajan's district central, an area of rolling hillsides, open desert and a lot of compounds. The ANA were going to clear the compounds, as intelligence suggested that there were a lot of Taliban in the area. The Yorks would provide direct support to the ANA and we would provide overwatch to the whole operation.

I jotted down some notes in the small notebook that I always carried and went to find the troop leader. As I walked across the compound, a feeling of concern started to creep into my gut. I pulled out my map and had a really good look at the area we would be going to. What was bothering me was pretty straightforward. We were being asked to dominate a really large, complicated area with far too few people.

I caught up with Andy, who had already seen the orders, and had a chat with him. I voiced my concerns and he agreed. There wasn't much anyone could do about it, though, so it was a case of "suck it up."

Andy gave his orders that night. We would leave one of the Jackals behind to beef up the security of the compound, while the rest of us would head out to support the clearance operation. He would have half the troop with him to provide close protection, while I would take the remainder onto a high feature and provide overwatch. I would have three Jackals in total.

Once the boss had finished his piece, he handed over to me for my part of the orders. I went through the logistical details before wrapping up with an observation. "Keep thinking ten minutes ahead, as it takes twenty minutes for the Taliban to flank us."

The Taliban were always trying to get around us, so that they could come at us from an angle that played to their advantage, but it took them time to sort themselves out. From what I had seen, that was usually about twenty minutes. If we kept changing what we were doing every ten minutes, they wouldn't be able to get any advantage.

The lads nodded and then headed off to sort out their kit. Cliff, Wit and I checked our wagon over: fuel, radios, ammunition. Everything seemed all right so we decided to get an early night.

We were up at 0330 hours and drove out the front gate at 0400 hours, heading southeast and then west. It was freezing at that time of the morning so I tried to tuck myself into my duvet jacket and cover my face around my night-vision goggles. It didn't help much.

The going was initially good, the tracks fairly solid, but as we approached the high ground, the conditions started to deteriorate. The slope and the wet ground made the driving a challenge and the vehicles started to struggle. The lads worked through it and, as dawn began to break, we crested the high ground. I "circled the wagons" to give us maximum coverage in all directions. The poor terrain meant that the vehicles were closer than I would have liked—about forty yards apart—but sometimes you can only work with what you've got. I only had three wagons so I was struggling straight away to dominate all of the potential enemy approach routes.

Once we had parked I climbed out of my vehicle, pulled out my map and started orientating myself to the ground. The compounds were the usual Afghan affair: single-story buildings, sometimes two stories, surrounded by a ten-foot wall. There was usually only one way in and out—through the single gate.

As I scanned through my binos, I could see the Yorks' patrol base. I could also see the large three-peaked hill, almost two miles away, that they would be patrolling toward. "Three Titted Hill," as it was known in the Army, was covered in compounds and Taliban rat runs. They could sneak through this area with impunity and hit the patrol bases whenever they wanted. It also allowed them to extract their wounded without being seen. The Yorks and the ANA were going to try to clear this area.

I kept scanning the ground and spotted a Bedouin camp

about 160 yards to my right in a gully. There were the usual patches of green caused by irrigation and farming.

The whole area was crisscrossed with irrigation ditches, treelines and low walls. It looked like a right warren.

I'd just got myself happy with the lie of the land when I saw movement off to my right. It was the Yorks and the ANA leaving their base to start their patrol. I needed to get on with things. I hopped back into my wagon and continued to scan the area, all the while being fed updates over the radio. Intelligence had heard the Taliban relaying information about the patrol as soon as it had left the base, so we knew there were dickers out there. That really got me focused.

A glint off in the distance caught my eye. The old "sniper sense" started to kick in and I decided it was time to deploy some better optics. Ahead of me, I could see a low wall and some folds in the ground. The undulating land was now going to come in handy.

"Move the wagon twenty yards over, into that dip, so that only the grenade launcher is exposed," I told Cliff.

He moved the vehicle so that the bulk of it was protected. The remainder of my guys were scanning their arcs and manning their weapons, so I climbed into the back of my wagon where I kept my sniper rifle, secured in a hard plastic transit case just behind the roll bar. I unclipped the locks and slid out the rifle. The Schmidt & Bender scope would be much better for looking at things at distance. I passed the spotting scope to Cliff.

"Wit, you stay here and cover our rear with the grenade launcher. Keep relaying information to us on your personal radio or by shouting. Cliff, you and I are going to head forward slightly to that wall and use the better optics. Happy?"

Cliff and Wit nodded. Cliff and I trotted about twenty yards to our front and crouched behind the old wall. It was neck height; perfect for me to balance the rifle on. The downside was that the mud wall was in pretty bad shape and starting to crumble.

"Cliff, scan to the front while I sort myself out."

"Roger."

I put my rifle by my feet and pulled out my map. I needed to work out a hasty range card so I quickly identified compounds on the map, worked out the range and then relayed the information to Cliff. Once I was happy with that, I rummaged in the top of my daysack and pulled out my wind markers: tent pegs with para cord hanging off them. I put two out, one on either side of me. I always like to have wind markers as well as a range card, where possible. The wind can have such an effect on the bullet's trajectory that a sniper always needs to know wind direction and speed.

I kept scanning the map and ground, and started joining the two pieces of information together. There were about thirty compounds between us and Three Titted Hill. I made sure Cliff was identifying compounds and allocating them target numbers. This would speed things up if he had to dial me onto a target quickly.

Glancing over to where I last saw the Yorks and ANA patrol, I observed that they were making steady progress and were starting to head out into the open ground in the valley.

Once I was happy with the map and the ground, I picked up my rifle and balanced it on the wall by its bipod. A small chunk of baked mud dropped to the ground.

"Fuck me," I muttered to myself, "if Frank and Daz could see me now, they would not be impressed. They would definitely fail me on the sniper course."

I leaned into the rifle to stabilize it and grabbed the bipod with my left hand to try to stop it moving around. It would have to do.

Once I was comfortable behind my rifle, I turned my attention to the area where I thought I'd seen movement. We knew there were dickers out there; it was my job to remove them.

I was trying to get a good view through my scope but my helmet was getting in the way. It kept bumping into the scope and the straps were biting into my neck. I took it off and dropped it at my feet.

Now that I had a clear picture, I started to scan across the compounds. I could see Taliban stacking up behind compounds, AK47s and RPGs in their hands, clearly waiting for further directions. I was off at an angle to them and they were so focused on the patrol in the valley that they weren't paying any attention to me. I quickly counted thirty Taliban and relayed this information to the Yorks on my radio. Hopefully they wouldn't get ambushed.

I needed to find the dicker. He was the Taliban's eyes and ears, and without him they were headless. It was almost 1030 hours now and the sun was shining. There was a glint off in the distance, from the spot where I'd seen movement before. It was a long way off, almost at the base of Three Titted Hill. Movement caught my eye again in the same place, just to the left of a compound. I focused my scope in and scanned the area. Another glint. Finally, I could see a bearded, turbaned man. The glint was coming from the antenna of the radio he was holding.

"Cliff, got him."

"Where?" he replied.

"Lone compound almost on Three Titted Hill. I saw movement at the left-hand corner."

While Cliff got himself on target, I quickly looked at the map by my feet. I hadn't got time to measure it but I could see straight away that it was a long way away, about a mile, maybe further. Further than they had told me this rifle could shoot.

"I've got him," Cliff replied. "As you said, bottom left corner of the compound, behind the wall. I can see the fucker watching the patrol."

I reached over and began dialing clicks into the elevation drum of my scope. When you fire a shot through a rifle, the bullet flies on a parabolic curve; it doesn't fly straight. It gains height before dropping because of gravity. The sniper needs to know the range so that he can dial corrections into the scope to compensate for the bullet's flight path.

I dialed a massive correction into my scope. I was going to have a go. I'd never shot this far out, and, from everything I had been taught, the .338 round wouldn't go that far. You never knew, though, and if I could get a round in the general area, it might keep the dicker's head down.

There is so much to take into account with extreme long-range shooting: range, temperature, humidity, wind speed and direction, even flight time. A bullet takes around two seconds to reach 1,000 yards. That meant that, at this range, my round would be in flight for five to six seconds. During that period, the earth would have actually moved, what's known as the Coriolis effect. So I had to fuse all of this data together in my mind to try to make the best shot I possibly could. To start with, though, I was just going to attempt to get a shot in the right area.

I went through my preshot routine. I cleared my mind, regulated my breathing and concentrated on keeping the rifle as level and as stable as possible. I took up the slack on the trigger and exhaled. I had the Taliban; at this range he was a very small object in the scope, right in the center of my cross hairs.

At the peak of my exhale, I took up the 4lb of pull and

the rifle barked into my shoulder. I quickly recovered from the recoil and the scope settled. I waited six seconds and didn't see anything, except a very much alive Taliban. I had no idea where the shot had gone.

"Miss," said Cliff.

"I can fucking see that; where did it go?"

"Low, very low, about one hundred and fifty yards below him."

This was where it was great having a spotter. Two sets of eyes are better than one but the spotting scope also gave him a much wider field of vision than mine. He could see a lot more of the surrounding area. I quickly dialed more adjustments into the scope and fired again.

"Low," he said.

We repeated the process eight times, the dicker oblivious to the fact that someone was targeting him and that he wasn't just hearing stray shots on the battlefield. Each time Cliff spotted the impact and I made an adjustment to my scope. By the ninth shot, I had run out of clicks in the scope and was at the bottom part of the central pillar of my cross hairs. I was literally out of scope. The ninth round struck the wall just below the dicker, though, sending him sprawling for cover. Finally, I was now in the field of vision for my scope—so I could see where my bullets were hitting and more precisely calculate the adjustments I needed to make.

I made my own minor corrections and as soon as I saw the dicker's head I fired again.

Miss.

I fired another four rounds, none of which gave me the spray of red mist I was desperate to see, but at least I was keeping his head down.

"Craig," Wit shouted from the wagon. He had an intelligence update. "That dicker is getting a right bollocking from the Taliban in the valley. They want information on the patrol but he says that he can't see as someone is shooting at him."

"Perfect," I thought to myself.

"Look at the Taliban behind the compounds," said Cliff.

I pulled my head away from my scope and looked down into the valley. I could see Taliban milling about aimlessly. Without the dicker they had no way of knowing where the patrol was—and they didn't want to risk bumping into the Yorks, with their much better drills and firepower. In a one-on-one fight, the Taliban lost every time, which was why they liked to ambush.

Out of the corner of my eye, I saw two Jackals start to drive down the center of the valley. Straight into the potential kill zone of the Taliban ambush.

I quickly got on my radio to higher headquarters.

"Zero Alpha, this is Maverick 41. Why are you driving into terrain that is a potential ambush site? Over."

"Roger, this is the only available route in and out and we need to keep it open for the patrol. Out," was his response.

Now I had to try to keep the dicker's head down, provide overwatch for the patrol *and* provide cover for the vehicles.

Then it all kicked off. The Yorks patrol got attacked on multiple flanks. Jonesy, the troop leader's gunner, saw a Taliban on the flat roof of a compound and stitched him with the belt-fed grenade launcher. I watched as the body flew twenty yards back.

Wit was shouting at me from my Jackal.

"What?" I shouted back.

"The Bedouin; they've fucked off."

I glanced over and saw their camels kicking up dust as they ran off into the distance. They'd left their tents, everything, behind. Even the fires were still burning. That was not a good sign.

I switched my focus back to my front, starting to worry about my ten-minute rule.

"Wit, keep watching our flanks. I don't want any Taliban sneaking up on us!"

"Roger," he called back.

Cliff started pointing out targets to me. "Craig, compound two, I've just seen two Taliban moving into a position to attack the patrol."

I would have to deal with the dicker later; this was a more pressing threat. I glanced down at my range card. Compound two was 830 yards away. My scope was set for 2,000-plus yards so I needed to dial it back to the correct range. I knew that I could hit with my first round at these shorter ranges— but only as long as my scope was adjusted correctly, and it seemed to take forever to click the elevation drum back to the correct setting. Once I was happy, I got the rifle as stable as possible on the crumbling wall and looked through the scope, scanning right to left without disrupting my position too much.

I saw clearly what Cliff had spotted: two Taliban crouching behind a wall, positioned so that they had a compound between themselves and the patrol in the valley. They had no idea that I was off to their flank and could see them. See them and, more importantly, hit them. I went through my preshot routine, keeping the cross hairs as steady as I could. I exhaled and took up the slack in the trigger. It felt like time stood still.

I squeezed the trigger. *Bang.* The round impacted the first Taliban's chest and he dropped instantly. I rapidly cycled the bolt with my right hand while trying to disrupt the rifle as little as possible. I got the cross hairs onto his pal.

The shock of the bullet impacting the first Taliban had

stunned the second guy. This only lasted a split second and then he quickly came to his senses and started running. I tracked him with my cross hairs, gave the usual slight lead for a moving target and then squeezed. *Bang.* His leg shot, he dropped, howling. Moving targets are always a challenge as there are even more variables that you have to take into account.

Again I rapidly cycled the bolt and placed the cross hairs on his head. He had hold of his weapon so he was still a threat. I paused, squeezed and watched as his head exploded.

"Hit," I thought to myself.

As I took out the second guy, I caught more movement through the scope. I couldn't be completely sure, but I thought I saw a shadow moving behind the compound.

"Wit, two down in the area of compound two," I shouted back to the vehicle. "I saw a shadow so I think there is probably a third near the compound."

Wit relayed this information to the patrol but I didn't know if they were listening, as they were firmly in contact and having to fight their own battle. More and more Taliban were swarming into the area and the sound of gunfire and explosions in the valley was increasing by the second. It looked like the Yorks, the ANA and the remainder of my troop were getting further and further into the shit. I had to help in any way I could and right now that meant neutralizing as many insurgents as possible. I would have liked to nail that dicker, but for the moment I was going to have to concentrate on the direct threats to my front.

I switched my focus back to the area where I'd seen the shadow, right near to where I'd nailed the second Taliban. I tracked back to a second compound, just behind the one I'd been observing, and saw a Taliban crouching behind a wall, holding an AK47. I glanced down at my range card and saw that this compound was one thousand yards away. I decided not to dial the adjustment into my scope to save time. Instead, I would use the mil-dot reticule to "hold off" if necessary.

I knew that these guys usually worked in pairs, so I fought the urge to shoot him straight away and instead waited to see if he was joined by anyone. I would rather get two than one and he wasn't currently firing on the patrol, so I could afford to bide my time.

After a minute, the Taliban started getting twitchy and then he was up and running to his front, heading toward another compound. After a minute he reached the back wall. According to my range card this compound was 800 yards from my position. Good thing I didn't make any adjustment to my scope.

I kept watching and suddenly another head popped up. A second Taliban—and this one was holding an RPG. These guys definitely needed to be taken down. I settled into my rifle and controlled my breathing, exhaling and taking up the slack. I had my cross hairs on the insurgent with the RPG.

I fired . . . and missed. The round passed between their two heads. "Fuck," I cursed to myself, rapidly cycling the bolt.

The round passing between them clearly made them jump and they started moving in different directions, the Taliban with the RPG heading into the open while the other one stayed behind the wall. I had time with the one in the open, who was exposing himself and giving me a clear shot, so I switched back to the other Taliban. I quickly fired again and watched as the round struck him in the hip. He literally spun round four times before collapsing to the ground.

I cycled the bolt and got the cross hairs back onto the guy with the RPG. Cliff had been tracking him and quickly talked me on. I fired. Perfect hit. His body jerked as the round slammed into him.

There was movement back where the other guy was, his leg twitching. The hip shot had put him down but not taken him out. He started trying to get to his feet, using his AK as a crutch. He was still a threat to the Yorks so I placed my cross hairs on his chest and fired. He almost snapped in half.

Back at the vehicle, Wit was relaying all of my shots and the targets to the Yorks. Things were really heating up for them in the valley and they were getting pummeled with rifles, machine guns and RPGs.

"Craig, compound five. Taliban trying to get on a motorbike," Cliff shouted out.

I picked up a bearded Taliban with an AK47 slung over his shoulder, settled the cross hairs on him and fired—but instantly realized that I had rushed the shot. When you shoot enough you know when a shot is good or when you have "pulled it."

The round hit the bike. The .338 bullet is big and travels with a lot of energy, so the bike slammed into the Taliban and pinned him to the floor. I cycled the bolt and fired again, hitting his left arm. He was trying to get his AK up with his right hand so I took my time, placed the cross hairs on the center of his face and fired. His head exploded, splattering the wall behind him with blood.

I suddenly remembered that Cliff was new to all of this and watching everything through the spotting scope. I turned to him.

"Mate, are you all right with all of this? I know it's probably the first time . . ."

He looked me straight in the eye and winked at me, before turning back to the spotting scope. He was clearly all right, so I got my attention back to the chaos in front of us. It was a relief that he was okay as I couldn't stop now and I needed him more than ever.

I was starting to get a feel for what was going on in front of us. The Yorks patrol was 650 yards away in the valley, with the Taliban between 100 and 650 yards in front of them. The Taliban were using the rat runs between buildings off to their right flank to effectively "shoot and scoot" at the Yorks and the ANA, who were scattered in small pockets across the village. While the rat runs were obscured from the Yorks, they were perfectly exposed to me at my oblique angle, so this was going to be a target-rich environment.

I told Cliff to start scanning 100 to 650 yards in front of the Yorks and to shout out any targets that looked like they were a direct threat.

Then I jumped slightly, as I heard the rhythmic thump of the belt-fed grenade launcher being fired on my wagon. I glanced back and saw Wit firing three-to-five round bursts.

"RPG team. They're setting up to fire," he shouted.

I traced an imaginary line from the grenade launcher off into the distance and started looking in the area where the rounds were landing. I could see the Taliban team 1,100 yards away and fired at the man holding the RPG.

"Miss, low," said Cliff.

I reached to the scope and dialed two clicks into the elevation drum, settled back into the rifle and took up the slack. *Bang.*

"Hit," said Cliff.

The guy went down and the other member of the RPG team picked up the weapon and started trying to drag his mate to safety. I placed the cross hairs on the second guy and fired. The round hit his leg and he went down. I fired again, hitting him squarely in the chest. He stayed down.

Cliff was using the wider field view of the spotting scope to scan as much of the area as possible and point out targets to me.

"The dicker's back up," he suddenly said.

"What?" I replied.

"The dicker is back toward Three Titted Hill."

"Right, bring me back on and let's nail this guy," I said, while rapidly dialing clicks into my elevation drum. At least the calculations were simpler this time: dial in maximum elevation until there were no clicks left, then use the very bottom of the cross hairs, and I'd be in the right area.

Once the rifle was adjusted, I grabbed the bipod with my left hand, settled the rifle on the wall and tried to reacquire the target. "There you are," I muttered to myself, as I spotted the same guy with the walkie-talkie in the same place as before: just behind the wall. I placed the cross hairs on his chest and once I was happy that things were as stable as they could be, I fired.

Six seconds later, I saw the round strike.

"Miss, low. You hit the bottom of the wall," said Cliff.

I was happy with this now, having pretty much worked out exactly where I needed to be aiming in order to get my rounds on target.

The shot had sent the dicker off into cover again so I glanced back into the valley. I could see the Yorks starting to assault some compounds. They were in a pretty rubbish position, right in the kill zone of an ambush.

"Craig, intelligence has intercepted the enemy saying that there's a sniper off on the left on the high ground," Wit said from the vehicle.

"Fair one," I thought to myself. "They were going to work it out in the end."

In the sniper world, we constantly move after firing. A sniper will fire one to two shots, possibly three, from one position, before having to move. If you stay still, you will be identified—and if you are identified, you will be taken out. I had no idea how many rounds I had fired from this position, but it was a lot more than three. I should have moved a long time ago. I didn't have much choice though. I needed the Jackals on the high ground so that they could use their weapon systems. I couldn't push away from the vehicles and I really was in the best position to provide support; there was nothing better than this wall in my immediate surrounding area.

Even so, I was in the process of looking for a new position to move to when Wit started shouting behind me, "Craig, Taliban!"

I followed the direction that he was pointing in, but Cliff had beaten me to it. "One Taliban by a water pump on the far right," he said.

The target was 830 yards away: I hit him and watched him go down. Then I spotted a guy on a motorbike, with an AK47 slung across his back, coming from Three Titted Hill toward the water pump. I gave him a three-mil-dot lead as he was a moving target and fired. I missed.

"Go four-mil-dot lead," said Cliff.

I fired again and watched with satisfaction as the rider tumbled off and disappeared behind a sandhill. I continued to scan the area in case he got back up.

"Troop leader is starting to bring his vehicles back," shouted Wit.

The only way for the troop leader to get his vehicles out was to bring them back the way they had come: through the kill zone. The place was crawling with Taliban and the vehicles would be really exposed, but with all the ditches and the treelines, any other route was practically impossible, the ground too hard-going.

I watched their movements through my scope, all the while scanning the surrounding area for enemy. All of the vehicles suddenly stopped and I could see one of lads, Mark, dismount and start to walk round his vehicle. I knew I wouldn't stop in the middle of a kill zone.

"Wit, talk to me. What is going on?" I called.

"One of the Jackals is bogged in," he replied. "It looks like the Taliban have been flooding the fields to trap the vehicles. That's why that bloke was standing by the water pump."

"Tell them to hold on while I scan the area."

I'd just started to search around the vehicles when a large weight of fire started up. All of the lads hit the deck.

"Contact, contact," Wit shouted, relaying what he had just heard on the radio.

Dust was kicked up all around them and I could see Mark trying to get back into his vehicle to get the machine gun to bear, but the fire was just too heavy around him and he was forced to jump into a nearby ditch. Both wagons were pinned down and the lads were really in the shit. We needed to act fast or they were going to start taking casualties. Once you have a casualty, the whole situation gets ten times worse. I needed to work out where all the fire was coming from and I needed to work it out fast.

"Cliff, help me check all of the firing points. We've got to help the guys," I said.

We both started searching all of the previous firing points but they were clear.

"Fuck, fuck, fuck," I thought to myself, as the fire got worse around the vehicles.

I needed to stay calm. I could feel my heart rate rising and my muscles tensing. I was desperate to help my lads, but would be no use if I couldn't shoot properly. I took a deep breath and forced myself to relax.

"Where the fuck is that machine gun?" I muttered.

It suddenly occurred to me that the only place we hadn't

checked was around the dicker. My brain was processing a lot of information very quickly and I started to think about enemy weapon systems. If the fire wasn't from any of the previous close-in firing points, it must be coming from further away. The machine gun with the longest range that the Taliban had was a PKM, a belt-fed machine gun capable of shooting out to 1,600 yards. The RPK, their other machine gun, was magazine fed and wouldn't be capable of such high rates of fire. That meant that they had to be . . . on Three Titted Hill.

I brought my rifle round, scanned the area of the far compound where the dicker had been and suddenly I saw them. A Taliban machine-gun team was up on the right-hand side of the compound, pouring fire down on my lads. Whereas I had been happy just to keep the dicker's head down, I knew I had to get these guys—or they were going to kill one of mine. This time the rounds had to count.

I could feel the pressure and the stress mounting, but I pushed that to the back of my mind. Now, I started factoring in everything. I glanced at my wind markers. They were hanging limply; good, no wind. I was already at maximum elevation on the scope but I dialed twenty clicks left to take account of the spin drift, then factored in the earth's rotation.

I lifted my head up an inch and then placed it back down, checking my eye relief (how far back my eye was from my scope). I ensured I had a good cheek weld to the stock. The sponge that I'd put on the stock the other day was doing its job, even though it was soaking wet with sweat. My left hand was getting sore from holding on to the scope for so long, but I just had to push through it. The rifle was comfortable in my shoulder and I could feel that I was getting into the most stable position that I possibly could. I still wasn't happy, though. I was standing on a small incline, which meant my right knee was slightly bent. By now it was trembling with strain.

"Cliff, grab a rock and shove it under my right heel. I need to get my foot as flat as possible."

Cliff scuttled over and shoved a rock under my foot so that I was nice and even. All of this activity took mere seconds. Finally, I was ready. I placed my aiming mark on the machine gunner, took up the trigger slack and started to exhale. I paused on the trigger's break point and a sense of calm washed over me. I continued the squeeze and fired.

Then, all I could do was watch intently through the scope for six long seconds. Miss.

"Shit, fuck," went through my head.

I cycled the bolt again. The machine-gun crew were looking around. They knew that a round had just passed very close to them.

I fired again.

Six seconds later, I watched the machine gunner slump down on the PKM. Hit. *Hit.*

I couldn't believe it and had to fight an almost uncontrollable euphoria.

"Keep calm," I thought to myself. "Take out the other one."

I quickly got another round into the chamber and fired at the machine gunner's number two. Miss.

The second gunman picked up the PKM and started to turn. I cycled the bolt, setting myself up for the next shot.

"He's moving," shouted Cliff.

It was now or never. I knew what I needed to do, I knew where I needed to aim, I knew everything that I needed to take into account. In the blink of an eye, I fired. And six long seconds later, I watched as the second gunman collapsed.

For a minute or more, I scanned the area, checking that there were no more threats to my men.

"Cliff, check all of the firing points; check that they're all clear. We need to be sure," I told him. After a minute, Cliff confirmed they were all clear. Once I was happy that there were no other threats out there, a sense of relief washed over me. My mates were out of danger.

"Wit, tell the troop leader that it is all clear," I shouted back to my Jackal. "They're safe to get the bogged-in wagon out."

I kept scanning the area as they moved the wagon and started to pull back. The Yorks and the ANA had continued with their clearance patrol and a general calm was descending. I was quietly chuffed with myself. "That was some pretty good shooting," I thought.

An hour later, the remainder of the troop pulled up onto our little piece of high ground. The lads were all pumped with adrenaline and started thanking me.

"Did you really get those guys from here?" Andy, the troop leader, asked, with disbelief in his voice. He thought that I'd just scared them away. I gave him my rifle and he looked through the scope. The two bodies were still there.

"Fuck me," he said, in his posh Cavalry officer tone.

I just grinned.

While we sorted ourselves out, the ANA patrolled all the way up to the machine-gun position as they wanted to collect the weapon. I was told over the radio that the PKM machine gun was gone but the bodies were still there. One was shot in the gut and one through the side. Upon closer examination, they recognized one of the Taliban's faces; it turned out to be a local commander.

By the time we were heading back to our crappy little compound, I was absolutely shattered. My mind and my body had been working very, very hard today.

News of my shooting soon spread. An Apache was in the area later that day and it hovered over my firing position and, using its laser range finder, measured the distance to the machine-gun position. It was 2,705 yards. I had made the longest confirmed kills in the world.

But, of course, I didn't know that at that stage. I just knew that I'd done some good shooting, some of it at extreme range. I also knew that if I hadn't done what I'd done, eight of my lads would either be dead or injured. That was all that mattered to me and I was just very happy with the calls I'd made.

13. Bullet Magnet

About a week later, all of the commanders crowded into the ops room. As usual, the officers got the chairs at the front so the NCOs had to stand at the back. This meant that we got information secondhand, which pissed me off. The CO walked in and started chatting to the officers, ignoring the rest of us. That's the Cavalry for you. It's more like an officer's club. The lads bust their balls and the officers get all the glory. It's a shame. We do get some good officers now and then, but they never seem to stay for very long.

The CO started his briefing. The mission was to build a new patrol base on the top of a hill, west of a village that had been named Mindon. Of course, the Taliban would need clearing from the area before the patrol base could be built, which was the infantry's task while we provided assistance and cover. The infantry would be coming in by Chinook. The CO then gave the commanders their individual orders.

"Corporal of Horse Harrison," he said to me. "You are to locate and secure three helicopter landing sites by first light. Once that is done, move southwest and block west."

"Sir," I replied, before looking at my map. The area he had asked me and the lads to operate in looked flat, but the maps weren't that good so I couldn't see much detail. I headed off to find my lads. Once they were briefed I went to bed, but I didn't get much sleep; I had a lot on my mind.

We left at 0300 hours. It was always a slow start when we headed off; today we were following C Squadron and were stuck behind their vehicles. It was freezing and the driving was challenging. The concentration these drives required while staring through the green glow of night-vision goggles always gave you a headache. Cliff fed me Haribo while I alternated glances between the road and the GPS I had mounted to the dashboard. I looked down and then up again, into blinding light. "Fuck me, it's morning already," was what I thought to myself for a second. Then the shock wave hit us and we were pelted with stones. The rear vehicle of C Squadron—a Mastiff—had hit an IED. We ran over and it took us ten minutes to pry the rear armored door open.

"Is everyone okay?" I shouted into the back, once we'd got the battered door open.

There was a chorus of "yes, mate" from inside.

No one was hurt; the Mastiff did its job well, but it was wrecked.

After the wagon was recovered, we pushed on to our line of departure. Once we crossed this imaginary line, we had to be fully ready to engage in battle. We were now in a bowl surrounded by hills. I let the lads get some sleep, waking them up only when it got closer to H-hour—the time the op was due to begin.

I had been given a Navy guy called Brad for the op, who would communicate with the helicopters. He looked like a small Grizzly Adams with his beard and a bandanna on. We headed off and started securing the HLSs. Due to the poor maps, it took us two hours to locate suitable landing sites and secure all of them, with the CO constantly on my back. He had thought it would only take thirty minutes, but I kept telling him that I couldn't rush this. Predictably he didn't want to hear it.

"We have a timeline to stick to."

I knew that. I was also sure he wouldn't be saying that if a Chinook got shot down. I ended up leaving one vehicle on each landing site. I parked in the middle so that I could see all of the HLSs while Brad talked to the pilots.

"HLS secure," I said on the radio, before tossing a green smoke grenade as a visual signal for what I'd just said.

The first Chinook raced in, blasting us with hot air and stones. The second and third helicopters followed onto their HLSs. The CO was immediately on the radio asking for sitreps (situation reports).

The first Chinook was just lifting off and pulling away when, suddenly, there was a massive explosion.

"Shit, IED," I thought to myself. I felt sick. The color had drained from Brad's face. Under his beard he was as white as a ghost.

"Contact, wait out," I said on the radio.

The CO immediately started pestering me for updates. In the end I had to say again, slowly, as if I was talking to an idiot: "Wait . . . out." Which bit of "wait" and "out" did he not understand?

Brad and I started scanning the area, trying to work out where the explosion had come from. There were some Afghan Army in the area, so I wondered if they had had an accident with something. Then I heard screaming and, looking in that direction, we could see what had happened. The Royal Engineers had been told to carry detonation cord in their map pockets. Det cord looks like thick wire and is packed with explosives. It is used as a primary charge to set off a main charge. When these guys came off the Chinook, the det cord in one of their pockets went off, blowing a hole the size of a bowling ball out of the poor fucker's leg and hitting some of the others with shrapnel. Surveying the casualties, I couldn't see anyone doing anything to help them.

"Cliff, go over and give first aid."

Cliff wanted to become a medic after the tour, so now was his chance to prove himself. He rammed his fist into the hole to stop the bleeding and then got it all wrapped up with a field dressing. By the time the doctor arrived, the wound was dressed. The doc was impressed. The same heli that had dropped the guys off came back and picked up the casualty.

I looked over at Cliff, who was covered in blood, gave him a thumbs-up and then updated the CO on the radio.

Once the main operation was underway and the infantry had started to clear the village, we drove on and I stopped us on some high ground overlooking Mindon, so we could provide cover. I could hear C Squadron getting whacked in the wadi (valley) with RPGs and small arms. Scanning the area, I noticed a compound with six motorbikes propped against the wall, which didn't look right. One guy left the compound, got on his bike and rode off. Once he had gone, another one came out and did the same.

It was then that I noticed the glint of an antenna.

"Wit, pass my sniper rifle and give Cliff the spotting scope."

With the rifle on my shoulder, I scanned the area that the bikes had headed toward and located the riders, who all had rifles on their backs. There was an amazing-looking tree nearby—it looked like a Joshua tree and it really stood out: a useful landmark for a sniper. Observing the men, it was clear that these guys were dickers and were the ones coordinating the attacks on C Squadron.

I heard the firefight go quiet. The guys got on their bikes again and changed position. I got on the radio and explained what I had seen to the CO. This was clearly a dicking screen and it needed removing.

The map told me it was 1,000 yards to the Joshua tree. I got out my shot data card and started working out the elevation and deflection, then factored in spin drift. Even if I didn't kill the dickers, I could keep their heads down and stop C Squadron getting shot up.

"Nice and smooth," I reminded myself, placing the cross hairs on the dicker with the radio. I traced a line down his center of mass, stopping at a position on his spine, midway between his lungs. I could see the guy's mate with an AK in the background, looking around.

I was just about to take up the 4lb of pull when the CO piped up on the radio. "Watch and observe only. Do not engage."

"Fuck." I released the trigger slack.

One of the sniper's roles is simply to observe, but that does not feel good when your friends are being shot up. I thought back to the Sniper Mission we were taught on the course:

> The sniper's primary role is to disrupt enemy command and control by day and by night, in all weather conditions, in all phases of war. Destroy, suppress, neutralize.

> The sniper's secondary role is to act as an observer to produce additional battlefield information, with the ability to direct indirect fire as necessary.

"Why won't the CO let me carry out my primary mission?" I thought. I knew the top brass had to worry about the "hearts and minds" policy but it was frustrating for those of us on the ground who believed there was a place on the battlefield for some good old-fashioned violence.

C Squadron were hit again. In fact, I listened as they got hit another four times. Fuck this. I pushed down the pressel switch on my headset radio and tried again with the CO.

"I told you to watch and observe," he shouted at me.

Letting go of the switch I bellowed out, "Wanker," and passed my rifle back to Wit. What a waste of fucking time.

Then I heard a noise that sounded like firecrackers coming from the compounds to our front. I started to get a funny feeling in my gut about that, which solidified as the local women and kids walked out of the village and started heading north. Suddenly, there was a *whoosh* sound and an RPG screamed toward us.

"Contact," I shouted.

The RPG landed two yards in front of Jim's wagon and exploded. The driver—Simon—was having a piss and instead of diving into the vehicle he started running around it, trying to do his flies up. I couldn't help but start laughing. Jim reversed his vehicle next to mine.

"Did you fucking see that?" he asked. He was covered in sand and his eyes looked like pool balls. I could see that the vehicle had been struck by shrapnel.

"Yes, mate, but we need to hold the blocking line. Get back up there."

"What? You said that you saw that!"

I'd known Jim for years and we had been on a few tours together now. I just cocked my head; I didn't have to say anything. He moved his vehicle back to the forward position while I sent a contact report and let HQ know that the screen was back in place. Then Jim came up on the radio.

"I can see a pile of RPG warheads on the ground near to where that last one was fired. I can also see a male bobbing up and down behind a wall."

"Roger, keep eyes on," I told him. That male must be the fuck who'd fired the RPG at us.

I got everyone to move positions, to try to make the enemy's life a bit harder, and noticed that there was a ridgeline off to the flank that I hadn't cleared yet.

"Jim, cover me. I'm going to clear that ridgeline off to the left."

Cliff started to drive up the hill. As we got near the crest, we had the shock of our lives. There in a small gully were four Taliban with AK47s and a PKM, getting ready to set up an ambush. They immediately started firing, hitting my vehicle and Jim's as well. Wit—my gunner in the back—couldn't open up fire as his weapon, being mounted on the roll bar, wouldn't depress far enough to target them. I fired forward with the GPMG that was mounted in front of me.

Rounds were slamming into the vehicle and landing all around us; we found out later that the vehicle was hit 136 times. The Taliban were scrambling for cover but still managing to fire at us.

"Hold your position," I told Jim. Looking down, I saw Cliff in the footwell, trying to get in cover.

I had just leaned forward to fire another burst with the GPMG when my head was slammed to the side. It felt like a giant had punched me on the right side of my head. The world went black.

Twenty seconds later, the darkness started to clear. I was staring at sand. As my hearing returned too, I realized small-arms rounds were whizzing past.

"Where the fuck am I?" I groggily muttered to myself.

I started to crawl on all fours, but arms reached out and grabbed my body armor. That's when I saw that I was outside the wagon, on the ground, and Cliff was braving the gunfire while trying to drag me back in. With his help I scrambled back in the wagon and felt my helmet, my fingers running all over the smash mark left by a bullet. The force of the impact had launched me out of the vehicle. I picked up my radio and talked to the ops room.

"I would just like to confirm that the helmet works."

Jim's wagon had now pulled alongside us and they were also getting rounds down. I went back to firing my GPMG at the enemy to the front, until it jammed. I cocked it—but still nothing. The ammo box had been hit.

"Cliff, more ammo."

Cliff passed up a box of ammo from the footwell, shouting in pain as he did so. He'd dislocated his shoulder trying to pull me back into the vehicle.

A sudden thud threw me back into my seat. I had now been shot in the front plate of my body armor.

I saw red. "Who the fuck do these people think they are?" I thought angrily to myself. I got a new belt on, cocked the GPMG and started hosing the fuckers down. I watched with satisfaction as two of the original four dropped under my fire.

"Cliff, we need to go. Start reversing the wagon."

"They're dead, Craig."

"Just go," I replied. There could have been more Taliban out there and we were still in a vulnerable position.

Jim moved his vehicle off first, then Cliff gunned our wagon and started reversing at speed. We hit a small ditch that slammed us to a halt and I could suddenly smell burning. Cliff had left the handbrake on and it had caught fire. We put the fire out and then realized that we were still getting hit by small-arms fire from our left. I threw a smoke grenade to try to cover our extraction, but it went high so I moved

round to the side and threw a phosphorous smoke grenade as well. The firing stopped.

"Right, Cliff, get us out of here. Drive to the other wagons."

The odd, single shot was still fired at us but we made it back to the other vehicles and relative safety. I clambered out and unbuckled my helmet. As I turned it over in my hands, I couldn't believe what I was seeing. There was a strike mark slap bang on the side. "One inch lower and I would be dead," I thought to myself. My neck hurt and my ears were ringing.

The doctor came over and I told him to check out Cliff first.

"I'm fine," Cliff insisted, so the doc switched his attention back to me. He diagnosed concussion and whiplash, and made me spend the night in the ambulance while the lads joined C Squadron. The next morning I felt terrible—as though I was suffering the world's worst hangover. The doc checked me out again.

"So how do you feel?"

"Fine," I replied. I just wanted to get back to my lads.

The doc stared at me, clearly not believing what I was saying. After a moment he said, "Go on, then. Rejoin your patrol."

As soon as my feet hit the floor outside the ambulance, I felt like I was going to collapse. Plus, it sounded like a tuning fork was ringing in my head.

The lads looked pissed off, but pleased to see me. They were pissed off because they had been told to fire illumination rounds the night before—and when they did, the Taliban shot back at the firing point. The order was given to stop firing flares but one of the lads had fired some more anyway and shitloads of tracer came flying back in their direction. They'd been harassed by enemy fire all night.

As we drove off, I couldn't stop looking at the bullet holes in the vehicle and thinking about my helmet. I couldn't believe how lucky I was.

"How's your shoulder?" I asked Cliff.

"Fine."

"Look. Thanks for saving me yesterday, when you dragged me back into the vehicle."

"That's all right. Tanya would have killed me if I'd let you die."

He's a modest man.

As we drove into the district center, the padre was there to meet us.

"So did you see God?" he asked me.

"No, sir," I replied. "I saw my granddad."

I'm not a huge believer in God. My granddad used to smoke cigars and whenever something bad is about to happen, I smell cigar smoke. Right before we'd got contacted I'd smelt the faint whiff of cigar smoke and I knew then that the shit was going to hit the fan.

We sorted ourselves out and were then tasked to head back out to look after a damaged Jackal that had been hit by an IED. The lads were a bit fed up with what appeared to be a pretty crap tasking, but it was important that the locals weren't allowed to get near our kit. We ended up waiting for four days for an inspection team to come and work out exactly what blew the vehicle up. We camped next to the damaged vehicle and fortunately were left alone.

At night, we ended up firing quite a few illumination rockets as we were always convinced that we could see movement. On what turned out to be our last night, Rocky popped

a small flare; the wind caught it and blew it into a neighboring field.

"Watch where you fire those things," I shouted out to him, annoyed.

After about twenty minutes, smoke started to drift over us. Rocky had definitely set fire to something. The smoke smelled slightly sweeter than burning wood. Oddly, I was getting light-headed and the lads were giggling. Standing up in my vehicle to get a better look at what was going on, I saw about an acre of field on fire. Grabbing my binos, I confirmed it was a field of cannabis. We were all getting high! The smoke started to get really thick so we had no choice but to move downwind.

We pushed south for 500 yards while maintaining eyes on the damaged vehicle. We were really wary of mines so took our time and did the drills properly. The next morning, the inspection team rocked up with a recovery truck and we were soon on our way back to our main base. The lads had the serious munchies and everyone laughed when I told them what had happened.

I had just stepped out of my vehicle when one of the signalers came and found me.

"Commanding officer wants you," I was told.

I went and found the colonel.

"The Americans are starting a major new offensive to retake previously held ground. They are going to take Nowzad and they've requested some support to prevent the Taliban escaping," he told me. "I want to put your troop up north to search cars and cover the roads."

"How long is the op?"

"Nine days."

"Roger that."

I gave the lads the "good" news and some time to sort out their admin. The vehicles needed preparing; we needed food, water and ammunition. A couple of the lads headed off to the cookhouse to see what they could scrounge. I dished out our mail, which cheered us all up, and just a few hours later we were ready to head north.

We positioned ourselves next to a massive wadi, which was used as a kind of motorway by the locals. We had good eyes on the wadi and were in position four days ahead of the main assault to prevent any enemy escaping.

When the main op kicked off, it was like the Fourth of July. The Americans put about a hundred snipers in the mountains and had an incredible amount of firepower. Watching the main assault, as the troops moved into the town, was like watching someone stamp on a tube of toothpaste: stuff squirted everywhere. Civilian vehicles quickly started pouring out of the town.

Some of our vehicles were on the high ground to provide fire support and the remainder were down in the wadi to do the searching; a female RMP joined us to search females passing through. We had a simple set-up of a "dirty box," where people waited to be searched, and a "clean box," into which they were moved once they had been searched. Their vehicle was checked at the same time. We got a lot of disgusted glares during the process.

It took a few days before we found anything. On the eighth day, the lads were searching a few men when the interpreters found pictures on their phones of them posing with AK47s. We "tagged and bagged" them and drove them back to the FOB to be flown on to Bastion for interrogation.

Then, on the last day of the op, I saw a white car off in the distance really shifting. It blasted straight through our checkpoint and nearly ran the lads over. Rocky and I started

to give chase in our vehicles and I requested permission to open fire.

The Jackal is an awesome vehicle both on and off road and we comfortably matched the car's speed of 50mph. Of course, there was a delay while my HQ had to ask their "higher," but eventually I was told we could engage.

"Rocky, open fire," I told him over the radio.

I watched as he fired a small flare, which, at our speed, was just whisked away.

"Use your fucking GPMG," I snapped.

"I can't. It's too bumpy!"

Before we could continue the conversation, the car screeched to a halt next to a cliff edge. By the time we had closed in, the occupants had bugged out into the wadi.

Looking over the edge, we saw a nomad camp and realized the Taliban must have gone in there. We searched the car and found some duffel jackets and a prescription for medication. When the interpreter read the name on the prescription, his eyes widened.

"This is the name of a Taliban leader."

"Fucking jackpot."

If we could bag this guy, it would be a huge tick in the box for the troop.

We kept eyes on the nomad camp while we sorted ourselves out. At dusk, I left some of the lads with the vehicles and the rest of us headed down into the wadi. I put guys at each end of the long beige tent, all equipped with night-vision goggles, to make sure that no one escaped. It was getting dark, so I asked the artillery guns back at the FOB to start firing illumination rounds for us. Once we had some light, I got the interpreter to call out for the elder.

A small, white-bearded man appeared through one of the tent flaps and we had a chat with him and then started our search. Two of the guys in the tent really stood out. They had new dishdashes and shoes, plus they smelled of aftershave while everyone else stank of goat. The problem was that there was no evidence to justify lifting them and the elder was sticking to his story that he could vouch for everyone.

In the end, we had no choice but to return to our vehicles and head off, dragging the white car with us so that it could be forensically checked.

Back in FOB Edinburgh a few hours later, I told the lads to sort out their kit in case we had to go out again, and then headed off to the colonel's office to give him a rundown on the op.

"Good, very good . . . Do you think your lads could be ready to move out in four hours?" he asked, once I had finished.

I thought, "Only four hours?" but I said, "Of course."

"Good. We're going up north to do some patrolling near another FOB."

I walked wearily back to my tent, sat on my camp cot and dropped my head into my hands. It had been a long few weeks and the pace was relentless. We never seemed to get any downtime. It was flattering in some ways, because I had the impression that the colonel liked my troop and knew we got the job done, which was why he was giving us so many ops, but we could still do with a break.

Ten minutes before we were due to depart I had a brainwave and went to find Billy, the head storeman, who lent me a satellite phone to take out with us. That way the lads could ring home at least. I shoved it in my pocket and got back in my vehicle just in time. The colonel pulled off in his Panther and we followed.

Night fell quickly and we drove in darkness for about two hours before arriving at a small FOB, where we were briefed by a Yorks officer. The Yorks and the Afghan Army were going to be patrolling in the nearby green zone and they wanted us to provide support from the high ground. Once he was finished, we got some time to sort ourselves out and get some much-needed sleep.

At first light we headed out and about half an hour later were in position. The colonel kept his vehicle slightly back on the high ground and I brought my troop forward. Once I was happy with where we were, I pulled out my sniper rifle and moved forward to a wall. Using this as a rest, I started scanning my arcs. I quickly identified the patrol and did a scan of the area around them.

Off to the right was a wall about five yards high and twenty yards long. It had four window holes cut out of it, but all without any glass. In one of the windows, I noticed a shadow.

I cranked up the magnification on my scope and zoomed in. I saw an arm and could swear I also saw a rifle. The colonel's vehicle had really good optics on it so I asked him to check it out.

"It's just a shepherd looking after his sheep," he told me.

Four hours later, I could hear small gun battles starting as the Yorks came under contact, so I looked back to the window and scanned the surrounding area. There was a man next to some rubble, crawling backward, and then I saw movement again in the original window in the wall.

"Just continue to observe," the CO said when I got on the radio to him.

"I have been, for hours," I wanted to say. I walked back up the hill to the colonel's wagon. As soon as I opened the door, I was hit by a blast of cold air. "He's got the air conditioning on full blast while I'm down the hill sweating my tits off," I thought.

"There's definitely something iffy with that window; I want to fire some warning shots," I told him.

"Okay," he relented.

I headed back down to my vantage point, leaving Cliff to cover my rear. Once I'd found a decent spot I built up my position, working out the corrections I needed to make for wind, range and heat shimmer, and then dialing them into my scope. Once I was ready, I aimed to the right of the window, fired and hit the wall; I fired again and hit some rubble near the window. "That should let them know I can see them," I thought.

I didn't see anything for a minute, and then I caught movement in one of the other windows. I started to count in my head as I tracked between windows.

"One . . . two . . . three."

The walker appeared in the next window and now I could see he was definitely carrying a weapon. I started another count and tracked again to the next window. As he appeared in the window, I fired. He fell, but I knew I hadn't hit him; I wasn't aiming for him, I was aiming just in front of him. He must have felt the air break as the bullet cracked by. Now *that* is a warning shot.

Finally some air support arrived in the form of two Apaches, and they reported that they could see six Taliban sheltering behind the wall, all of whom were carrying weapons. They were waiting to ambush the patrol as it came back into the green zone. The colonel got on his radio and called in an Exactor rocket to fire down onto their position. It missed by about sixteen yards but still did a lot of damage. I could see a number of casualties, and motorbikes arriving to casevac their injured.

"I am in a position to engage further combatants," I told him over my radio.

"Negative. Just continue to observe."

It pissed me off, having to just watch as the enemy collected the injured, and all their weapons, and then headed off, so I was glad when we got the order to extract. I slid my rifle back into its case and got back in the vehicle. It was about 1630 hours as we headed off.

We had to drive through a small village with a lot of vulnerable points, including choke points for the vehicles, so I didn't want to hang about, especially as it was getting dark. The Taliban wouldn't be happy that they had taken casualties and would be out to get us.

Then the lead vehicle just stopped.

"I'm going to find out what's wrong," I told Cliff, as I jumped out of our wagon and walked over.

"What's going on?" I asked the lead vehicle commander.

"I've got a bad feeling about this one," he nervously replied. "And I've got a wife and two kids at home."

I just stared at him.

"Fuck it, we'll lead," I told him and headed back to my vehicle.

I briefed Cliff and we moved to the front. I decided that we would head left, out into a plowed field, rather than go down another alley. The field looked freshly plowed and we would be breaking "virgin tracks" as they are known. There were no vehicle marks and no footprints in the soil so there was minimal chance that the Taliban had laid anything for us.

As we drove across the field, the sun was starting to set, and it was actually quite peaceful. I'd just noticed that I hadn't seen any locals for a while when—

There is a blinding flash on the right-hand side of the vehicle and time just slows down. Everything happens in slow motion and I feel like I am an observer rather than actually in this real-life "movie."

I am leaving my seat and I feel the impact as my shoulder hits the roll bar and my right leg hits the GPMG. I can see Cliff smashing into the steering wheel and then catapulting back into his seat, before he slumps forward and drapes himself over the dashboard.

As I fly out of the Jackal to the left, I watch Wit pass me in mid-air and connect with the front of the vehicle. He comes to rest on the hood, his desert combat uniform blending in perfectly with the paint of the vehicle.

I hit the ground with a thud and roll, before coming to rest. My ears are ringing badly and I can hardly see. I try to stand but my right leg won't work. I desperately start crawling toward Cliff, but first my wrist and then my arms give out. My head is really hurting and it feels like I am on a rollercoaster ride. Waves of nausea and dizziness wash over me.

I can't make it to Cliff and I just want to scream.

Then everything goes black.

I come round and have no idea where I am. I am looking at gray cladding and red webbing seats. The noise is loud and I become aware of lots of movement around me; people in surgical gloves holding drips and needles.

I realize I am in the back of a MERT—a Chinook helicopter with a medical team onboard. The pain starts to overwhelm me and I scream out.

"Hang on there, buddy," one of medics shouts, while holding on to me. "Get some painkillers in him," he instructs his team.

"We can't find a vein. He keeps going in and out of shock," someone else shouts back.

"Drill into his shin."

I feel an intense pain in my shin, which continues to build and build.

"Fucking batteries have gone on the drill; give me the hand drill."

The pain increases to an almost unbelievable level; I can't feel my other injuries as these guys butcher my shin. Every turn of the drill bit as it cuts through my bone is agony.

Once down to the marrow, they insert a needle. The pain starts to subside and I black out again.

I open my eyes and I can't see anything except blinding white light. The intensity decreases a bit as I blink, but everything remains white. "Bollocks, I'm dead," I think to myself.

I can see movement around me. Must be angels.

I reach out with my left arm to try to catch one of them but they keep weaving just out of reach. I expect my arm to pass straight through them. I suddenly manage to grab one and pull it in close.

"Am I dead?" I ask the angel. "Please just do one thing for me. Tell my wife, Tanya, I'm sorry and that I should have listened to her."

"You can tell her yourself, mate," the angel replies, before injecting something into my arm. I pass out again.

The next time I came round, I could see in color. I could also see I was in hospital. It must be Bastion as that was our only hospital in Helmand. The angel I'd been talking to was a medic who had injected me with something to counteract whatever they gave me on the Chinook, which had made everything look white.

I looked over to my left and there was an empty bed with Cliff's name on it. The bed had been made up and a feeling of panic and nausea washed over me.

"No . . . no . . . no . . . He can't be dead," I started saying to myself. "Please, not Cliff."

An hour later, they wheeled him in from surgery, where he'd been rushed as soon as they'd brought us in. When I saw him, my heart sank: he looked in a shit state. "I'm so sorry," I said to him, shaking my head. I didn't think he could hear me. He looked so out of it. He'd had dreams of becoming a medic, of advancing his career. Now he looked like he might not make it through the night.

Within hours of being in hospital, my arms and hands really started to hurt. The doctors passed through the ward every few hours, so I told them—but they said it was just side effects from the morphine. Four hours later, I was in agony, so I talked to the doctor again.

"Look, my arms and hands really hurt; I'm sure something is wrong."

"There's nothing wrong; it's just the side effects."

I kept badgering him and eventually he relented, I think just to shut me up.

"Look, we'll bring up a mobile X-ray and *show* you that nothing is wrong," he told me.

They wheeled over the X-ray machine and turned it on. The medical team surveyed its picture wordlessly. Then: "How did we miss *that*?" the doctor said to one of the nurses. It turned out that my arms were broken after all.

They strapped up my arms to immobilize them (they couldn't put on casts, in case my arms swelled up when I was on a flight back to the UK). My leg looked bad as well—all black with bruising from where it had hit the GPMG. I was nowhere near as bad as Cliff though. I watched him as if it was a dream. Every few hours they changed his sheets due to blood loss and general oozing from his wounds. It turned out he had broken every bone in both of his legs.

All I could say was sorry.

Cliff and I got a steady stream of visitors, although he was knocked out and didn't know. I had a morphine pump, which was handy if someone arrived I couldn't be arsed to talk to. A few presses on the morphine button and I was out for the count.

Harry, the sergeant major, came in to see me a few days after the mine had blown us up, by which point I hadn't pissed for a couple of days, as morphine tends to slow things down. Now, my bladder was bursting.

"I need a piss. Can you help me?" I asked Harry.

"Sure thing," he replied, and grabbed a papier-mâché beaker.

He helped me get set up and then stood back. You're supposed to take your knob out as the water level increases but Harry just left mine in and stood there laughing. There was nothing I could do; he was just trying to cheer me up. I tried to stand up and blood poured out of my shin where they had drilled into it. I loved it when Harry came to visit.

He told me that the colonel had brought the rest of the troop back to the main base as we had been hit pretty hard. The troop was just too small to operate effectively now. It turned out that we had hit a seventy-pound anti-tank mine.

The next day, there was a commotion down the other end of the ward. The Yorks had shot a Taliban fighter out in the field, who had been treated by our medics and then put on the same ward as us. Understandably, things kept kicking off. To make matters worse, Cliff and I were at the end of the ward closest to the toilets, so they had to bring him by us every time he needed the toilet. The next time he went by,

I managed to scoop up a Rubik's cube with my left hand and hurl it at him. It was a perfect hit—straight off his head. The doctors rushed over to help him and surprisingly didn't tell me off. I just wanted him to keep the noise down; some of us were trying to rest.

It did bother me—how well we treated them compared to how they would have treated us. I certainly didn't think he should be on the same ward as us.

It didn't take long—just four days—for them to fly us in a Hercules straight to Birmingham, where we were transported to Birmingham Hospital. I was drugged up to the eyeballs so I missed most of it; I woke up in a new ward with a nurse shaking me and calling my name.

I looked up to see Tanya walking toward me and I just started crying.

It was such a breath of fresh air to see her; she literally breathed life into me. Her legs buckled a bit as she approached and she gave me a cuddle and a kiss.

"Oh, Craig," she said, hugging me.

I couldn't speak.

I spent a week in rehab and physiotherapy while Tanya stayed in a hotel nearby. My dressings were the same ones from Afghanistan and were soon starting to smell. Tanya complained to the medics and very quickly I was in nice new blue casts. All very pretty—but now I couldn't do anything for myself. I was reliant on Tanya for everything, even wiping my arse. Tanya and I had different theories on how this was supposed to be done and I was not convinced my ring cleanliness was as good as it should have been.

The next person I really wanted to see was my mum, but she didn't come. My parents-in-law, Paul and Sue, were fantastic and went to a lot of effort to visit and to be there for me.

Within three weeks of being injured, I was back at home. I spent the next six weeks transitioning from wheelchair, to crutches, to walking, working through my leg injury. I also started to become aware of other issues—what I now know was post-traumatic stress disorder (PTSD).

I found myself going into rages with Tanya and losing it over the smallest things. I hated the stupid casts and smashed them into the walls.

Body armor can stop shrapnel, but nothing can stop a blast wave. In fact, I'd been in two IED blasts, the second of which got me. I'd also been shot in the helmet and concussed by an AK47 short round on the right side of my head, the same side that took the impact of the IED blast. The pain I'd had since I was concussed had increased to a constant pounding on the right-hand side of my skull. I couldn't sleep because my brain hurt so much I couldn't even put my head on the pillow. I constantly felt like my face had prolapsed on the right side, there was pressure behind my right eye that built up from the top of my spine to behind my head, and there was a black dot behind my eyes. At this point, my brain injury hadn't been diagnosed, and when I tried to talk to the civilian doctor about my symptoms I felt as if he wasn't really listening and didn't want to make a decision that would step on the Army's toes. Our regimental doctor, who had more experience with these injuries, was in Afghanistan. I started taking a lot of painkillers, over-the-counter ones as well as the ones the hospital gave me.

When the doctor at Birmingham finally took the casts off my arms, I was shocked at the pale, flaky, noodle limbs I was now looking at. I went to the cafeteria to get some food and as I leaned over the hotplate, a load of skin flaked off into the dish. There was a collective sucking-in of breath as the chef looked down at a Bolognese sauce seasoned with a nice hint of Harrison.

"Sorry," I said to everyone. We had to wait for an hour while they threw the Bolognese away and made some more.

A week later, I went to see the physio in camp. I was high as a kite on painkillers.

"Can you do ten push-ups?"

"Sure thing."

I got in the position and banged out sixty. I couldn't feel anything and the whole experience was quite trippy.

After that, I was called up to the admin offices to see the duty clerk.

"You're flying out on Wednesday," he told me.

This was a Friday. "Fuck me," I thought, "they didn't waste any time." I was standing there feeling like half the man I used to be and didn't feel physically or mentally ready to go back, so I tried explaining all of the symptoms I'd told the civilian doctor about.

"Even normal physical activity like walking, driving, shaving is hard," I added. "My short term memory is bad, so how do you expect me to write down orders?"

"The physio cleared you and you did ten push-ups, didn't you?"

"Yes, sir. I'm not a silly man. I know that I don't just have PTSD. This is a brain injury," I said.

"Are you a doctor?"

"No," I said biting my lip.

"And you think you've got PTSD," he said not even looking at me.

"Yes, sir. I have nightmares and I shake like a pissing

dog." I lifted my hand up to show him. "Plus I feel like a time bomb."

"Good," he said, "go and take it out on the Taliban. And that shaking is because you just had your casts off. That will pass."

I felt like saying, "Are you a fucking doctor, prick?" He didn't mention the nightmares, but I didn't want to bring it up again as it looked like he was getting pissed off with me moaning.

"You'll be fine, Harrison. Have this time off to clear your head. You'll feel better on Wednesday."

"Will I?" I said, walking out rubbing my aching wrists and closing my right eye as the pain rose up behind my eyeball. I was shitting myself, not because I was going back out or because I didn't feel right, but because I didn't know how I was going to tell Tanya. She deserved better than the wreck I'd become and I had this constant fear she'd realize it and leave me. I got the duty driver to take me home to face the music.

14. On Panda's Ridge

Tanya didn't say goodbye to me. "Sorry, baby, I need this," was all I could manage as I left to get in the taxi back to camp.

From there I was driven to Brize Norton in a minibus, traveling with some other lads returning to Afghanistan. For most of the journey I was silent, feeling really bad that I was putting Tanya through all of this again. She didn't know that I didn't feel ready to go back. I loved the army and didn't want her to end up hating it so I told her that I wanted to finish the tour with the lads.

The RAF's fleet of aircraft was in a shit state, so inevitably we got delayed heading back. The two days spent kicking my heels at Brize Norton actually did me some good, though. It gave me time to get my head round things and work out what I needed to do to see me through the remaining six weeks of the tour. My arms felt better but I still had constant headaches. My plan was just to tough it out with a combination of willpower and medication.

Finally the RAF found a working plane and I was on my way. As we came in to land at Kandahar, we were all told to put on our helmets and body armor. This is standard procedure when landing in a "hostile" zone—although a fat lot of good they would do if we got shot down. It didn't feel right wearing someone else's helmet and body armor; mine had been left at Bastion.

Of course, getting to Kandahar was only one leg of the journey. I had to wait around for another plane down to Bastion, and then a helicopter to take me back to the front line.

Things didn't feel quite right. I was slightly skittish, over-reacting to bangs. Even a door slamming would make me flinch or cringe. I also found myself getting agitated in the queues in the mess hall, not liking people standing behind me or close to me. I just wanted to be on my own and spent most of the time fighting the urge to go into one of the toilet cubicles and cry. A couple of times, when I'd been sitting on my own, staring off into space, I'd looked down and realized that I was holding my Browning pistol. I couldn't even remember how it had got into my hand. I couldn't understand what was happening to me and it scared me.

At Bastion, I was issued with my weapon, ammunition, morphine, first-aid dressing and sniper rifle. I told them that the body armor I'd been given was too small so Paul, the storeman, took me round to the shipping container that was used for storage. As he pulled out some boxes, I could smell stale blood.

Paul was rummaging around among bits of old kit. He held up Cliff's bloody boot.

"Is this yours?" he asked.

I just stared at the boot. Paul asked again but I couldn't answer, choked with guilt and sorrow.

Then I realized that the storeroom was full of boxes marked with names I recognized: Jones, Wardy, my troop leader's—who'd been injured while I was away and flown back to the UK—and many others.

"Is this where all the kit from the injured soldiers goes?" I asked.

"Yes," said Paul, still rummaging around in boxes.

"Here we go," he exclaimed. "Is this yours?"

He lifted out my old body armor, dried blood all around its neck. I just took it and walked off, somehow ending up back in my tent, sitting on my bed, mindlessly tracing my fingers over the bloodstains on the armor. I started to cry.

A corporal major I used to work for walked into the tent so I quickly stood up and faced the other way, pretending to sort out my kit. My hand reached for the pot of painkillers that I'd brought with me. I was taking about eight to ten tablets a day as my head hurt so much. That was double the recommended dosage but it was the only way I could keep the pain under control.

I was a mess and I knew it. I even found it hard to lift and hold things, and struggled with tasks involving coordination.

I finally got the message that a helicopter would be taking me north in two hours so I had a shower to freshen up, popped some more painkillers and headed down to the HLS.

Two hours later, I was flying over the stunning Afghan scenery, heading to Mount Carla, where my troop was currently stationed. As we came into land, for some strange reason I hoped things had changed. Of course they hadn't. Same smell—weapon oil, rations, body odor and smoke— same layout, same people.

I felt terrible. I really, really didn't want to be there. I also really didn't want to see anyone. After dumping my kit in the tent I tried to find out what was happening on the base at that moment. It turned out that my lads had been moved to another FOB. Apparently the colonel had said that he wanted to use them for protection.

That night I went over to the fucked wagons, which were all dumped round the back of the base. I found the one that I was blown up in and peeled back the cover. It was a real mess. Cliff's blood was still all down the front of the hood. I rested my head on the bloodstains, whispering, "I'm so sorry." I started to cry.

There was a gentle tap on my shoulder. It was Billy, a mate of mine, who worked in the stores. "Are you okay?"

"Yes, mate," I replied, roughly wiping the tears from my eyes with my hands.

"If you ever need to talk, I'm here."

"You never saw this, okay?" I told him, before heading back to my tent. I appreciated his kindness, but I didn't want to talk about it.

That same night, I got word that I'd be leaving in the morning to join the rest of my troop. C Squadron were going to take me up there in a Mastiff patrol. I took out my .338 rifle and decided to do some training drills without ammunition. It felt good to pick her up again, the familiar drills bringing focus and calm, plus a degree of normality, as I lay behind her and built up my position. I opened and closed the bolt and aimed at an imaginary target through the scope. I squeezed the trigger up until the breaking point and then added the 4lb of pull. The hammer fell on an empty chamber. I closed my eyes and then opened them again. My point of aim hadn't shifted.

I did this for forty-five minutes then loaded all of my magazines with ammunition and gave the rifle a good clean. I didn't know if the scope had been knocked when I was blown up, so I still needed to do a test fire before I would be happy to go out on patrol with it.

Since being back in Afghanistan, I was having nightmares where I kept reliving the blast. After another crappy night's sleep, I was chewing the fat with a small group of men clustered around the vehicles, all waiting for our lift, when I got a message that the colonel wanted to see me. I headed over to his office and knocked on his door.

"Come in. Have a seat," he said, gesturing to the empty chair in front of him. I sat down.

"How is everything? Everything okay?"

"Yes, I'm fine."

"Really? Because you don't look okay."

"Shit," I thought to myself, "my mask must be slipping."

"Honestly, I'm fine," I said. "I just want to get back out there, be with my lads and do my job."

"Okay then. If you say so."

We made idle chit-chat for a few more minutes before the conversation dried up and he dismissed me. As I walked out of his office, I saw Billy and strode over to him, wanting to be sure he'd kept his mouth shut about seeing me break down.

"I haven't told anyone," he said hurriedly, when I confronted him.

"Okay. Thanks, mate."

I headed back to the Mastiff vehicles, which were waiting for me.

It took about sixty minutes to get to the FOB on a good run—and about four hours on a bad one. Fortunately, we had a clear run and just over an hour later I was back with my gang. There were some new faces as "battlefield casualty replacements" had been sent out to fill in where we had lost people. The lads looked generally pissed off, but pleased to see me.

As I walked in, Jim was just leaving, going back home for his much-needed R&R. We said hello to each other.

"Sorry for the state of things," he said, before heading off to a waiting helicopter. That was all the chat we had time for.

I didn't really know what he meant—until I saw the shit state all the vehicles and kit were in. There were vehicle parts everywhere, plus the lads' discipline and fitness were starting to slip. It was lucky I was back, just in time for me to sort things out.

The commander of the FOB was Major Carly, whom I'd known for years, ever since he was a sergeant. He was an "old sweat," a gravelly voiced old-school officer who had been through the ranks before commissioning. I organized a meeting with him as soon as possible and quickly found out why the lads were so pissed off. After all the losses we'd taken, it looked like the colonel had decided to wrap them in cotton wool. No patrols over 900 yards from the FOB. Since the FOB had five watchtowers, which provided cover out to 900 yards, the lads were under no threat while patrolling.

We'd push our vehicles out into this 900-yard security bubble to extend the cover over the resupply route. These were long hot days, sitting in the vehicle, providing overwatch down into a wadi that the supply convoy moved through once a week.

It wasn't all bad, though. We were on our own and pretty much left alone. I got to dry-fire my rifle and I could feel myself getting my eye back in and the muscle memory returning. One day, I grabbed an old gas can from the scrapheap and placed it 200 yards away from my firing point. I let everyone know what I was doing so they wouldn't think we were under attack, went through my routine and fired a round. I then fired five more shots in rapid succession. All six rounds were tightly grouped together, exactly where I was aiming. It felt good—good to be back in the game.

Once I finished shooting, Major Carly called for me and told me that I had been selected for a mission and had to take a Javelin (anti-tank rocket) operator with me. I picked J, a hard little Scotsman with the world on his shoulders. He was from another troop but I'd heard that he was good with the Javelin. The pair of us were taken into the ops room and given a set of orders. Well, almost a set of orders. We were told that we were going to a place called Panda's Ridge and that we would get a full briefing once we were up there.

We jumped on a departing convoy and were taken out to the transfer point, where we were handed from one unit to another. A British Army officer (I had no idea what unit he was from) gave us a quick brief that we were there to stop the Taliban using a resupply route with China, hence the name Panda's Ridge. I was taking over from a sniper who had been out there for a few days.

There was a huge ridgeline and large rocky outcrops in front of us. I was told that the outgoing sniper was over by a Mastiff vehicle I could see parked. I found him underneath the vehicle, asleep. I kicked his feet and he clambered out, rubbing his eyes.

"I need a ground brief, firing points and hot spots," I told him.

"There are loads of places to fire out there," he replied unhelpfully, grabbing his kit and fucking off.

I was told by the officer who had briefed me earlier that I could pretty much do what I wanted as long as I stayed to the right of the ridgeline. A composite protection force (so made up of a hodgepodge of different units) would stay on the ridgeline and dominate the area from there. J was given a separate brief and I didn't see him again. I was to push off the ridge itself and cover any blind spots, as well as keeping an eye on a village that was the focal point of the resupply route. I sorted out all of my kit and then waited for nightfall.

The landscape was bathed in an eerie green glow as I scanned through my night-vision goggles. There were gullies and rocky outcrops all over the place. Vegetation was sparse but there were plenty of rat runs—places the enemy could hide and move in. Over the previous two hours I had very cautiously patrolled forward on my own. I was about 550 yards to the right of Panda's Ridge and quite a bit forward of my support.

Once I was close to where I wanted to set myself up, I slowly lowered myself down onto the ground and started crawling forward on my belly. My sniper rifle was in my padded drag bag, attached by a cord. I had my SA80 assault rifle in my hands—but at the moment my night-vision goggles were my main weapon. I reached a small outcrop that I wanted to use as my firing position, dragged the bag in and retrieved some small wind flags that I'd made. Cracking an infrared marker, a Cyalume light stick, I left it on the bag so I could find my kit again easily in the dark. As the enemy didn't have night-vision kit the infrared stick didn't risk giving away my position. Then I crawled out about a hundred yards to the right, and then the left, and placed the little flags. Next, I pulled out my ghillie suit and hat and put them on. I'd covered them in dust so they blended in well with the rocks.

I swapped over my sniper rifle and the SA80, draping some spare scrim over the rifle to break up its outline before pushing the case behind me. My map went next to the rifle so I could quickly scan it if I needed to. My pistol went under my arm, so that if anyone ambushed me I'd have quick access to it.

I dug myself a little trough between my legs to piss in and positioned my daysack within arm's reach. Inside were my radio, food and water. Reaching into the top pocket, I took out some painkillers and gulped them down. Everything was hurting.

Then I settled into position and started scanning. Morning broke and the heat started to build. Before long, the sweat started to pour off me. Of course with the heat came the flies. The really annoying kind—the ones that climb in your ears and your eyes. I couldn't swat them away as that would be an obvious movement so I just had to accept them.

Fortunately, the Taliban quickly took my mind off the heat and the discomfort. As I scanned the terrain, a Taliban fighter appeared on the outskirts of the village. I glanced at my range card and estimated he was 800 yards away. I dialed the clicks into the rifle scope and then checked that my wind flags weren't moving. Once I was in a position to fire, I got on my radio to higher HQ on the ridgeline.

"Hello, Zero. This is Maverick 41. Can you see a lone male gunman 800 yards to your front? Over." I would rather not give my position away by firing if they could take him out.

"Maverick 41, this is Zero. Negative, it's too steep an angle for us to see him. Over."

"Roger that. Out."

I started to build up my firing position, getting everything as stable as possible. My breathing came under control and I gently started to take up the slack in the trigger. I exhaled halfway and squeezed. The Taliban was hit in the chest and slammed back into a tree.

As a sniper, there's an inner freeze when you shoot someone. It's as if time has slowed down and all of your senses are heightened. There is also an excitement that all snipers know and love. I felt it again, then; like a drug coursing through my veins. I'm no psycho, nor a butcher. I don't crave the killing. I just love the exultation of a job well done.

I cycled the bolt again and kept the cross hairs on the slumped body, waiting for any sign of life. I saw him start to move. "This fucker must be hard as nails," I thought to myself. "He's been hit with a .338 round and he is still functioning."

I hit him again. He moved again. "Fuck me!"

Then I saw that someone was pulling his feet from behind the mound he was slumped over. I fired a round into the mound to discourage them but could only watch as the body disappeared. I marked the point on my range card and captured all of the firing data. The Taliban liked to use the same points over and over so it might get used again in the future.

I started to have a good look at the village. There was a large square building, which was probably a mosque as there were speakers on it. I marked it on my range card as a point of interest and calculated the range and firing data. Bar that, not much happened for the rest of the day. I had two pisses, which the flies loved, and a one-hour catnap over an eight-hour period.

I awarded myself another catnap at the end of the day but I was woken by a massive explosion off to my right and immediately started scanning the area. There was a lunatic local 650 yards to the right of me, screaming like he was high as a kite. He had a smoking RPG launcher on his shoulder and it looked like he had just fired an RPG down into the village.

Through the scope I could see where the rocket impacted—and a man in a white dishdash covered in blood. It looked like one of his arms was missing. His face was so clear I could see he was talking to himself while staggering along. Then he fell to his knees and pitched forward; his back was covered in blood. His eyes were open but he had stopped moving. He was dead.

I watched as people started to come out. One looked like his wife, as she was screaming and wailing as she knelt next to the body. I got on my radio and told those on the ridgeline what was going on and started describing what I could see.

The villagers were pointing up at the ridgeline and once I traced where they were looking I could see enemy crawling all over the place. "The shit is going to hit the fan," I thought to myself, getting behind my rifle.

It wasn't long before I was proved right. One of our Scimitars up on the ridgeline pulled forward and started engaging the Taliban with its 30mm cannon. I watched and identified the enemy firing points and then cross-referenced them on my range card. Once I was sorted, I started engaging as well. The beauty was that the enemy didn't even know I was there due to the noise and the confusion.

I lost count of how many Taliban I killed. It was just "shoot, hit, move on." I saw blood spray everywhere; up in the trees, down in the sand. Over a two-hour period, we killed a lot of people.

As darkness fell, I felt numb. Through my night-vision goggles, I could see the dead bodies being collected by the locals.

I drifted off again and I was woken by a burst of 30mm cannon fire. I grabbed my radio.

"What the fuck are you firing at?" I asked the guys up on the ridgeline.

"It's not us."

There was another burst of fire. It wasn't us; it was the enemy. They'd brought up a Soviet SG17 anti-aircraft gun and were hammering the ridgeline! It turned out that the Taliban knew there was a sniper on the ridge somewhere; they just didn't know where. They were determined to try to track him down—or, rather, blast him to kingdom come with the SG17.

I could just about see what was going on from my position. Most people had battened down the hatches in the armored vehicles, all apart from an interpreter, who was running around screaming. Suddenly, he went down; he had been hit . . . in the arse, it turned out, by shrapnel. Some of the lads broke cover to help him while I tried to scan for the firing point. I couldn't see where the cannon was firing from, so an Apache was called.

Once the Apache arrived, the pilot thought he could see the firing point, a shape that looked like a barrel, and let rip. The firing stopped so he must have been close.

The lads on the ridge secured an HLS to casevac the interpreter and bring in a replacement. Meanwhile, I got my head down and tried to catch some sleep.

Although it felt strange being without my spotter, I managed to sleep fairly well through the night. I knew the lads on the ridge were watching over me and the temperature was quite pleasant.

Come dawn, though, the heat quickly became unbearable. The flies were doing my head in. I started to get really bad shakes and my focus was all over the place. I lifted my right hand up, trying to make a fist. I flicked my vision from my hand to the ridgeline in order to get my focus going again. My body was a mass of pain I was trying to ignore. There was also a raw ammonia stench from my piss and I needed a dump, but I knew I would have to wait until nightfall.

I heard on the radio network that the lads on the ridge had received intelligence that the enemy had brought a DShK up. This is a Soviet .50 cal belt-fed heavy machine gun and it can do some serious damage, so I was determined to find it. A building grabbed my attention so I continued to watch it. It had speakers on it, so it might have been another mosque. I switched radio networks and spoke to higher headquarters, in case they had some more info on the building, but they didn't. Then locals started to walk in and out of it, carrying rifles.

"Positive identification of enemy; do I have permission to engage?" I asked higher HQ.

"Negative. Wait and observe," I was told.

"Fuck this," I thought to myself and started to build up my position. Higher came back up on the radio. "You are clear to engage."

"Happy days," I thought to myself and settled into my preshot routine. Then I saw a young fighter carrying something heavy. I couldn't quite work out what it was so I cranked up the magnification on my scope.

"Fucking hell."

He was carrying two RPG warheads and a green bag full of machine-gun link. I considered letting him go but realized I couldn't. If one of those RPGs killed one of our guys, it would be on my head. Plus, I had a job to do. I fired.

The round knocked the male off his feet and must have passed straight through him because I saw the splash on the compound wall before the body hit the ground. The machine-gun ammunition tumbled out of his bag.

Another young-looking fighting-age male appeared out of a doorway and ran toward the body, shouting. He glanced at the lifeless form and then back through the doorway he had just come from. He nodded, like he had just been told to do something, then bent down and picked up the warheads and ammunition. He took two steps before my next round hit him straight in the chest, spraying blood up the wall.

After that, they decided to leave the ammunition where it was.

All of this was a very personal experience. A sniper watches everything through a powerful scope. I saw facial expressions, feelings. I saw the moment that life passed from someone. It is godlike. I had the power to take another human's life. But I am only human myself. And I will carry that last instant of their life in my mind forever. I know it will never leave me.

The guys on the ridgeline came up on the radio and told me that the Taliban were going mad on their radio network, screaming about a sniper and that he wasn't on the ridgeline but somewhere in the hills. They wanted to get me. It's not a nice feeling, being hunted.

Finally night fell and I could move around a bit. First things first: the painkillers in the top of my daysack. I popped a couple of pills and then sat back, giving myself half an hour to relax and let them kick in. I stared at the sky, which was so clear, and thought of home. I thought about how much I missed Tanya and Dani, and how I couldn't wait to see them again.

"I love you," I whispered to them.

After a while, I realized that my hand had stopped shaking and the pain in my head had ceased. Then I took care of the second order of business and had a crap in some cellophane, wrapped it up and placed it in a Tupperware box, tucking that into my daysack. A sniper leaves no sign that he has been somewhere. I had a quick wash with an old rag and then I was sorted.

I grabbed my pistol and night-vision goggles and pulled back about five yards from my firing point, waiting for my prearranged resupply. Before long, I saw two of the lads scrambling toward me. I let them know where I was and they closed in.

"Fuck me, Craig, you stink," one of them said as he got close.

"Cheers, fellas. I love you too."

They left me some more water and ammunition and then pushed off. It's funny, but when you are on your own even the briefest of human contacts is pleasant.

When day broke, I was back in position. I was scanning my sector when someone kicked my foot. I grabbed my pistol.

"Corporal of Horse Harrison, what are you looking at?" a booming voice asked me.

Out of the corner of my eye I could see it was the colonel. There was also a camera crew on the crest of the ridgeline, waiting to come forward. I continued to scan to my front.

"If I were you, I'd get down," I told him.

He knelt down, right where I'd pissed. That made me smile.

"I've come to get some pictures of the ridgeline," he said.

God knows who had briefed the colonel but he clearly wasn't aware of the situation. That was about to change! The incoming started almost immediately, an anti-aircraft cannon with rounds the size of an AA battery, blasting in our direction. I grabbed my kit and started crawling backward while the CO ran off down the hill. The camera crew weren't so lucky; they were hit in the opening burst.

The rounds started to head my way, impacting about two yards from me, throwing earth and rocks into the air while I just put my head down. I desperately wanted to run off, but I realized that it was the CO who had given the position away and they might not actually be able to see me.

The firing stopped and I tried to calm myself down and gather my thoughts. That was way too close for comfort. I needed to move but I also knew I would have to wait until nightfall to set up a new position.

On the ridgeline, the camera crew were receiving first aid. Poor fuckers. I did a complete 360-degree check to make sure no one was sneaking up on me. I could see a lone figure off in the distance, near a derelict compound. This fucker was the one coordinating the anti-aircraft cannon.

"I need smoke in three separate points to my front," I told the ridgeline over my radio. They fired a number of smoke grenades and mortar rounds, and I started running for the ridgeline. Once at the top, I looked back and I saw that the dicker was still there. I ran over to the nearest Scimitar.

"Traverse right. Derelict compound a thousand yards away. Lone dicker," I shouted at the gunner, fighting to get my breath back.

He traversed the turret, picked up the target and fired a three-round burst from the 30mm cannon. That took care of that dicker.

In the end, all the commotion gave me the cover I needed to relocate to the other end of the hill, so I didn't have to wait till nightfall after all. I managed to get down to a new firing point without being noticed and settled in. I got out my range card and reoriented myself. I could still see a lot of the old hot spots so it was just a matter of working out the new range.

I was told on the radio that I had one more day on the hill as the Americans were coming to take over tomorrow.

But what a last day it was. It was like the gates of hell had opened.

I watched with a grin as my old firing point was smashed to bits by enemy fire. They were hitting the ridgeline with everything they had and were obviously now convinced they knew where I was. Scanning to my front, I picked up two fighters in the dead ground, 700 yards to my front. They were following a small berm, constantly looking up to see if they could be seen by the ridgeline. They couldn't. On their heads were the little round hats that were normally worn by the local youths.

"Please not again," I said to myself, taking my eye away from the scope and shaking my head.

I cleared my mind and refocused on the job at hand. I could see that the insurgents had RPG warheads on their backs and were both holding AK47s. I suddenly realized that I needed to act fast. They were walking forward toward some scrub that was only about fifty yards away. Once they reached it, I wouldn't be able to see them anymore.

I built up my firing position and got my left hand under my rifle stock. I slowed my breathing and glanced down at my range card just to check the distance. I didn't have time to make adjustments to the scope so I was mentally calculating where to hold off. My plan was to shoot the lead guy and then swing onto the other, hoping that he froze when the first one was hit.

I took up the trigger slack and squeezed. Felt the 4lb of pull . . . *Bang*. The first lad was hit in the leg and dropped. The other started running around like a headless chicken.

I reloaded, fired and missed.

I reloaded again, gave it a two-mil-dot lead in the scope and fired. This time I hit. It looked like the fighter had suddenly slipped on ice as he flew off to his left with the force of the impact. The first lad was screaming, crawling up the bank, trying to get into position to shoot. His screams went right through me. I fired again and shot him straight through the throat.

Blessed silence, just for a short spell—before it all started again.

The enemy started spraying the ridgeline with an AGS17, which is an old Soviet belt-fed grenade launcher. This time they were on target and I could see my mates scrambling for cover. I scanned to my front and saw Taliban heads bobbing up and down.

"I don't fucking believe it." Two fighters had crawled past the dead lads and were trying to get to the ammunition that they'd dropped. "Don't you fuckers think about anything but war?"

There was a small gap in the berm that these guys were going to have to crawl past if they wanted to get to the ammunition. I would ambush them there. It was just a matter of placing the cross hairs in the middle of the gap and waiting for someone to crawl into view.

I had to wait twenty minutes before a hand appeared in my scope. All the while the ridgeline was being hit by incoming. Obviously the enemy thought they were keeping our heads down by hitting the ridgeline.

Back at the gap, there was no further movement and I was starting to think about shooting through the berm when a head bobbed up and down, then a second. A moment later I saw a third. I fired a round at the next head that bobbed up. I missed.

I cycled the bolt and when the head bobbed up again, I tried again. Miss.

"Fuck," I said to myself. I had been on target all day so I couldn't work out why I was now missing. I decided to do a miss fire drill and picked a piece of sandy area away from the targets, where I knew I would be able to see the splash of my shot. I fired a round and watched as it impacted to the right of where I was aiming.

"Dickhead." I hadn't been watching my little wind flags. The wind had picked up and it was pushing my rounds to the right. I made some corrections and then fired again. I was still not happy, so I made a further correction to the scope and then swung the rifle back onto the targets.

A head bobbed up. *Bang*, miss; reload; *bang*, hit. Finally! It was a neck shot and the guy's body crumpled onto the berm.

The body spent the entire day out in the sun—the body and the ammunition. I watched, sweltering in the heat, hoping that some fighters would try to retrieve the corpse or the weapons. That way, I could bag a few more of them. Unfortunately, they didn't.

Finally, the sun started to set and the temperature dropped. I was told that we were sending a patrol out from the ridge-line, down into the dead ground to our front, and that I should keep an eye on them and provide overwatch. I was in a good position to observe further than they could see and engage any threats. I had comms with the patrol and tracked them as they moved tentatively down the ridgeline. They quickly came under fire but it was just a lone burst, probably a "shoot and scoot." I didn't even have the chance to swing into a firing position.

I could hear a motorbike engine, though, so I started scanning and quickly picked up a guy in a brown dishdash sitting on a bike with the engine running. He had an AK47 slung across his back and was clearly waiting for someone. There was another burst of fire at the patrol and then a guy appeared from between two compounds, carrying an AK47. He jumped on the back of the motorbike and they sped off.

I told the patrol that it was a shoot and scoot and tried to vector them onto the motorbike. They couldn't see it—but I could, catching glimpses as they whizzed between compounds. The cover of the various buildings gave me only a very small time window in which to fire. As they came into the open briefly, I shot a round toward them, but missed.

"Fuck this." I decided to do "rapid bolt." This is where you place the rifle in your left shoulder and rapidly cycle the bolt with the right hand, pulling the trigger with your left.

I found the next gap between compounds, where I thought they would appear, and started counting.

"One banana, two banana, three banana—" The bike shot through the gap. "Right, so it is going to take three bananas."

I pointed my rifle at the next gap, placed the cross hairs in the middle at about waist height, and started counting. Once I got to three banana, I started firing rapid bolt, intending the bike to ride into a hail of bullets. The magazine held only ten rounds, so the timing still had to be accurate; on my sixth round I hit the bike. I cycled the bolt and quickly swapped the rifle back to my right shoulder, just in time to see the bike hit a wall and the two guys go sprawling.

I nailed the passenger and then turned to the rider. He unslung his AK47 and started crawling toward the wall. I took my time, watching him through the scope, and then hit him with a head shot.

And then I started to lose it. I was hit by a wave of emotion. In a split second, I realized that I'd lost the ability to switch off my humanity, to be no more than a weapon waiting to be fired. I started to shake and the faces of my lads rushed into my mind. I rolled over, looked at the twilight sky and started crying.

"I'm done . . . I'm done," I kept repeating to myself.

"Are you all right?" I was suddenly asked on the radio. The guys on the ridgeline could see me.

"Yes, just a bit of cramp," I replied, rolling back over and wiping my eyes. "Guys, keep an eye on me. I'm going to get some sleep."

I circled into the fetal position and started to drift off. I had racked up a fair number of kills in the last four days, so many I had lost count. I had a beard, I stank of piss and I had a daysack full of little bags of crap, but overall it had been a successful operation.

Once asleep, I started to dream. I saw all of the families of all of the people I had shot over the last couple of days. They were closing in on me, crying and wailing, until they had me surrounded. Their arms reached out for me . . .

I jolted awake and sat bolt upright, pistol in hand. It was only after I'd swept the pistol around me that I understood it was just a nightmare. I lay back down and stared at the sky. It was a cold night and I suddenly realized how hungry I was. But I couldn't do anything about that now. I catnapped through the night, drifting off and then waking up shivering.

Morning arrived and fortunately the temperature started to rise. I rummaged around in my daysack, but I was totally out of food. Glancing up at the ridgeline, I saw that the Americans had arrived. Time to go.

I sorted out my kit, making sure I hadn't left anything behind, and then crawled out of my firing position. Once I was clear, I stood up and tentatively started walking back up the hill. I hadn't really moved much in the last few days and my legs were stiff. Once at the top, I met the US officer and briefed him about the firing points I had been using.

"Where are your snipers?" I asked him. "Do you want me to brief them up as well?"

"They're not here yet," he replied.

"Fucking hell, the one place you want snipers is on this ridge."

He just shrugged and headed off to brief his men. I started to walk down the other side of the hill. Lord knows what I looked and smelt like, but the Americans all parted like the Red Sea for me. Fair enough.

I threw my kit into the back of the waiting vehicle and was driven back to the FOB. My small part in the battle for Panda's Ridge was over.

15. Behind the Mask

It was March 2010, and I was coming home at last. One minute I was on the front line fighting, and the next minute I was on the bus heading back to Windsor. It was all behind me and I should have been happy, but I didn't feel right. Everything seemed to happen in slow motion, as if the movie of my life was being played at the wrong speed. I felt slightly nervous and out of place.

The bus pulled onto the parade ground, where all of the wives and girlfriends would be waiting to meet us. Tanya didn't drive so she wasn't planning on coming. I was going to grab a cab and meet her at home.

As I stepped off the bus and watched all of the hugging and kissing going on, though, I couldn't help but feel a bit left out. I'd just turned to find my bags when I heard a little female voice behind me.

"Craig? . . . Craig?"

I looked round—and found myself staring into Tanya's beautiful eyes. I could feel a knot tightening in my stomach. She'd got a lift down with a friend. God, I loved her so much. I dropped my bags, ran over and she jumped into my arms.

I knew how hard this had been for her. She hadn't wanted me to go back to Afghanistan for a second time. She'd seen me come back injured and then return again; her fears for me were that much worse, having seen me smashed up by the mine. She'd spent months wondering if she would get that dreaded knock on the front door, an officer and a chaplain standing there ready to deliver terrible news. She is stronger than anyone realizes and I am blessed to have met such a wonderful woman.

We were not allowed to go straight on leave; we had to spend a week in camp as part of the "normalization" process. There was a lot of shit rolling around in my head but I made sure I hid it from Tanya and work. Years ago when we'd got back from operations, you just walked into a room and a woman asked you if you "felt all right." Now, SOP was that we had to spend a week in camp getting used to being back in society.

Well, we would have been getting used to being back in society—if it wasn't for the fucking drill. The "brains" had decided that a useful way to spend this week would be marching around in circles, practicing for the parade where we would all be presented with our Afghan medals. In fact, this just made the contrast even worse. One minute you were on the front line, the next you were on a parade square being shouted at.

We were all pissed off. We just wanted to get on leave, have a nice month with our families and spend the money we had saved. The medal parade was eight weeks away, so it wasn't even like we didn't have time to prepare for it.

Tanya had already told me that my mum couldn't make it. Despite the advance warning, this came as no surprise. Unless there were dogs in the medal parade, she was never going to come. Paul and Sue were planning to attend, however; they never let me down.

Thursday 10 May was a lovely sunny day. The parade started behind one of the accommodation blocks and we marched onto the grass and halted in front of the officers' mess. In my heart, I didn't want to be there. There were just too many people around and all I wanted to do was be on my own. As ever, though, I "wore a mask" and got on with it. I didn't want Tanya to see how much I was struggling or that I had cried most nights since I'd got back. There was just a hurt and a pain in my head that I couldn't make go away.

The band struck up and, as the drum banged, I had a flashback to the vehicle being blown up and my lads being hurt. It caused me to freeze and I put everyone out of step.

"Sorry," I shouted and got my shit together. We all got back in step.

As soon as we approached the officers' mess I searched for Tanya. Once I saw her I immediately felt calm. Then I caught sight of my injured lads in the crowd—the troop leader, Wardy and Cliff were there. I immediately felt guilty. Then I spotted that their families were standing with them. That made me feel even worse. I just hoped that my mask could stay on.

The local MP, who was an ex-Cavalry officer, handed out our medals. Afterward, we marched down to the memorial and sang a hymn and said a prayer for those who weren't coming back. After that, we were dismissed from the parade.

The plan was to go to the NCOs' mess for a drink and some food. I started searching for my family, but hadn't yet found them when the adjutant—the CO's military secretary— walked up to me with two men in tow.

"Corporal of Horse Harrison. These men are from the press. As your troop had the most contacts and injuries out in Afghanistan, they want to do a story on you and your lads," he said.

"Will these stories get censored?" I asked.

"Yes," he replied. "They all have to get cleared through the MOD."

Another officer standing with him backed this up, so I went to find the lads. Once they were all assembled, I explained the situation to them and finished off by saying, "You can tell them anything you like as everything will be run through the MOD. No personal details or anything like that will be mentioned."

I then handed them over to the reporters. Cliff went first and told one of the journalists about the very long shot I had made, balanced on the old wall. The reporter turned to me.

"You know that you broke the world record with that shot?"

I gave Cliff a slightly bemused look. "Oh . . . er, okay," I replied, taking it with a grain of salt. I hadn't heard that one before. (It turned out that the MOD had told the reporter I'd broken the record, but they hadn't bothered to tell me.)

Out of the corner of my eye, I could see that all of our families were getting restless. I turned to the adjutant. "Why don't we all go to the mess and the journalists can walk around and talk to people?"

He thought that was a good idea, which enabled me to shake him off. I wanted to talk to the families of the injured lads. What should I say? "Sorry?" "How are things going?" I just didn't know, but I still wanted to talk to them.

In the end I had a really nice chat with the families and it went better than I'd expected. After an hour, the same journalist came back to me and asked if he could take some pictures. I looked over to the adjutant and he confirmed that this was all right. We went behind the officers' mess and they started taking my photo. I felt like I was posing for some sort of gay magazine.

"That's it, Craig. Work for the camera," the photographer was saying.

I had to bite my lip.

"How about you lie down on the grass?"

"How about you fuck off?" I thought to myself, lying down. After I stood up again, I glared at the photographer.

"Sorry, Craig. I was getting a bit carried away."

"No shit," I replied. "I thought you were going to ask me to take my clothes off."

After the porn pics, I headed back to the mess. My head felt really bad; I had a crushing headache. I found Tanya and took her arm.

"That's it; I just want to go now," I said.

"But you haven't said goodbye to people," she replied. Then she looked at me, properly, and she could tell that things weren't right. "Come on. Let's go."

On Saturday morning, the phone rang.

"Hi, Craig. It's the reporter from the other day."

"How the fuck did you get my number?" I asked.

"The guardroom gave it to me."

Good old Cavalry; they never fail to fuck up.

"Look, I just wanted to let you know that your story is going to be in the papers tomorrow."

"Right. Thanks for the heads-up."

The next day, I bought the papers and started flicking through. My story was in about four of them. I felt sick. I wanted the stories to be about my lads; instead they were all about me. I couldn't give a fuck if I broke the world record; I just wanted my lads to get the recognition that they deserved.

"Should they have used your real name? How come your face isn't blurred out in the photos?" Tanya asked, worry clear in her voice.

"That should have happened when the MOD censored it," I replied.

It clearly hadn't. Like Tanya, I started to get a bad feeling about the articles. But when I chatted to friends and family on the phone, they all said the same thing. "Don't worry about it and enjoy the moment."

On Monday, the story appeared in the *Sun*. Mid-morning, I got a phone call from the welfare officer at the regiment. He explained that there had been a mistake and that we had "really kicked the hornets' nest." Mine and my family's details should never have been released. Some people from the MOD needed to come round and see me. An hour later, a guy from Military Intelligence with a briefcase handcuffed to his wrist—and four police officers in tow—arrived at my front door.

The MI guy pulled a single piece of paper from the brief-case. I filled the form in and handed it back to him. He never explained what it was and I never saw it again. Fucking Army, always covering its own arse for its cock-ups. He went on to explain that our details never should have been released to the public. The MOD hadn't had the opportunity to censor the pieces at all and, because of this, there was now a potential threat to our lives from extremists. Fucking brilliant.

Once the clown from MI left, the police explained that they were going to step up patrols in the area. They did, as did the MOD police. Over the next few days, our suburban close was crawling with police. Of course, this actually drew even more attention to us. Tanya and I were keeping our mouths shut, but other people were starting to talk.

Then Military Intelligence came back to us and said it might be best if we left the country for a bit. We were in complete agreement. Dani's school was brilliant and gave her some homework to take with her, and we headed away for three weeks. The break did us all some good and helped us forget about what was going on at home. Snipers are never usually identified in the press as they are seen as "killers"—as if we are any different from anyone else in a combat role.

When we got home, Tanya went back to work. She came home crying at the end of her first day. She had lost her job. Her employers didn't want any form of negative publicity and had decided it was best to let her go.

Paul kept reading the papers cover to cover and updated me on what was being written. He rang to tell me about an article that he had just read, with the heading "Plot to Behead a Hero." It turned out that one of the Taliban I'd killed in Afghanistan was a leader—and now they wanted revenge. They had put all my details on the internet. Al Qaeda had been planning on kidnapping a serviceman and then beheading him. Now that my details were out there, I had made it onto their "shit list."

Then a car was found up North with a photo of me in it. The boot was lined with plastic and it looked all set up for a kidnap. From that point onward, our lives really started to unravel.

Once I was told about the kidnap car, I was straight on the phone to the military welfare office, asking them to move us. We were given a small flat in camp that was a right dump. Workmen continually wanted access. There were ants' nests and cockroaches in the apartment, which was also overlooked by the HQ and a couple of accommodation blocks, so there was no privacy. We were living out of suitcases.

Dani was doing her GCSEs and having a terrible time. A welfare driver took her to and from school and while she was taking the exams she had to have a police escort. The other kids started picking on her, too, telling her that her dad was a killer and showing her things they had found on the internet.

Then the police told us that we couldn't return to our old

house. Tanya and Dani spent the whole time crying. I tried to stay strong, as I thought they needed me to, but in the end the day came when I broke. It was hard enough trying to process everything that had happened in Afghanistan—but now this? I buried my head in my hands and started sobbing. Tanya had never seen me cry before, but on that day my mask properly slipped off. Initially, she didn't know what to do, but quickly ran in and gave me a hug. I realized that I needed to go to the medical center and try to get some help.

On the way to the doctor's, I bumped into the quartermaster who was responsible for the welfare flat that we were staying in.

"Harrison, have you got dogs in the flat?" he asked.

"Yeah, two little ones."

"Well, they are going to have to go. No pets allowed in the flat."

Anyone who knew us well understood that our two little dogs—Betsy and Winny—were our world. There was no way we would be separated from them.

I turned around and walked off. My rage was building. I didn't go to the med center. I went back to the flat and got a lump hammer. Then I went to wait for the quartermaster. Once he'd left work, I followed him home. I had a look at his house and started working out how I was going to gain access and kill him. My plan was pretty simple: get in and smash his head in until the selfish fucker was dead. I just didn't care anymore.

It was only the thought of Tanya and Dani, and all they had been through already, that stopped me. That fucker has no idea how close to death he came on that day. In the end, I realized what I was doing and forlornly walked home. We asked Tanya's mum to pick up the dogs and look after them.

The next day, I got myself to the med center and I ended

up breaking down again. Rage, anger, guilt: it all flowed out. They referred me to the psychiatrists in Aldershot, who quickly came to the conclusion that I was suffering from severe PTSD, as well as brain trauma from being blown up. I came home with a big bag of pills.

A meeting was organized with the welfare office and the commanding officer, during which I told them that all this was not fair on my family—they were not in the Army.

"Don't worry about it," replied the CO in his posh, clipped tones. "It will all blow over. Today's news is tomorrow's chip paper."

Years later, it still hasn't blown over and we still get death threats.

Tanya also spoke to the welfare office and told them that she wanted to move. They treated her like she was an idiot, so the next day I politely rang up and complained. They said that they would look into it. The following day, while I was out, a minibus pulled up outside the flats. Two men in suits got out and rang our doorbell.

"Can we speak to Tanya Harrison?"

"That's me. What is it?"

The panic was building in her mind, as this was the same format of house call that the Army uses to inform the next of kin that someone is dead.

"Can we speak to you in private?"

Tanya was really panicking now, having seen the state that I was in. She started to assume the worst.

"What is it?"

"Can we speak to you inside?"

Once inside, they continued. "No. You can't move."

"What?" Tanya asked, confused.

"I'm the welfare officer. You asked if you could move—and the answer's no."

Tanya went mad, but they just turned around and left.

The following week, I was summoned to the CO's office. Once through the initial chat, he slid an envelope across the desk.

"What's this?" I asked.

"It's money back for the holiday you had to take and some extra for any inconvenience." There was an awkward pause. "It's not hush money," he continued.

"Right, sir."

He told me it wasn't hush money another three times before I left his office. It was clearly hush money; they were scared I would go to the papers.

The same week I got a call from the media officer of the Army's London district, who wanted to find out where it all went wrong—but this turned into a waste of time as he was leaving the Army in three days' time anyway. I went to see them regardless and a geriatric lieutenant colonel explained that the journalist who ran the story realized that he could make a lot more money by selling the uncensored version, and so went ahead and did it. He asked me to get a letter together, explaining the impact that everything had had on me and my family. I rang Tanya for some help, but I could tell that it was stressing her out, so I called Paul, who is good with words. Between us, we wrote the following:

> I have been in the Army for twenty years and have done
> many tours. I am well aware of dangerous situations,
> but the most recent events have caused me and my
> family, especially my wife and daughter, the most
> horrendous grief and severest problems imaginable.
> We have coped with not going out anywhere in case a
> situation occurs. My wife cannot sleep at night and has
> lost her job due to what was in the paper, and we had to

*take our daughter out of school at a crucial time in
her life.*

*Our financial situation has changed as there is now
only one income, which has created additional stress
and disruption to my family.*

*Life has been very emotional. To live in a community
with families in the Forces and not tell them anything is
extremely difficult; not being able to explain why the
police are in the area several times a day is hard.*

*My wife is beside herself every day and to have a
sixteen-year-old girl on the verge of depression as a
result is difficult, especially after I have just returned
from a tour. With the problems that occurred for me
out there—two near-death incidents—the tour should
have finished months ago. Instead, I feel I am still on
guard—for myself and my family. It is very draining.*

*To say that the situation is difficult for me and my
family is an understatement. I cannot put into words the
upset, emotion, pain and anguish that this has caused. It
has made me think about my, and my family's, future—
as every day we will be looking over our shoulders.*

Once I had finished the letter, I sent it on to the adjutant,
who was going to forward it to London district media operations.

Just take the time to read the letter again. Would you have
expected a response from someone? The adjutant? Media
ops? I would have. I did. But I got no response from anyone.

We stayed in the flat for three weeks, living out of suitcases, washing our clothes in the bath as there was no
washing machine. Then the Army found us a house and we
decided to live away from military quarters, so that hopefully
no one would know us. We were not allowed to return to our

old home, so the movers did all of the packing and we were reunited with our possessions at the new house.

Before we moved in, the police installed a panic room upstairs, put alarms on the doors and panic alarms in each room. Armed response was ten minutes away if we set off an alarm. They also put blast film on all of the windows.

We also asked for a fence to be put up, so that people couldn't see in. I thought the regiment would help with some of this, as did the police. They wrote to the CO four times and never got a response. Good old Cavalry. There was no help from military welfare or the regiment.

A week later, the phone rang and it was the welfare officer. I was in shock; I thought he was ringing to see how I was. He wasn't.

"You need to clean your old quarter so that it can be handed over," he explained.

I was utterly baffled. "But we've been told that we can't return there."

"Well, you'll have to pay £400 for the cleaning firm to do it in that case."

I just put the phone down, and then drove round to the house to clean it myself. As I got close, I could see three journalists waiting outside, so I just kept going. At two o'clock in the morning, when no one would see me, I went back and cleaned. Fortunately, Tanya keeps a clean house so it didn't take long. I handed the quarter back over the phone.

I was sent on medical leave—basically, don't return until you are better—but at least the new house was okay. Tanya kept the blinds shut and we rarely went out. After a few months, we decided to brave it, and headed out to the local town to go shopping. Unfortunately, I was recognized. A youth ran into a shop and reappeared with eggs, which he threw at us, yelling that I was a murderer. We made it back to the car and Tanya broke down crying. Dani started getting funny calls on her mobile, so we had to buy her a new one.

I booked Tanya in to see the doctor, hoping he would give her some happy pills and something to help her sleep. I was on a lot of pills myself: happy pills, panic pills and sleeping tablets. They helped a little bit. I just wanted to find my mask again. For my own and my family's sake.

Anger, guilt, rage, depression. These are just words on a page; the descriptions are in the dictionaries. Let me tell you, though, that the words do not do the feelings justice. I know, because I have experienced all of them.

It was autumn 2010 and the whole regiment was on parade outside the Naafi—the camp shop. The operational honors and awards list was out, and the colonel was going to read it out. I had been told that I would be getting a Military Cross and had been asked what ceremony I would like. I'd gone for the private option at Buckingham Palace. It would be a closed ceremony with no media access—I really didn't need any more attention from them.

The colonel started reading down the list, calling out people's names and the award they had received.

"Corporal of Horse Harrison . . . Mention in Dispatches."

You could have heard a pin drop. I could hear some of the lads muttering as they felt I should have got more. I just stared to my front.

After the parade, the colonel came to find me.

"You would have got the Military Cross, but I turned it down for you," he told me. "I just didn't think your family could cope with the pressure."

I was too dumbfounded to say anything. However well-meaning he'd been, surely that should have been my choice.

I noticed that he hadn't turned down the OBE he had been awarded. In fact, all of the "decent" awards had gone to the officers, proving yet again that the Cavalry is an officers' regiment.

My life continued to go downhill from there—so far and so fast that I hit points where I thought about ending it all.

We lived in an area where no one knew who we were. When we were in the house, with its alarms and panic room, we had to keep all of the blinds shut. I had a GPS tracker built into my phone and Tanya carried a little black rubber box called a "buddy." If you squeezed it, it sent a GPS location to the police, to let them know where you were.

I was walking with Tanya one day when a car drove by and people shouted out of the window at us. It was just innocent, but the scare caused Tanya to pass out. I ended up carrying her into a nearby graveyard where no one could see us, holding her until she came back round. She just sat there sobbing; she couldn't speak.

I didn't have anyone to talk to. When the regiment had told me, "Don't worry about it; it will be tomorrow's chip paper," it had almost broken me. I was still seeing the Army's psychiatrists and medical officers, but I never got the sense that anyone cared.

I might not have seen eye to eye with the law in the past, but the police were great. The head of Surrey Police continued to write to the regiment for assistance, such as asking for a new fence for us, and continued to be ignored.

There was a fifty-foot tree in our new garden. Each day, I looked at it and thought about putting a rope on it and hanging myself. I wondered when that point would be reached, when the day would come when I'd know it really was all too much for me.

Fortunately, in the end the landlord cut the tree down,

as it was dead. It didn't stop me planning, though. I spent a lot of time looking for other trees that I could use instead. I started carrying a rope around with me in a small daysack, in case I found the perfect tree. I even modified the rope, adding a cable that would go over my head, so that people couldn't cut me down, and a small rubber ball that would sit under my Adam's apple and push back into my throat. I really thought things through.

I had fucked up so many lives and killed so many people that I didn't deserve to walk on this earth. Sniping isn't a job; it's a curse.

I know that people say that suicide is the coward's option, and that you only hurt the ones that you leave behind. I understand that—but people couldn't see what was swirling around in my mind. I could see every kill that I had made; I could feel every life that had been impacted by what I had done.

Every day was a hell on earth. I couldn't bear to see myself in the mirror and I hated my skin. I stopped shaving, as every time I put the razor to my face I wanted to keep pushing until I'd stripped off my skin.

I started praying to my granddad—but I guess once you're dead, you're dead, as he didn't help me. Neither did God.

I drove out to a country lane and parked in a lay-by. I put a hose on the exhaust pipe and fed it in through the window. Back in the car, I sat with my fingers on the ignition key and stared out of the window. I just wanted to turn the pain off. I wanted the pressure to go from within my head. I wanted to stop fucking up my family's life.

I turned the key. At the first click, only the lights on the dashboard came on. I turned the key again . . . and the fucking car wouldn't start. I beat the steering wheel with my fists.

"Piece of fucking shit," I screamed.

I tried again, but the car still wouldn't start. I don't believe in God and I am not religious, but I do believe in fate. I sank back in my seat and cried for two hours.

As soon as I removed the hose, the car started. I headed home.

Each morning, I woke before Tanya. I would roll over and look at her beautiful face and whisper to her how sorry I was.

A single voice started to grow in my head. It just said two words: "You're vile." Every time I smiled or laughed, the voice got louder. I really did start to think I was going mad.

"How are the voices?" the doctor would ask me.

"It's not voices, it's a fucking voice."

I started to believe the voice and it started to become more real—like someone was standing behind me. I actually started looking over my shoulder.

I had no idea why Tanya stayed with me. She spent the whole time walking on eggshells around me as I was liable to explode. I was hell to live with; I hated tapping, clicking, people eating, rustling. I was like a coiled spring and any of these noises sent me over the edge.

When I'd first met Tanya, she was the life and soul of the party. When she walked into a room, it glowed. I fell in love with her the first time I saw her. But now she looked like a shadow of herself; the glow was fading, the sparkle gone from her eyes.

One day, I was called into the medical center.

"Corporal of Horse Harrison, we are downgrading your medical category," the doctor told me. Being downgraded meant that my medical leave was now indefinite. I wasn't considered fit for service, like some useless piece of kit being chucked on the scrapheap. "This means that you don't have to come into work anymore. Come in Friday, sign some papers and that's you. Just stay at home."

I was in shock. Just a complete and utter sense of rejection. The fuckers didn't even want me at work anymore. I'd served my regiment for twenty years. Regiment first; family second. What a fool I'd been. I'd given them everything, even my own sanity. I had hideous PTSD, a brain injury, and these people didn't even want me coming into their camp anymore.

Two years went by, and not a single person from my regiment's welfare chain got in touch with me. In fact, none of my lads who got injured were looked after. They all went through the Army's "trauma and risk-management process," but after a year it just stopped.

I rotted and festered at home. I had been taken off my regiment's roster and I now belonged to one of the regional recovery units. As far as I was concerned, that was where fucked soldiers went, so I wanted nothing to do with it. I felt so unwanted and such a failure, abandoned by the organization I had been with since I was sixteen.

I was on a lot of medication to keep me sane, but when I closed my eyes I could still see all the people I had shot. I stopped taking the medication, to see if I was "better," but I crashed—big time. Even when I was back on my meds, I could see no light at the end of the tunnel. The temptation to hang myself was there all the time.

Tanya said I had to start behaving as if I was out of the Army now, but I still had my ID card and I still got paid. I didn't want it to be over. I missed the lads, I missed the life, and I missed the Army. I didn't miss the Cavalry though.

People say that when you're in the Army, you're just a number. Now, I was just a number full of drugs.

I needed to take the drugs so I could sleep. I felt like I was trapped in a reverse nightmare now—because it was the day-time, and being awake, that was a living hell. Night-time and sleep were my only respite.

Thank you, Army. Thank you, Cavalry.

Be the best?

Fuck off.

Epilogue

Tanya is my blessing and my savior. She has stayed by me through everything. Her family are just great, far better than my own. They have been there for me ever since I was blown up.

But despite their love and support, each morning when I woke up I still found it hard to get into the right frame of mind. Each day I forced myself to "man the fuck up"—but by the afternoon it felt like my heart was in my stomach. By the end of each day, I was still overcome with guilt, grief and loneliness. I just wanted to be alone.

I was not a bad person, but I found myself repeating the words "sorry" over and over again. I am so sorry . . . for everything.

Everyone's life has the potential for unlimited happiness, but all I saw was an empty box. Each night I fell asleep with a black heart and no feelings, just emptiness.

This cycle repeated itself day after day.

I was thirty-eight and I felt exhausted, like an old man.

But gradually over time, things improved. It was a slow process, so slow I almost didn't notice it happening. In 2012 I had a job interview with a firm that makes kit for snipers. I should have been a good fit, but I started worrying about whether the guys in the firm would see straight through me.

Straight through the mask and into the bag of chaos that was now me.

On the day of the interview, I shaved, something I hadn't done for a long time. I looked in the mirror and accepted what I saw, some of the self-hatred gone.

Tanya couldn't believe I'd shaved.

I made myself look presentable, and Paul, Tanya and I drove to the firm's headquarters. Tom and Dave, the owners, met us and made us feel so welcome. They have hearts of gold and anyone who has met them knows that they are straight down the line. They showed me around the whole setup, including the range, where Paul got to fire a .50 cal rifle. I knew what the kick was like . . . but Paul didn't. He fired from a chair with wheels on it and the recoil sent him rolling across the room, weapon still in hand. He looked at me open-mouthed as if to say, "What the fuck happened there?"

I surprised myself by laughing.

Later, we saw some of the guys grinning at the CCTV screen. They replayed the footage and you could clearly see Tanya jumping about ten inches out of her seat every time a gun went off. We all had a good laugh at that as well.

Just as we were about to leave the range, they presented me with a model miniature rifle mounted on a plinth. Tom and Dave made a short speech, thanking me for all that I had done for this country. It was the first time I had felt appreciated in a long time.

It was the first time I felt hope.